DATE DUE

DEMCO 38-296

States of Sympathy

States of Sympathy

Seduction and Democracy in the American Novel

Elizabeth Barnes

Columbia University Press
New York

New York   Chichester, West Sussex
Copyright © 1997 Columbia University Press

Library of Congress Cataloging-in-Publication Data

Barnes, Elizabeth.
    States of sympathy: Seduction and democracy in the American novel. / Elizabeth Barnes.
    p.   cm.
      ISBN 0-231-10878-8 — ISBN 0-231-10879-6 (pbk.)
      1. American fiction—19th century—History and criticism. 2. Sympathy in literature.
3. American fiction—18th century—History and criticism. 4. Domestic fiction, American—
History and criticism. 5. Didactic fiction, American—History and criticism. 6. Politics and literature—United States—History.
7. Sentimentalism in literature. I. Title.
PS374.S97B37 1997
813.009'358—dc21   96-53284
                                                                                           CIP

Casebound editions of Columbia University Press books
are printed on permanent and durable acid-free paper.

Printed in the United States of America
c 10 9 8 7 6 5 4 3 2 1
p 10 9 8 7 6 5 4 3 2 1

For my family

Contents

Preface   *ix*

Acknowledgments   *xv*

1. The Politics of Sympathy   1

2. Natural and National Unions   19
    Domesticating Sympathy
    The Metapolitics of *Common Sense*
    The Erotics of Common Sense: *The Power of Sympathy*
    The Man Within the Breast

3. Seductive Education and the Virtues of the Republic
    Conventional Rebellions   40
    The Art of Seduction: *The Crimes of Love* and *Wieland*
    "Female Education" and Its Discontents
    The Authority of Representation: *Charlotte Temple*
    "This Man Will Seduce Me Into Matrimony": *The Coquette*

4. Changing the Subject: Domestic Fictions of Self-Possession   74
    Domestic Reformations
    The Conversion to Love: *A New-England Tale*
    Corporate Individualism: *The Lamplighter*
    Reimagining the Familiar Body: *Uncle Tom's Cabin*

5. Mothers of Seduction   100
    The Lessons of Womanhood
    Literate and Literary Daughters: *The Wide, Wide World*
    Mirroring the Mother Text: *Love's Progress* and *Ernest Linwood*
    Conclusion: *Billy Budd* and the Critique of Sympathy   115

Notes   127
Index   147

Preface

Almost thirty years ago Leslie Fiedler began his landmark text, *Love and Death in the American Novel*, by declaring that "the American writer inhabits a country at once the dream of Europe and a fact of history." The book I have written seeks to reconsider Fiedler's claim but shifts the burden of dreaming from Europe to America. That is, this book stresses not Europe's dreams about America but America's dreams about itself. From the late eighteenth through the nineteenth century America was as much an act of the American imagination as a (f)act of history. Such an idea informs my methodology as well as my argument. In attempting to retell some of the stories that American writers told about themselves and their country, I have chosen to focus on representations of American culture offered to us by the literature of the time—to emphasize, in other words, American *imaginings* over American history. Implicit in my argument is the idea that the cultural imaginary can be as powerful a political tool as material facts and events. Rather than treat specific historical or political incidents, I investigate the ways in which sociopolitical discourses intersect with popular literary themes to construct a compelling and coherent image of America. In doing so I have found that what most preoccupied American authors was imagination itself. Sympathetic identification—the act of imagining oneself in another's position—signified a narrative model whereby readers could ostensibly be taught an understanding of the interdependence between their own and others' identities. In a time when American national as well as individual identity was in question, it is not surprising that American literature brought such issues as identification, unification, diversity, and autonomy so directly to the fore.

Despite the fact that I talk in terms of what is "distinctly American" about these texts, this is not a comparative study. I do not place English and American texts side by side in order to prove what is unique about American literature. Interestingly enough, such a study might show that there are more similarities than differences between American and English sentimental fiction of the same period. For example, one need only think of Richardson's *Pamela* and *Clarissa*, MacKenzie's *Man of Feeling*, or Goldsmith's *The Vicar of Wakefield* to see that the interest in states of feeling did not originate in America. In American fiction, however, seduction and sympathy take on decidedly political connotations. Moreover, I would contend that America's debt to English sentimental fiction becomes in some sense the catalyst for claims to narrative authority. The obvious similarities between English and American cultures, in terms of language, dress, literature, and government, etc., made it all the more imperative for American writers to either emphasize or invent some essential difference between their own creations and those of their British counterparts. In light of the current critique of American Studies—the idea that such a field is founded on an erroneous idea of American Exceptionalism—it is necessary to distinguish between my own and these early authors' ideas about what constitutes "Americanness." I would say that what is distinctive about late eighteenth- and nineteenth-century American letters is the pervasive and insistent need of American authors to prove that distinctions exist. It is therefore less *my* claim than the claim of American authors themselves that their work embodies something peculiarly or distinctively American.

One of the distinctions American authors emphasized, and one of the tools with which they attempted to forge their new identity, was, ironically enough, sympathy. Sympathy was to be the building block of a democractic nation, and democracy, so the story goes, was a defining element of the United States. Sympathetic identification—one of the foremost elements of sentimental literature—works to demonstrate, even to *enact*, a correspondence or unity between subjects. In American literature sympathetic identification relies particularly on familial models. Readers are taught to identify with characters in such a way that they come to think of others—even fictional "others"—as somehow related to themselves. At the same time, the family analogy generates a myriad of problems for an emerging national audience. For example, the long-standing metaphor of England as America's "parent country" raises questions as to how America can both glorify family and reject the "parent" that has so profoundly influenced its culture. For how does a nation repudiate that which has brought it into being without repudiating an essential part of itself?

One can identify this literary, cultural, and political "anxiety of influence" in all the early popular texts with which I deal. Thomas Paine's *Common Sense*, for example, argues the need to reimagine the notion of family in order for colonists to transfer their affection and affiliation from the "parent country" to their own flesh and blood. William Hill Brown's *The Power of Sympathy*, as Cathy Davidson has shown, was marketed as "the first American novel," a title earned by virtue of geography (its author and publisher lived in America) rather than by its original theme. Hannah Foster's *The Coquette* is rife with the rhetoric of liberty and independence and what these concepts might mean for an unattached American woman. Even *Charlotte Temple*, written by the Anglo-American author Susanna Rowson, has its eponymous protagonist lose her virginity, and thus her familial identity, on a voyage from England to America. By the latter half of the nineteenth century the effort to construct and maintain the integrity of an "American" character reaches its climax. Both echoing and inverting Paine's argument nearly a hundred years before, Harriet Beecher Stowe's *Uncle Tom's Cabin* insists that to be truly American one must be able to conceive of others as if they were part of one's own family. To be able to do so is—to use Paine's words—to put on the true "character of a man." In *Uncle Tom's Cabin*, however, we see what sentimental fiction has all along been teaching us. For men to be *truly* American, that is, truly sympathetic, they must learn to be more like women: more suggestible, more seducible, more impressionable readers of both literature and human relations.

In this book I argue that American culture's preoccupation with familial feeling as the foundation for sympathy, and sympathy as the basis of a democratic republic, ultimately confounds the difference between familial and social bonds. This accounts in part for why so many American stories center on the distinction between licit and illict love and why incest and seduction become recurrent themes. Although it is tempting to read these stories as proof of anxieties about national corruption, I believe that incest and seduction represent the "natural" consequence of American culture's most deeply held values. Both can be read as metaphors for a culture obsessed with loving familiar objects. In making these arguments, I challenge three long-standing critical assumptions in American literary, feminist, and cultural studies: the notion that American individualism represents the hallmark of the American novel and American identity, the contention that "women's" sentimental literature is principally for and about women, and the idea that civic republicanism and liberal humanism represent chronologically distinct ideologies of the postrevolutionary and antebellum periods, respectively. To demonstrate these claims,

I have concentrated for the most part on "noncanonical" novels, novels that, by virtue of their popularity and their stylistic or thematic similarities to one another, prove central to the imagination of the age. The point is not only recuperation but representation: these works best exemplify the ideas and values that helped construct a notion of American identity based on a model of affinity. Since I am arguing for a reorientation of the field of "American literature" itself, to concentrate on more canonical works—while it might constitute a very "American" enterprise—would ultimately prove self-defeating. It would be simply to reiterate what is known and loved—and loved because it is known.

Having said this, I must also acknowledge that I have chosen texts based on their familiarity and availability to the public as well as for their pertinence to the subject at hand. With two exceptions, *Ernest Linwood* and *Love's Progress*, all the novels I treat have been reissued by major presses in the last ten to twenty years. In some cases I have eschewed the standard edition of novels in favor of those editions I believe most people—students and critics alike—are apt to read. In addition, most of the novels presented here, including *The Power of Sympathy, Charlotte Temple, The Coquette, Wieland, The Wide, Wide World, Uncle Tom's Cabin, The Lamplighter,* and *Ernest Linwood*, have all received critical treatment by such critics as Richard Brodhead, Cathy Davidson, Ann Douglas, Philip Fisher, Mary Kelley, and Jane Tompkins. What this book does differently is to read these works in relation to each other, proposing a theory of sympathetic reading that has both literary and political implications. By offering detailed analyses of these novels I hope not only to make clear their significance to the fields of American literature and culture but also to demonstrate their potential for critical debate in the classroom and in the academy at large.

In his own preface Fiedler, in an uncanny echo of Hawthorne's "The Custom-House," writes that the "cautious" reader has every reason to expect a prefatory word, and "the author (if he is I, at least), [will be] delighted to explain himself, to welcome the kind of audience he has all along desired, and to warn off the unsympathetic." Although Fiedler expresses here what is unquestionably the quintessential sentiment for a book on American literature, I must release my audience from any such readerly contract. After all, as a critic I myself must (try to) remain relatively unmoved by the seductive manipulations of the literature with which I am engaged. If at times I seem unduly critical of the works I have chosen to study, I can only say that, as any good reader of American literature will eventually discover, sympathy has its limits. It has not

been my intention to argue that the sentimental strains evident in these philosophical, political, and literary texts are either good or bad, liberatory or dangerous, but rather to show that they are unambiguously pervasive and influential. To this end I offer as many insights as I can into the "power of sympathy," to try to make apparent sympathy's central place in the American
imagination. How successful I am in this endeavor, or how sympathetic my
audience will be to these claims, remains to be seen.

January 1997

Acknowledgments

This book grows out of my involvement with two academic communities: the English departments at the University of California, Santa Barbara, and the University of Michigan, Ann Arbor. I would like to express my gratitude to the University of California for the humanities fellowship that gave me the opportunity to develop my ideas for this project while it was still in its early stages. My warmest thanks to Giles Gunn, Garrett Stewart, Christopher Newfield, and Julie Carlson, friends and colleagues at UCSB who generously guided and encouraged me in this endeavor. Special thanks to Zelda Bronstein, who first introduced me to the rich mine of popular culture; without her example and influence this book would never have been conceived. Thanks as well to the department of English Language and Literature at the University of Michigan for the one-term sabbatical that allowed me to complete this book.

I would also like to thank certain individuals whose critical insight, professional advice, and personal encouragement saw this book through to its conclusion: Jonathan Freedman, Julie Ellison, Nancy K. Miller, Steven Mullaney, Robert Weisbuch, June Howard, Kerry Larson, Gordon Hutner, Carol Singley, Elizabeth Sweeney, Eric Sundquist, Patricia Meyer Spacks, Kathleen Woodward, and Martha Vicinus. I owe a special debt to Patsy Yaeger, whose expert advice at a critical time helped bring the book's argument more sharply into focus. Thanks to Mako Yoshikawa for her practical talents in putting this book together, and to Michael Sowder for helping me come up with the book's title. I would also like to express my appreciation to Jennifer Crewe, publisher for the humanities, and to the helpful and expert staff at Columbia University Press: Susan Pensak, Anne McCoy, Leslie Bialler, and Linda Secondari.

Not to be ignored are those friends and colleagues who have generously shared their time, talent, and sense of humor with me over the years. They continue to exemplify for me the crucial connection between the intellectual and affective life: Anne Krook, Aline Flower, Kris Miller, Brian McCuskey, Yopie Prins, P. A. Skantze, Matthew Fink, Philip Blumberg, Rebecca Egger, Bill Weinberg, John Kucich, Linda Gregerson, Elessar Tetramariner, Shelley Doran, and Adela Pinch.

This book is dedicated to my family: Doris Sherbano Barnes, William Henry Barnes, Patricia Barnes Hecht, Kevin, Joshua, and Daniel Hecht, Jeffrey Harold Barnes, Jasmin Barnes, Lorie Pellizer, and Helen and Harold Sherbano. Their unflagging faith, sympathy, and counsel have given me the courage and determination to do my best work—not only on paper but in those personal relationships in which both my life and scholarship gain truth and meaning. I must include in such a category those whose extraordinary combination of rigorous criticism and unwavering support have turned this project into a labor of love: to Tresa Grauer, Anita Norich, Athena Vrettos, Christopher Flint, and Suzanne Raitt I offer my gratitude for being not only my most trusted and valued friends, but my lifeline to the riches of the world outside my mind. You, too, are my family, and when I'm with you I feel that I am home.

States of Sympathy

1

The Politics of Sympathy

In a definitive example of American sentimental politics, Jefferson's Declaration of Independence exempts Americans from the constraints of British authority on the grounds of a democratic consensus yet to be realized in the author's own country: "We hold these truths to be self-evident, that all men are created equal, that they are endowed by their Creator with certain unalienable rights. . . . That to secure these rights, governments are instituted among men, deriving their just powers from the consent of the governed." Beginning with a description of the "unalienable rights" of the individual body—namely, the right to "life, liberty and the pursuit of happiness"—Jefferson goes on to extend those rights to the political realm, claiming "the people's" power to "alter or abolish" any government threatening to infringe on their personal rights. What results is a surprising conflation of the personal and the political body—a vision of "the people" as a single and independent entity, asserting its liberal privilege in a body at once collective and individual.[1]

I would argue that this body—and particularly the principles and sentiments attached to it—becomes in a measure Jefferson's own. Writing as he does in the first-person plural, Jefferson creates rather than articulates the personal and political identity Americans are to fashion for themselves.[2] His claims *personalize* and thus in a measure unify "the people" whom his writing represents. One could say then that what is specifically "sentimental" about this foundational document lies in its methodology as well as its message—its attempts to construct as well as to celebrate union. In an effort to make real the political consensus he envisions, Jefferson recurs to a strategy of identification characteristic of sentimental narratives. By depicting "the people" as equivalent to himself, Jefferson projects onto the body politic the thoughts, feelings, and privileges with which he himself is invested. His claim that "all men are created equal" epitomizes the power of sentimental representation—a power to reinvent others in one's own image.

Jefferson's declaration exemplifies the ways in which representations of American democracy rely on models of identification to promote political union. The idea of the American people as a single unified body is made possible by imagining diverse individuals connected in a sympathetic chain. But, in eighteenth-century constructions of it, sympathy—the act of imagining oneself in another's position—is contingent upon familiarity. In order for the reader to engage in sympathetic identification, others must be shown to be *like* the reader. In other words, sympathy is both the expression of familiarity and the vehicle through which familiarity is created. Popular narratives of the eighteenth and nineteenth century reveal the ways in which sentimental constructions of sympathy in particular allow readers to imagine themselves both represented by and representing others, encouraging readers to participate in a fantasy of democracy that would fulfill its promise of equality by negating diversity in the cause of union.

This book calls for a new approach to reading early American fiction and politics, one that recognizes sympathy as crucial to the construction of American identity. Sympathetic identification emerges in the eighteenth century as the definitive way of reading literature and human relations. For disgruntled colonists, it defines national interests as well: to read sympathetically becomes synonymous with reading like an American. Examining philosophical and political texts alongside literary ones, we see the extent to which sentiment and sympathy pervade early national culture. In all three genres, sociopolitical issues are cast as family dramas, a manuever that ultimately renders public policy an essentially private matter. The conversion of the political into the personal, or the public into the private, is a distinctive trait of sentimentalism; its influence is made plain in the postrevolutionary and antebellum eras where *family* stands as the model for social and political affiliations. In American fiction and nonfiction alike, familial feeling proves the foundation for sympathy, and sympathy the foundation of democracy. For American authors, a democratic state is a sympathetic state, and a sympathetic state is one that resembles a family.

States of feeling are exactly the issue in the American novel. Paradoxically, sympathy, while touted as the emotional foundation of a democratic republic, also proves that feeling cannot be controlled. Not surprisingly, then, the distinction between licit and illicit love, exemplified in a score of stories about incest and seduction, becomes a preoccupying theme in American literature. Such stories have traditionally been read as a manifestation of cultural anxieties about corruption in the young republic. Far from subverting the goals of national union, however, incest and seduction represent the logical outcome of American culture's most cherished ideals. In holding up the family as a model for sociopolitical union, sentimental rhetoric conflates the boundaries between familial and social ties. The result is a confusion of familial and erotic attachment: one learns to love those to whom one already feels related. Incest can thus be read as a metaphor for a culture obsessed with loving familiar objects. Similarly, seduction, while ostensibly representing a breach in legitimate union, actually serves as a model for the ways in which political union is effected after the Revolutionary War. In the typical story of seduction, protective fathers become indistinguishable from the seductive lovers whose power they seek to supplant. Rather than challenging national values, incest and seduction become the unspoken champions of a sentimental politics designed to make familial feeling the precondition for inclusion in the public community.

Rhetorical evocations of sympathy abound in sentimental fiction across the North Atlantic, thus one can identify similar narrative patterns in both British and American literature. In American literature, however, sympathetic identification takes on a particular political significance. In writings spanning nearly a hundred years, and including authors as diverse as Tom Paine and Harriet Beecher Stowe, sympathy—expressed as emotional, psychological, or biological attachment—is represented as the basis of democracy, and therefore as fundamental to the creation of a distinctly "American" character. Paine's *Common Sense* (1776), for example, presents the evils of "external" authority as embodied in the person of a distant, unapproachable, and hence tyrannical monarch, while it locates "natural" authority in those "feelings and affections" that, on every level, lie *within*—within the individual but, more precisely, within the affective (e.g., familial), structures that define both individual and national "common sense."[3] Paine's treatise shows as well the political expediency of setting limits on the sympathetic imagination; for Paine, sympathy is reserved for those who inhabit the same geographical "domestic" sphere. In an artful reconfiguration of the bonds of filial loyalty, Paine contracts the parameters of familial sympathy to alienate colonists from their outmoded perceptions of Britain as the "parent country" and to unite them in a vision of a national nuclear family, one based on the shared values and investments of a democratic people.

What becomes clear in the narratives that follow, however, is sympathy's dangerous capacity to undermine the democratic principles it ostensibly means to reinforce. By displacing a democratic model that values diversity with a familial model that seeks to elide it, sentimental literature subordinates democratic politics to a politics of affinity, employing a method of affective representation that dissolves the boundaries between "self" and "other." By contrast to critics who view sentimentality as distinctly democratic in nature and practice,[4] I suggest that sentimental literature teaches a particular way of reading both texts and people that relies on likeness and thereby reinforces homogeneity. In the sentimental scheme of sympathy, others are made real— and thus cared for—to the extent that they can be shown in *relation* to the reader.

Feminist political theorists have argued that through the rhetoric of disembodied persons American constitutional language obscures the power accruing to the white male body alone.[5] This book addresses the ways in which rhetorical figures are *embodied* for readers through the power of readers' sympathetic identifications. That this is exactly the point of a sentimental education is made clear in the preface to Susanna Rowson's 1794 novel *Charlotte Temple*. In it, the novel's pedagogical efficacy is seen as proportionate to its ability to make the story real for readers: "For the perusal of the young and thoughtless of the fair sex, this Tale of Truth is designed; and I could wish my fair readers to consider it as not merely the effusion of Fancy, but as a reality."[6] The novel's tale of seduction becomes its own method of education, for in reading Charlotte's unhappy story it is assumed the "fair sex" will avoid the errors that ended poor Charlotte's life. What is significant is that the novel's "female education" is inextricably linked with the novel's claim to verisimilitude; the lessons readers learn are dependent upon the author's ability to contract the distance, or, rather, to *obscure the difference*, between reality and representation, reader and character. One of the questions this book seeks to address is *how* it is that readers are made to conceive of themselves in relation to static fictional characters.

The logic of literary sentimentalism depends on the conception of sympathy as fundamentally grounded in, and bounded by, the human imagination. While many Enlightenment theorists posit sympathy as the affective tie that holds a society together, they also present sympathy as an epistemological conundrum to which only the individual's imaginative capabilities can attend. As Adam Smith argues in *The Theory of Moral Sentiments* (1759), we can have no conception of what others feel "but by conceiving what we ourselves should feel in the like situation. Though our brother is upon the rack, as long as we ourselves are at our ease, our senses will never inform us of what he suffers. They never did, and never can, carry us beyond our own person, and it is by the imagination only that we can form any conception of what are his sensations."[7] Conversely, self-scrutiny is possible only by imagining one's actions as viewed through the eyes of another. Sympathy thus proves a mediated experience in which selves come to be constituted in relation to — or by relating to — other imagined selves, while those other selves are simultaneously created through the projection of one's own sentiments.[8]

Smith's theory of sympathy represents individual sense as the epistemological basis of "fellow feeling," offering a model of sympathetic relations as both fundamentally self-interested and imaginative in nature.[9] Sentimental literature exploits the latter idea by attempting to both represent and *reproduce* sympathetic attachments between readers and characters. In fact, "sentimental" literature can be defined by just this intention. Sentimental narratives typically foreground examples of sympathetic bonding in their story lines as a model for the way in which readers themselves are expected to respond. One could say then that for sentimental writers like Rowson the mediating function of literature mirrors the mediating function of the human imagination. Acts of sympathy depend upon such mediation: that is, one's apprehension of another's experience is understood to be achieved through the mediating influence of one's own emotions. As one subject views another, she must imagine how the other feels; this can only be accomplished by projecting onto the other person what would be one's own feelings in that particular situation. According to this model, personal feeling becomes the basis of both one's own and the other's authenticity.

Novels published even a hundred years after Smith's writings reflect the ways in which seventeenth- and eighteenth-century liberal theories of sympathy inform nineteenth-century methods of discipline. In Hawthorne's *The Scarlet Letter* (1850), for example, sympathy proves the ruling principle of narrative education; it denotes the single most important criterion for a pedagogically succesful reading experience. Hawthorne opens his novel with the conventional claim to the novel's veracity and, from there, goes on to suggest how a sympathetic reading will make even fiction a reality for readers: "It will be seen . . . that this Custom-House sketch has a certain propriety, of a kind always recognized in literature, as explaining how a large portion of the following pages came into my possession, and as offering proofs of the authenticity of a narrative therein contained." It is in fact the desire to put himself in his "true position" as editor that Hawthorne now assumes a "personal relation with the public."[10] In order to establish such a relation, however, an author must first feel that he is meeting with sympathetic minds. Hawthorne therefore self-consciously addresses his work to the "few who will understand him." Unless the author stand in some "true relation to his audience," writes Hawthorne, able to "imagine that a friend, a kind and apprehensive, though not the closest friend, is listening to our talk," no tale can be told. Rather, the author will be seized by a verbal paralysis, where "thoughts are frozen and utterance benumbed" (22).

Sympathy's power to identify us with others is reinforced in the novel proper. For example, we are told that the scarlet letter Hester wears—a symbol of her experience—becomes the vehicle through which she is able to sympathize with others: "Walking to and fro, with those lonely footsteps, in the little world with which she was outwardly connected, it now and then appeared to Hester . . . that the scarlet letter had endowed her with a new sense. . . . that it gave her a sympathetic knowledge of the hidden sin in other hearts" (80). Hester's experience—her "sin"—allows her a new interpretive authority; it becomes the basis upon which she identifies, and identifies with, the sins of others. Hester's letter—as text as well as experience—affirms literature's role as a medium through which disparate individuals are brought together. Its effect becomes a gloss on the pedagogical power Hawthorne envisions for his own *Scarlet Letter*.

As if to model for his audience the sympathy his readers are to feel, Hawthorne himself takes on the role of reader near the end of the introductory section. Claiming to have stumbled upon the literal scarlet letter in the second story of the customhouse, Hawthorne then goes on to relate the somewhat mystical transfer of identity that occurs:

> While thus perplexed,—and cogitating, among other hypotheses, whether the letter might not have been one of those decorations which the white men used to contrive, in order to take the eyes of Indians,—I happened to place it on my breast. It seemed to me,—the reader may smile, but must not doubt my word,—it seemed to me, then, that I experienced a sensation not altogether physical, yet almost so, as of burning heat; and as if the letter were not of red cloth, but red-hot iron. I shuddered, and involuntarily let it fall upon the floor. (43)

In this moment, Hawthorne communicates the effect his entire novel is to have on his readers. Ideally, author, reader, and subject will be shown in "true relation" to each other through the process of sympathetic identification. Such relations are not accomplished through reason but through the faculty of feeling; as Hawthorne reports, even before he put the scarlet letter on, its signficance was "subtly communicating itself to [his] sensibilities, but evading the analysis of [his] mind" (43). Thus from the outset Hawthorne makes clear the impression his story is to have on sympathetic readers. It is, moreover, an impression that has its *physical* effects, a point made most clear by Dimmesdale's increasingly wasted body.

Dimmesdale's complicity in, and identification with, Hester's experience manifests itself in a kind of fleshly sympathy, turning his own body against him. In the years that follow their affair, Dimmesdale's health deteriorates. This is in keeping with Dimmesdale's nature; his body, as Roger Chillingworth laconically observes, is "the closest conjoined, and imbued, and identified, so to speak, with the spirit whereof it is the instrument" (114). Although Dimmesdale's pain is real, it is also for his own benefit. In fact, it is the power of Dimmesdale's feeling that confirms his materiality. For "in so far as [a man] shows himself in a false light," declares Hawthorne, "he becomes a shadow, or, indeed, ceases to exist. The only truth that continued to give Mr. Dimmesdale a real existence on this earth, was the anguish in his inmost soul, and the undissembled expression of it in his aspect" (121). In keeping with the sentimental principles of the age, Hawthorne demonstrates that the material cannot be divorced from the mental or emotional: in the sympathetic experience, body, mind, and heart are inextricably connected. Acts of sympathetic identification are bound to make one feel not only another's but one's own reality more acutely.

This last point explains in part Hawthorne's own ambivalence toward sympathy, and why, in the middle of his introduction, he retreats from the gaze of his readers. While acknowledging the autobiographical impulse that compelled him to write "The Custom-House," Hawthorne reminds his audience that it is not the "real" man about whom they read: "We may prate of the circumstances that lie around us, and even of ourself [*sic*], but still keep the inmost Me behind its veil" (22–23). For Hawthorne, sympathy is essentially an *act*: its double logic lies in the affective connection it establishes between individuals and in the necessarily theatrical nature of that connection.[11] That is, even in the act of communicating with others, we find ourselves confirmed in our own subjectivities. Rooted as it is in our projections of the other, sympathy ultimately brings us back to ourselves.

For Hawthorne, sympathy bridges the gap between the "Actual and the Imaginary" (46) and brings fiction one step closer to the material world. The notion that sympathy is equally as imaginative as affective in nature allows us to consider the ways in which sentimental literature contributes to a broader cultural discourse that obscures the difference between real and fictional bodies and attempts to dramatize anxieties about the material body through fictions that replicate the sympathetic process. As *Charlotte Temple* and *The Scarlet Letter* suggest, it is the feminine (and *feminized*) body in particular that carries the burden of early literature's ideological work.

If political rhetoric habitually locates patriarchal authority in the disembodied unspecified male who stands for both the individual and the collective at once, sentimental fiction works out sociopolitical questions and conflicts through a gendered body—the woman's. This can be accounted for in part by women's precarious position in the new republic. Immune to those economic motivations ensuring republican "virtue" and "independence"—e.g., entitlement to property and the vote—women embody what most endangers republican structures. Perhaps even more significant, however, is the fact that in this period women represent both the physical and psychological vulnerability crucial to the goals of a patriarchal state. Cathy Davidson has argued that in the late eighteenth-century sentimental novel of seduction female sexuality becomes "nationalized," and even "fetishized," as a symbol of republican virtue and innocence. The successful assault on the woman's chastity would therefore be read by postrevolutionary audiences as a metaphor for the debasement of American character and the corruption of national integrity.[12] While sex is unquestionably at issue in stories of seduction, the conflation of material and fictional bodies characteristic of sentimental narratives suggests that we must read beyond the woman's physical condition to the psychological condition that chastity signifies. The woman's body serves as a synecdoche for the *emotional susceptibility* at issue in an increasingly literate and fiction-centered republic: e.g., one of the central questions raised at this time is how readers are going to be *affected* by narratives without being *misled* by them. The burgeoning number of novels written by, about, and ostensibly for women signals in part a growing interest in affective forms of disciplinary control.[13] Liberal constructions of feminine sensibility play a key role in establishing both the methods and the motivations for these controls.[14] In the postrevolutionary period, women become increasingly associated with the dangers of psychological penetration; they embody, both figuratively and literally, the suggestibility requisite for sympathetic identification.

In effect, women represent ideal readers in the most positive and the most negative sense: they are open to influence and eminently seducible. Rather than attempting to root out the tendency to identification, seduction novels exploit it, justifying the novel's methods on the grounds of its contribution to "female education." What results is a confusion of legitimate and illegitimate authority, in which sentimental narratives reproduce the seducer's verbal arts. While warning young women to avoid the passionate urgings and sentimental naïveté to which its female protagonist has fallen victim, the typical seduction novel relies on the loaded language of sentimentality to drive home its point. The language and design of the seducer is overshadowed only by the more persuasive language and manipulative design of the novel, leaving authority to reside in whatever agent has the more convincing speech. Seduction thus denotes not only what the story is about but also what it does: it breaks down distinctions between parent and lover, moral guide and criminal influence, and translates "female education" into another form of seduction.

By evoking readers' feelings in order to modify readers' behavior, sentimental fiction effectively bridges the gap between internal and external authority, rendering the latter—represented by the novel itself—virtually indistinguishable from the reader's own "instincts." The meaning of seduction can thus be seen as effectively defined by the uneasy relationship between coercion and consent. As will become clear in what follows, sentimental strategies of seduction are exemplary of postrevolutionary politics at large. That is, seduction not only signifies the threat of illegitimate influence to the vision of democratic union, it indicates the particular mode by which patriarchal authority regains access to the American imagination after the fact of revolution.

In typical sentimental fashion, seduction fiction puts sociopolitical anxieties concerning the nature of authority into a personal context, where private interpersonal relations intersect with public concerns. In the postrevolutionary story "Amelia, or the Faithless Briton,"[15] for example, the young American woman's seduction by an English soldier is set against the backdrop of the Revolutionary War. Having taken the wounded soldier, Doliscus, into their home, the family is then betrayed when he takes advantage of Amelia's sympathetic nature: after a sham marriage, Doliscus abandons Amelia, leaving her pregnant and disgraced. Amelia's brother confronts the libertine in an effort to defend his sister's honor but dies in the attempt. This anonymously authored story, appearing in a magazine in 1787, does not attribute the family's tragedy to the corrupted tendencies of British aristocracy alone but to the compounded effects of "anarchy and war" as well. In such a chaotic age, American innocence has little or no chance to flourish. The breakdown of traditional patriarchal structures attending revolution signals the dissolution of Colonial security and the necessity of rebuilding protective structures from within the new republic.

The question of how innocence can survive the machinations of an educated but profligate male constituency informs the politics of the early novel of seduction, which posits patriarchal authority as, alternately, a threat to and the redemption of a young and innocent nation. The solution, depicted in fiction and political rhetoric alike, was the conversion of national into natural relations. For centuries, the family had provided an analogue to political order, with the king representing the "father" of his people. During the American revolution, the association between patriarchy and tyranny became crystallized in the figure of the British monarch. Citing seventeenth- and eighteenth-century literary, philosophical, and educational treatises, Jay Fliegelman chronicles American attempts to domesticate paternal authority through representations of filial relations as naturally affectionate, cooperative, and egalitarian.[16] The ideological shift from a coercive to a consensual view of paternal rule informs my reading of sentimental family narratives as well, but I argue that the move from coercion to consent ultimately bolsters patriarchal claims to domestic authority. As Carole Pateman observes, "The contract theorists' aim was theoretical parricide, not the overthrow of the sexual right of men and husbands." Both patriarchalists and contract theorists agreed, "first, that women (wives), unlike sons, were born and remained naturally subject to men (husbands); and, second, that the right of men over women was *not political*."[17] While seduction proves the unhappy consequence of political upheaval, the solution to such upheaval is offered in a vision of domestic relations that stands beyond the boundaries of political affairs. Similarly, although the woman's body can be seen as an icon of national vulnerability, the structures by which women are imagined rescued from their predicament are depicted as domestic, "natural," and apolitical. The problem of women's political status becomes represented as a problem of character and of emotional, rather than physical or material, susceptibility. Why reform social and political structures when one can reform the woman herself?

The translation of political into domestic issues—and the problems attending such conversions—plays a central role in Hannah Foster's popular story of seduction, *The Coquette* (1797). At the outset of the novel, the protagonist, Eliza Wharton, announces her intention to bask in the "liberty" of her youth and to put off marriage as long as possible. In doing so, Eliza is insisting not only on her freedom, but on the right to pursue her own happiness. As Carroll Smith-Rosenberg has noted, Eliza articulates her goal in language drawn from "that primer of American republican rhetoric," the Declaration of Independence,[18] demonstrating her faith in the democratic dream. "Throughout the novel, Eliza Wharton will insist that pleasure can be wedded to a desire for independence and liberty," writes Smith-Rosenberg, "that marriage without such a 'wedding' will destroy happiness."[19] What the novel ultimately reveals, however, is a culture's failure to conceive of liberty outside the constraints of republican union. Conjugal and political forms of authority and privilege are shown inextricably connected in a republican framework that would subsume the political in representations of the personal. Such a strategy, though made to appear for the woman's own good, has devastating consequences for Eliza. After internalizing the social censure brought on by her "coquettry," Eliza succumbs to the advances of a married man and dies in childbirth. Apropos of the patriarchal culture in which it was written, *The Coquette* shows husbands and fathers as the woman's only protection from a patriarchal system embodied by these same males.

Whereas seduction constitutes a breach of republican union and the subversion of national identity, the concept of marriage represents the ideal in social relations. In the domestic sphere, the politically unrepresentable become represented through the men who love them. Such love dresses necessity in the guise of free will and influence in the guise of instinct. Affectionate marriage, a hallmark of republican political rhetoric, obscures the violation of democratic principles through models of affinity that would subsume one person's identity in the identity of another. Though depicted as antithetical models of heterosexual relations, both marriage and seduction symbolize the complicated relationship between coercion and consent characteristic of democratic disciplinary agendas. Each presents a relational paradigm based on an *im*balance of power, but an imbalance rendered temporarily invisible or moot by the language of affection that represents even divided interests as compatible, if not identical. While ostensibly telling stories about that which threatens a harmonious republic, seduction fiction in effect tells the story of how that republic came to be, revealing the seductive techniques that republican social contracts must employ in order to be consummated.[20]

In arguing the intimate relationship between seduction and marriage, I am seeking not only to illuminate the ways in which patriarchal authority reenters the national body (through the fictional "bodies" of women) but also to resituate nineteenth-century domestic fiction within the history of seduction out of which it arises. Nina Baym has shown that popular seduction fiction declined in the first two decades of the nineteenth century, to be superseded by the domestic novel's female bildungsroman of legitimate love and happy marriage. According to Gillian Brown, Baym has established a critical trend for reading domesticity as a "value scheme for ordering of all life, in competition with the ethos of money and exploitation that is perceived to prevail in American society."[21] Seen in the context of late eighteenth-century sentimental fiction, however, domestic novels signify more than a response to a capitalist system. Rather, these stories illustrate early national culture's attempts to reconcile conservative republican values of duty to others with a liberal agenda of self-possession.

Whereas eighteenth-century seduction fiction traces the fall of the ingenue to the verbal manipulations of the persistent, charming, and better educated male, nineteenth-century domestic novels typically chronicle a young woman's triumph over physical hardship and rebellious pride to gain the security of a newfound family. In best-selling novels like Susan Warner's *The Wide, Wide World* (1850), such triumph occurs through religious conversion. In Warner's story, the young heroine, orphaned and sent to live with her mean-spirited aunt, rises above her circumstances to achieve the emotional independence God alone can give.[22] Where "virtue" was once associated with the woman's virginal body, it becomes linked in the domestic novel to the spiritually regenerated heart. The shift in focus from flesh to spirit, from the protagonist's attempts at protecting her body to saving her soul, has been viewed by many critics as a progressive movement in women's fiction. After all, such self-control not only betokens a degree of independence, it results in a cult of womanly influence. One could add that the woman's conversion redirects the focus of woman's value from what can easily be appropriated through contract or force to that psychological space more difficult to penetrate. The spiritual Father's initial entrance into this domain—usually at puberty—prevents a more substantial suitor from moving in. What remains unspoken in this formulation, however, are the political implications of abstracting issues of liberty and self-possession. In the transition from seduction to domestic plots, classical republican theories of a material independence succumb to more transcendental notions of freedom and equality. The domestic heroine's psychospiritual empowerment, while seductive in its claim to provide an alternative to physical exploitation, actually serves to facilitate the process by which seventeenth- and eighteenth-century liberal theory is made compatible with nineteenth-century forms of discipline. In surrendering herself to an irresistible paternal influence, the domestic heroine represents not only the ideal woman but the perfect liberal individual, self-mastered and ultimately reconciled to her domestic situation.

In effect, domestic fiction aims to perfect sentimental strategies of affective representation through the successful conversion of the material body into the immaterial soul. In doing so, it converts sympathy as well: the sentimental story now offers a heroine with whom the reader can safely identify. The difference in story line between seduction and domestic fiction has led many critics to treat these subgenres as unrelated. Cathy Davidson and Michael

Warner, for example, have opened up inquiries into the relationship between early national republican agendas and the cautionary tales they engender, while Gillian Brown, Richard Brodhead, and Jane Tompkins have made important contributions to the reevaluation of nineteenth-century domestic fiction by illustrating its significance in formulating concepts of individualism, discipline, and the public sphere.[23] The story that waits to be told is the one that connects postrevolutionary with antebellum sentimental narratives and that recognizes the relationship between the republican and liberal agendas with which these respective periods are associated. In telling this story, I consider both the ways in which aspirations of "domestic" union (and the conflation of political and private spheres implicit in this concept) work to organize narratives of seduction and the extent to which seductive practices inform domestic stories.

Reconsidering sentimental literature in light of its ideological roots in the eighteenth century also allows us to rethink our understanding of sentimental literature as a genre written exclusively by, for, and about women. Critics from the eighteenth through the twentieth centuries have historically equated sentimentality with femininity, aligning both with an antirational and overly emotional state of mind.[24] This book aims to complicate such equations by demonstrating the importance of sentimentalism to the construction of a patriarchal state. Thus I seek to move beyond readings of "men's" and "women's" fiction as separate but equal strains in American letters by demonstrating the extent to which sympathy contributes to a sentimental vision of union that eventually becomes the ideal for both men *and* women. Though sentimental fiction often features female protagonists, these stories depict more than the woman's condition in early American culture. Rather, as Nancy Armstrong has argued in relation to British literature, sentimental literature articulates a culture's preoccupation with particular "qualities of mind."[25] In American literature, these qualities—including sympathy, suggestibility, and filial devotion—become foregrounded in narratives by and about men as well as women. In making this claim, my intention is not to devalue literature by women, nor to obscure the importance of women's roles in American history, but to suggest the central place of women in the development of a *national* sensibility. Moreover, the importance of sympathy in American politics demands that we reinvestigate our notions of American "classics" in relation to popular noncanonical works. The myth of classic American literature—the idea that an autonomous individualism (and a specifically *male* individualism) represents the hallmark of the American novel and American identity—breaks down in the face of early American culture's prevailing concern for promoting sympathetic relations between individuals. In the sentimental scheme of sympathy, the boundaries of identity—for women and for men, in the personal and the political realms—are shown as distinctly flexible.

Sympathy's power to construct permeable national and personal boundaries is the focus of my next chapter, where I examine Anglo-American Enlightenment views of filial sympathy as the foundation for sociopolitical allegiance. Philosophers as diverse as John Locke and Francis Hutcheson posit the filial bond between parent and child as the affective cement for all future social relations. Although sympathy is popularly represented by philosophers and politicians as a stabilizing force in liberal society, what we find as well are examples of sympathy's potential to destroy the family it was meant to bring together. The "first American novel," William Hill Brown's *The Power of Sympathy, or The Triumph of Nature* (1789), illustrates this point with dramatic effect. Brown's story of seduction and sibling incest challenges political as well as moral theories of natural domestic attachment and its social efficacy. By eroticizing the concept of "common sense," *The Power of Sympathy* underscores the confusion that develops from conflating familial and social attachment. Given this model, it becomes increasingly difficult to distinguish those individuals one wants to marry from those to whom one is already related. Incest is thus shown as the "natural" conclusion to a society built on the power of familial love. *The Power of Sympathy*'s focus on incest and seduction also exemplifies the problem of sentimental education itself. While attempting to discipline its readers about the dangers of seduction, Brown's novel reveals that it cannot control the sympathy it evokes. In other words, *The Power of Sympathy* teaches its readers to desire the very thing it has forbidden them to have.

In chapter 3 I consider the ramifications of seductive methods of education in terms of gender and the body politic. This chapter argues that in their construction as keenly susceptible to influence women represent not only ideal readers but potentially ideal citizens as well. Plots that center on the dangers of seduction and the importance of the novel's "female education" help frame a myth of republican union that aligns marriage with nationalism. Although contending political parties like the Federalists and the Democrat-Republicans vehemently disagreed about the function of government and the common man's role in it, both sides clung to a familial model of government in making their case. Early literature reflects this model: for example, works as dissimilar as Mason Weems's fictional biography, *Life of Washington* (1800) and Charles Brockden Brown's tale of murder and insanity, *Wieland* (1798), posit the state as father, protecting his naive children from deceitful influences, including the child's own heart. At the same time, popular magazines held up the private institution of marriage as a symbol of republican virtue and of lasting political union. What is most interesting to note, however, are the ways in which the categories of husbands and fathers intersect, so that, ultimately, the concepts of paternalism and eroticism become indistinguishable from each other. Paradoxically, the ambiguity between paternalism and eroticism becomes a key feature in the very texts that claim to distinguish legitimate from illegitimate love. Rather than depicting "female education" as an antidote to seduction, novels like Susanna Rowson's *Charlotte Temple* and Hannah Foster's *The Coquette* reveal the extent to which seduction proves an indispensable element of a patriarchal education.

The decline of seduction fiction and the rise of the domestic novel in the early decades of the nineteenth century signals a radical shift in the representation of affective bonds; what remains consistent in the story, however, is the conversion of political issues into personal ones and the emphasis on family feeling as the basis of sociopolitical allegiance. Ironically, in the novel of seduction, sympathetic identification became the means through which readers were to internalize the negative consequences of loving attachments. Story lines of incest compounded the erotic charge, revealing the oftentimes fatal effects of familial sympathy. In chapter 4 I argue that the domestic novel tries to offer a positive model of familial bonding by reconfiguring the boundaries of the family unit. The domestic heroine, often orphaned at a young age, learns to reconstruct her filial relations from among those men and women with whom she experiences an intellectual, emotional, and spiritual kinship. Whereas seduction fiction depicts the middle-class family as a closed system — a nuclear and potentially incestuous unit based on the affiliation of blood ties — the domestic story represents the family as a collection of shared values and emotional experiences. These stories emphasize nurture over nature, the *act* of familying over the fact of it.

One of the most significant effects of redefining the family in this way is the broadening of patriarchal authority's scope and appeal. In novels ranging from the first domestic novel, Catharine Sedgwick's *A New-England Tale* (1822), to Maria Cummins's best-selling novel, *The Lamplighter* (1854), father figures are *chosen* rather than received. The power of paternalism is no longer dependent upon the kind of father one has, as failed fathers can be supplanted by more suitable ones. In fact, *A New-England Tale*'s protagonist, Jane Elton, *marries* the paternalistic Robert Lloyd at the end of the novel, while Gertrude Flint marries her surrogate brother, Willie Sullivan, at the conclusion of *The Lamplighter*. These novels reflect a new development in organizing society on the family plan: now heroines can legally marry the men with whom they have developed familial sympathies. By reconceiving the family in terms of volitional attachment, nineteenth-century novels perfect the conflation of familial, erotic, and social ties, at once legitimizing incestuous bonding and extending the parameters of patriarchal influence.

Fatherhood itself is transfigured in these stories, which reflect the nineteenth-century Christian ethos. God represents the all-knowing, all-loving Father who, by molding the individual's will to his own, renders sympathetic attachment both desirable and efficacious. The trope of Christian conversion can be read as a metaphor for the idealization of both patriarchal and narrative discipline: sympathy is made safe, and readers are encouraged to imagine a harmonious rather than a disjunctive relationship between their own desires and that which is desired for them by a protective parent. As if to highlight the movement from Old Testament thinking to New, domestic novels transcend the problem of blood ties, and the material conditions such ties represent, by a vision of the Father who resides *within* the individual. In a deft consolidation of conflicting interests, the domestic novel reconciles the struggle between autonomy and influence, between internal and external authority, in a vision of individualism that incorporates patriarchal rule.

The story I have been telling is meant to draw attention to the seductive implications of conflating the personal and the political. The sentimental narratives described here have this in common: they all stage political issues as personal dramas. From this we might assume that the converse is true as well—that, as Jane Tompkins has argued, personal feeling has its own political power.[26] At the conclusion of chapter 4 I examine Harriet Beecher Stowe's *Uncle Tom's Cabin* (1852) to consider the limits and dangers of this assumption. Stowe's novel represents a culminating point in the sentimental novel's attempts to create a national "common sense" by demonstrating the necessity of grounding political principle in personal feeling. By employing a familial model to construct a more liberal democratic state, however, personal differences are elided in favor of a homogeneous family image. Sameness, rather than difference, offers the key to democratic equality and, hence, to national identity. Stowe's version of political correctness—epitomized in her call for readers to *"feel right"* by sympathizing with others—turns out to be an ultra-conservative move. Although, according to Stowe, right *feeling* engenders right *politics*, the rightness of both is contingent upon how similar to oneself others can be made to appear.

Thus far I have been talking almost exclusively about what might be called the heteroerotic construction of the body politic—that is, about the ways in which both sentimental literature and political rhetoric constructs its reader-citizens as wives and daughters of a patriarchal system. In chapter 5 I look at how patterns of seduction and identification inform the relationships between mothers and daughters in domestic narratives. Domestic novels such as Caroline Gilman's *Love's Progress* (1836), Susan Warner's *The Wide, Wide World*, and Caroline Lee Hentz's *Ernest Linwood* (1856) incorporate the seduction narrative through the lessons mothers offer to their daughters. In *Ernest Linwood*, seduction reenters the woman's story via the mother's autobiography: her written history of seduction and betrayal represents the textual legacy the daughter, Gabriella, inherits; it also supplies a protagonist with whom Gabriella "naturally" identifies. The idea of filial feeling as the basis of sympathy is conjoined with the seductive practices of sentimental narration to offer a mother indistinguishable from the lover she seeks to supplant: while warning Gabriella against male machinations, the mother psychologically seduces Gabriella with her own story of betrayal, leaving the daughter unable to distinguish between her own and her mother's identity.

As the domestic novel's literary predecessor, the seduction story itself figures as a kind of "mother-text" for a new generation of readers: it provides the narrative model both against and by which the domestic story constructs itself. What these novels point to is the impossibility of gaining independence through filial identification. Such identification reinforces the idea of sympathy as sameness and similarity as the basis of all love relationships. *Love's Progress, The Wide, Wide World*, and *Ernest Linwood* illustrate the destructive effects of this psychology by underscoring the difficulties involved in daughters extricating themselves from their mothers' stories. My reading thus ultimately challenges the idea that female bonding offers a new and liberating alternative to the seductive practices of a male-dominated culture. When tied to a familial model of politics, sympathetic identification inevitably traps the individual in a cycle of history bound to repeat itself.

Throughout this book, I consider the ways in which early American novels employ sympathetic identification to reinforce a familial model of politics that subordinates difference to sameness and that teaches readers to care for others as if they were reflections of themselves. Looking at the politics of early fiction in this light forces us to rethink the ideological gap we have created between republican and liberal notions of individual value. Gordon Wood has offered ample evidence of civic republicanism's subordination of self-interest to the general good, where " 'each individual gives up all private interest' " in the " 'interest of the whole body.' " What sentimental literature teaches us, however, is that the "whole body" is conceived by first imagining one's own. Wood's quotation from an article in the *Continental Journal* (1778) indirectly concedes this view: the anonymous author writes that true liberty is "liberty restrained in such a manner, as to render society one great family; where every one must consult his neighbor's happiness, as well as his own."[27] While Wood cites the article to make the point that, in American republicanism, self-interest is sacrificed to the common good, the family analogy upon which the sentiment relies works to reinvest the common good with the properties of personal attachment. This is consistent with a sentimental ideology that casts "republican virtue," and the disinterested benevolence associated with it, as inseparable from the sympathetic mechanisms that bind a people together. These mechanisms ultimately rely on an understanding of the feeling self as the foundation of democratic society.

Sentimental fiction's evocation of personal feeling becomes a necessary precondition for participating in the feeling of others; it also acts as a moral corrective to the reader's own behavior. As Adam Smith contends, we not only sympathize with others according to what we imagine they feel, we judge our own actions according to whether or not we can imagine others sympathizing with them. "We can never survey our own sentiments and motives," nor "form any judgment concerning them," says Smith, "unless we remove ourselves, as it were, from our own natural station" and "view them with the eyes of other people, or as other people are likely to view them."[28] In a move that anticipates Foucault's study of modern disciplinary forms, sympathy is revealed to be a self-regulating practice.[29] What we might call the conscience, and what Smith refers to as the "impartial spectator" or "the man within the breast,"[30] is an agent of disciplinary sympathy arising out of the psychological interplay of real and imagined feeling. Thus one could say that, by employing readers' sympathies in the service of modifying readers' behavior, sentimental fiction essentially puts self-interest to affective work, reconciling the seemingly irreconcilable division between internal and external authority, between individual rights and the needs of the community to which the individual belongs. It is sympathy's power in imagining such reconciliations, as well as the personal and political cost of such imaginings, to which I now turn.

2

Natural and National Unions

Near the end of Melville's tale of incest and paternal betrayal, *Pierre* (1852), the eponymous protagonist cries out what could well stand as an epigraph for the paradox of early American fiction: "If to follow Virtue to her uttermost vista, where common souls never go; if by that I take hold on hell, and the uttermost virtue, after all, prove but a betraying pander to the most monstrous vice—then close in and crush me, ye stony walls, and into one gulf let all things tumble together."[1] The "most monstrous vice" to which Pierre refers, of course, is incest, and his deep sense of frustration results from the fact that his greatest love is also his greatest crime: he has fallen in love with his half sister. *Pierre* was neither Melville's most critically acclaimed nor his most popular novel; it is, however, significant in one important respect: it represents a preoccupation with the power of familial love characteristic of American literature and politics. In fiction ranging from *The Power of Sympathy* (1789) to "The Fall of the House of Usher" (1839) to *The Lamplighter* (1854), familial attachment proves the bond that cannot be broken.

How a feeling so potentially good can go so wrong is the subject of this chapter. In it, I examine the liberal construction of familial sympathy as the foundation for social and political unity, ultimately arguing that the conflation of familial and social ties results in an eroticization of familial feeling of which incest is the "natural" result. What this suggests is the cultural cost of setting up the family as a model for politics. To demonstrate this claim, I must first reconstruct the ideological framework for eighteenth-century moral philosophy and political rhetoric on sympathy. I will then turn to the "first American novel," William Hill Brown's story of sibling incest and seduction, *The Power of Sympathy, or The Triumph of Nature,* to illustrate how the early novel engages the relationship between such issues as paternalism, eroticism, and narrative education. In many ways, *The Power of Sympathy* serves as a proto-type for eighteenth- and nineteenth-century novels; it sets the stage for subse-quent dramas surrounding the nature of filial feeling and its role in the new republic. Its sentimental strategies also reflect the politics of its time. In work-ing out political issues and anxieties through personal dramas, *The Power of Sympathy* unwittingly reveals the conflicts that ensue when the family becomes the model for social organization. Deepening the dilemma of sym-pathy is the sentimental novel's seductive method of discipline: in attempting to engage readers in a sympathetic attatchment to its characters, Brown's novel reproduces the confusion between licit and illicit feeling. At its most success-ful, *The Power of Sympathy* seduces its readers into a sympathy it has already taught them it is criminal to feel. What Brown's novel ultimately points to are not only the ways in which sympathy is used to construct a newly emerging American identity but also sympathy's power to destroy the identity it is meant to define.

One of the foremost philosophers on sympathy is the Scottish moralist Adam Smith, who, in his treatise *The Theory of Moral Sentiments,* devotes an entire section to the psychology of sympathy as a socially organizing senti-ment. Smith sets the philosophical terms for sympathy in the eighteenth and nineteenth centuries, and his theories offer insight into the confusion between familial and social feeling. As Smith describes it, sympathy is more than feeling for others; it involves a projection of the self outward, so that the viewer or reader imaginatively inhabits the minds of others. As we will see, Smith's theories of sympathy are crucial to the American sentimental imagi-nation, for Smith bases both sympathy and the society it produces on a prin-ciple of *relating.* Terms traditionally having public political valence—*sympa-thy, justice, mercy*—get inflected with personal bias, as sympathy becomes dependent on how well the individual can imagine himself in another's shoes or can imagine the other in his own. Put in this context, incest denotes more than the power of filial feeling; it becomes a metaphor for a particular way of relating to others, one that relies on likeness and familiarity as a precondition for sympathy.

Domesticating Sympathy

In an effort to explain the psychological mechanisms motivating citizens of a free society to coexist peacefully, Adam Smith offers a theory of identification in which reciprocal sympathy forms the basis of moral judgment and action. "We either approve or disapprove of the conduct of another man," writes Smith, "according as we feel that . . . we either can or cannot entirely sympathize with the sentiments and motives which directed it."[2] Conversely, our own actions will be judged by people who either can or cannot sympathize with *them*. However, since Smith has also claimed that we can never know what someone else feels "but by conceiving what we ourselves should feel in the like situation," it follows that our only hope of discerning another person's judgment is by putting ourselves in *his* place: "We either approve or disapprove of our own conduct . . . when we place ourselves in the situation of another man, and view it, as it were, with his eyes and from his station" (9, 109–110). Self-scrutiny is thus mediated by the projected sentiments of an objective bystander, but a bystander invested with our own subjective impressions. Smith goes on in this vein to suggest that because we can never adequately judge our own sentiments and motives we must "remove ourselves, as it were, from our own natural station" and view our actions "through the eyes of other people, or as other people are likely to view them" (110). In other words, we must enter into the sentiments of others before we can truly understand our own.

As Smith presents it, sympathy denotes both psychological attachment—or empathy, as we might term it—and psychological distance. That is, the self is constituted by acts of the imagination that simultaneously connect and distinguish it from projected images of other selves not unlike one's own. It is the tension between these two states—attachment and separateness—that affords sympathy its disciplinary function. For in imagining oneself under the constant scrutiny of others, one eventually comes to internalize that perspective. What follows is Smith's vision of an individual conscience that takes shape as a separate subject—a "man within the breast"—who, by temporarily adopting the other's perspective, manages to teach us the "most complete lesson of *self-command*" (153–154).

Smith's theories suggest that it is not individuals who create society but society that constructs the individual; a community of viewers must exist for the individual to be recognized or for the "self" to be conceived. The point is, however, that Smith's reasoning is ultimately circular. If we can only judge our actions through the eyes of other people, and we can only gauge their sentiments as we relate them to our own, we are still left with the self as our original point of departure. This, in fact, is the paradoxical crux of Smith's theory of sympathetic identification. Although Smith defines sympathy as "fellow feeling," such feeling cannot be evoked unless one is made to imagine *oneself* in the other's position: only when another's "agonies" are "brought home to ourselves, when we have thus adopted and made them our own," do they "begin at last to affect us" (9). Reading is one of the ways Smith sees identification being established, for in reading, our imaginations allow us to "become the very person whose actions are represented to us" (75). The link between reading, society, and subjectivity suggests several things at once: first, that sympathy requires mediation in order to operate; second, that an ability or inability to sympathize does not reflect on the viewer but on the one the viewer beholds; and third, that the self is constructed in relation to those with whom it feels an affinity, otherwise no act of the imagination will take place. This last point is especially significant. For returning to the original premise, that "we either approve or disapprove of the conduct of another man according as we feel" that we either can or cannot sympathize with it, the reader sees that the responsibility for sympathy lies not with the viewer but with the object of scrutiny who must elicit sympathy *from* the viewer. The viewer's ability to sympathize is an indication that the one beheld is operating within the realm of common human experience, a territory itself bounded by the viewer's own sentiments.

Thus, "fellow feeling" notwithstanding, for Smith, the self remains the epistemological bedrock upon which any evocation of sympathy must finally stand.[3] Although sympathy represents the avenue by which modern society might usher in a more inclusive sociopolitical atmosphere,[4] in terms of the way one is imagined viewing others, sympathy can as easily become a method of exclusion. Smith's use of the first-person plural is telling in this context. In attempting to delineate both the potential and the limits of sympathetic identification, Smith assumes, and in some sense engenders, readers' identification with his position by the consistent use of the term *we*. Such a gesture represents the power of sentimental rhetorical strategies to effect a connection between like-minded individuals while further distancing readers who remain skeptical of the author's premise. This reinforces the exclusionary principles of sympathy and of the sentimental structures that seek to employ it: while an individual may be taught to see others as her- or himself, what she learns is that difference is to be negated rather than understood. A sense of self is created through identification with others, but only those others who can be proven in some way related to *us*.

Smith's theory of sympathy as a process of bonding that is contingent upon one's perception of familiarity with the other is an idea crucial to American sentimental writing. It explains in part the prevalence of stories of incest and seduction in this era: in a period of national upheaval sentimental rhetoric is invested in the project of unification. Sentimentalism itself can be defined in just these terms. Something is "sentimental" if it manifests a belief in or yearning for consonance—or even unity—of principle and purpose. Sympathy complements the work of sentiment, for each can be defined as a set of registered impulses psychologically connecting an individual to things and people outside of him or her. Novels like *The Power of Sympathy* evince the work of sentimentalism by first representing sympathetic attachment in the story line and then reproducing it in the relationship between reader and text. In this way, sentimental novels of seduction reveal their affiliation with nonfictional revolutionary works as well as with eighteenth-century patterns of thought and articulation that depict social and political agendas in personal or familial terms. In this increasingly liberal era, growing distinctions between public and private spheres of influence were focusing greater attention on private life in general and the family in particular. The idealized sympathetic bond between parent and child both legitimated personal sentiment and guaranteed social interaction: according to the moral philosophy of the time, filial attachment formed the basis of sociopolitical allegiances. Thus, put in a cultural context, "the power of sympathy" refers not only to the power of personal feeling but to the importance, as well, of *inter*personal relations as necessary for the perpetuation of liberal social and political systems.[5] In other words, the very attempt to separate public from private obligations fostered new modes of personalizing authority, which further confused the boundaries between "public" and "private" agendas.[6]

Of course the invocation of family feeling as a model for political authority is not an Enlightenment invention. For centuries the family had been taken as the general model for social order, with the king representing the "father" of his domestic realm. Even Locke the rationalist, while asserting the difference between "a ruler of a commonwealth, a father of a family, and a captain of a galley," reaffirmed the relationship between politics and parenting by including his theories of child rearing in *Two Treatises of Civil Government*.[7] But Locke attempts to circumscribe parental power by limiting its duration: "Parents have a sort of rule or jurisdiction over [their children] when they come into the world," but at length the "swaddling clothes" of infancy "drop quite off, and leave a man at his free disposal."[8] The analogy was not lost on the "sons" and "daughters" across the Atlantic: as Jay Fliegelman notes in *Prodigals and Pilgrims*, Locke's pedagogical views provided the leading metaphor in the rhetorical campaign for American independence. Having argued that the teleology of parenting is its own superfluity, Locke offered frustrated colonists justification for political rebellion against the "parent country" on the basis of "natural" development.[9]

Locke's attempt to distinguish the "power of a magistrate over a subject" from that of "a father over his children, a master over his servant, a husband over his wife" is essentially an attempt to distinguish civil from domestic, or public from private rule.[10] A mark of liberal society lies in making just such distinctions. But, in the midst of revolutionary fervor, the term *domestic* necessarily takes on a public, even national, denotation. In the eighteenth century, revolution could not be imagined without a concomitant sense of national identity, and this new identity was closely connected with the development of an isolationist attitude. Both geographically and psychologically, Britain came to represent an authority disconnected from the interests and even the character of its political offspring, while America, reborn from the colonies, symbolized the beneficent and profitable politics of a self-created "home rule."[11] Put another way, the effect of imagining Britain as first "parent," then "bad parent," then "foreign" country is a consolidation of American sympathies around or within a new larger domestic space, one that, ideologically at least, encompasses private personal allegiances.

The translation from "colonist" to "American" entailed a reconception of familial ties, and the shift was not without its attendant anxieties. Locke's educational theories placed modeling at the center of proper character development, yet American officials were generally ambivalent over that political model with which they were most familiar.[12] Lockean psychology appears more like a threat than a warning in this context, as do Locke's guidelines for making the proper impression on a youthful mind: "Imperiousness and Severity is but an ill way of treating men, who have reason of their own to guide them, unless you have a mind to make your children, when grown up, weary of you; and secretly to say within themselves, 'When will you die, father?' "[13] The nominal "Founding Fathers" of the American revolution had occasion to witness firsthand just such an effect of tyrannical and arbitrary rule and doubtless had no wish to repeat the experience with themselves in the role of detested parent. The question remained, however, whether, given the model under which colonists had been quite literally impressed, American politics could be fashioned to a new design. Sentimental literature—including political, philosophical, and fictional texts—is to a certain extent a response to the cultural anxieties present in the question of patriarchal authority; more than this, sentimental literature shares in the process of creating a new cultural impression.

Locke's theory of modeling implies psychological and chronological distance as well as discretion: in the parent a child is given an image of future
maturity, a long-term goal to strive after. Sentimental ideology supplants this
hierarchical structure with the more intimate dynamic of identification.
Whereas modeling assumes the difference between subject and object, identification diminishes the distance between these categories, blurring the
boundaries between distinct identities, whether "parent" and "child," "fact"
and "fiction," or "reader" and "text." In fact, twentieth-century critics define a
work as sentimental in part by determining the extent to which the work seeks
to engage readers in identification with the main character or characters.[14]
Sympathy is a key component in this transaction, denoting, as David Marshall
writes in *The Surprising Effects of Sympathy*, "not just feeling or the capacity
for feeling but more specifically the capacity to feel the sentiments of someone
else."[15] Yet, as Marshall goes on to show, the experience of sympathy represents
"an epistemological and aesthetic problem: since we cannot know the experience or sentiments of another person, we must represent in our imagination
copies of the sentiments that we ourselves feel as we imagine ourselves in
someone else's place and person."[16] In other words, rather than rescuing us
from our isolated position as distinct individuals, sympathy reproduces our isolation by offering us a vision of unity while simultaneously confirming the
impossibility of its attainment. It is just this tension between union and alienation that provides the dramatic—and pedagogical—conflicts in Brown's *The
Power of Sympathy*.

As I have attempted to outline it here, the working out of sociopolitical anxieties in a newly configured domestic context is part of that sentimental structure of feeling in postrevolutionary America devoted to unifying public and
private demands and to liberating the concept of authority from its burden-
some past. The early American novel cannot be understood apart from the
sentimental ideology out of which it arises or from eighteenth-century theories
of interpersonal dynamics of which sentimentalism forms a core. Philosophers
as diverse as John Locke, Francis Hutcheson, and Thomas Paine theorized
and deployed models of sympathy in order to explain and create affective interactions between individuals.[17] Sympathy, as both felt emotion and cognitive
process, became the mode by which familial, social, and even national bonds
were reinforced; it represented the affective foundation of democratic society.
Participating in the sentimental equation of family and country, Paine's
Common Sense translates the act of "revolution against patriarchal authority"[18]
into an act of supreme filial loyalty. As a catalyst to momentous political

(dis)union, *Common Sense* reveals the double-edged nature of all acts of sympathy, thus providing a fitting introduction to the first American novel that devotes itself to tracing sympathy's tragic implications.

The Metapolitics of *Common Sense*

Relationships between pedagogy, parenting, and politics in the seventeenth and eighteenth centuries are difficult to untangle. As Enlightenment thinkers strove to identify and articulate differences between private and public allegiances, "patriarchal" political authority came under increasing attack. The notion that a political ruler served with a father's rights put the domestic sphere under civil jurisdiction and implied a natural lifelong commitment on the part of citizens to their sovereign. Yet, as liberal theorists pleaded the often conflicting interests of political and personal obligations, patriarchal authority in the domestic sphere came under scrutiny as well.[19] One of the effects of the separation of political from domestic governments was the greater responsibility imagined falling to parents, those domestic advisers who were warned, ironically, not to act like political tyrants. Thus, in *Some Thoughts Concerning Education* (1693), Locke argues that filial relations should be based on esteem rather than coercion, and that fathers should not only practice what they preach, but preach in love, inspiring affectionate devotion rather than fearful obedience. Locke opens his treatise by declaring that "men's happiness or misery is most part of their own making," and goes on to cite education as the chief reason "all the men we meet with . . . are what they are":

> It is [education] which makes the great difference in mankind. The little, or almost insensible, impressions on our tender infancies, have very important and lasting consequences: and there it is, as in the fountains of some rivers, where a gentle application of the hand turns the flexible waters into channels, that make them take quite contrary courses; and by this little direction, given them at first, in the source, they receive different tendencies, and arrive at last at very remote and distant places.[20]

It is clear from Locke's analogy that an effective early education consists not of the abstract lessons of a disinterested party but of the *personal touch* of an interested one: that is, only the "gentle" hand of the parent can adequately turn the tide of childish inclination.

The "power of a magistrate over a subject" may be qualitatively different from the power of a "father over his children," but parental power exists nonetheless. And that power is made all the stronger if the attachment is made early, with both force and consistency. Locke therefore charges parents "to establish the authority of a father, as soon as [the child] is capable of sub-mission, and can understand in whose power he is." However, as the child grows older, "fear and awe" ought to give way to "love and friendship"; "for the time must come," writes Locke, "when they will be past the rod and cor-rection; and then, if the love of you make them not obedient and dutiful; if the love of virtue and reputation keep them not in laudable courses . . . what hold will you have upon them, to turn them to it?" (33, 34–35). For Locke, love is its own discipline: the very familiarity of authority renders it ultimately indistinguishable from the child's character: "Every man must some time or other be trusted to himself, and his own conduct; and he that is a good, a vir-tuous, and able man, must be made so within. And, therefore, what he is to receive from education, what is to sway and influence his life, must be some-thing put into him betimes: habits woven into the very principles of his nature" (35).

As the last line suggests, Locke saw virtue as a matter of habit, reasonable actions made familiar in youth and continued in adulthood. This rationalist approach to virtue and principle was challenged in the eighteenth century by such Scottish Common Sense philosophers as Francis Hutcheson, who held that while the five senses may lead one to reason it is the sixth, the *moral* sense, that determines one's ability to act in another's best interest.[21] Thus, in section 2 of *An Inquiry Into the Original of Our Ideas of Beauty and Virtue* (1725), Hutcheson refutes the Lockean idea that virtue springs "from Self-love, or Desire of private Interest," for as soon as self-interest is involved, Hutcheson claims, action "loses all appearance of Benevolence."[22] It is therefore impor-tant to distinguish between moral and natural good, the latter being that which is to one's advantage but considered good only for that reason. Moral sense, by contrast, approves or disapproves of an action, sentiment, or character based on its intrinsic worth, not on its relative worth to the individual perceiver. According to Hutcheson, the problem with measuring goodness in terms of personal advantage is that it ignores the crucial distinction between material and immaterial pleasures and confuses self-interest with love:

> Had we no Sense of Good distinct from the Advantage or Interest arising from the external Senses, and the Perceptions of Beauty and Harmony; our Admiration and Love toward a fruitful Field or commodious Habitation, would be much the same with what we have toward a generous Friend, or any noble Character; for both are, or may be advantangeous to us: And we should no more admire any Action, or love any Person in a distant Country, or Age, whose Influence could not extend to us, than we love the Mountains of Peru, while we are unconcern'd in the Spanish Trade. (107)

Hutcheson juxtaposes commercial and interpersonal investments here in order to resist a commodification of "personal regard." Elsewhere Hutcheson makes a similar move by contrasting the joys and sorrows of parenthood with the gains and losses of "several Merchants join'd in Partnership," asking if such an investment is of the same kind as "that of Parents [and] their Children" and replying with the rhetorical quip "I fancy no Parent will say so" (145).

What is at stake for Hutcheson in differentiating between commercial and family models of shared experience is, paradoxically, the integrity of the larger community. That is, whereas cooperative ventures in business tend to reinforce one's inclination toward self-interest, filial love encourages that disinterested benevolence which will allow individuals to forego their private interests (including family interests) for the good of the whole. For Hutcheson as well as for Locke, then, it is filial attachment that makes social structures possible.[23] The "reciprocal sympathy"[24] between parent and child, which in Locke's view fosters a healthy, even loving regard for authority, provides for Hutcheson the theoretical lens through which one may imagine "weaker degrees of Love[,] where there is no tie of Parentage . . . extend[ed] to all Mankind" (146). Contracting his field of vision from the world at large to one's country in particular, Hutcheson ends the section by positing that it is in fact familiarity that forms the basis of "national Love." Since one's "Friendships, Familys, natural Affections, and other humane Sentiments" are associated with the "Buildings, Fields and Woods where [one] receiv'd them," it is inevitable that the "dear Idea of a COUNTRY" should become inseparable from the loving attachments first cultivated in that land (148).

As Hutcheson's connection between filial and national love suggests, familiar attachments form the basis not only of social ties but of political ties as well. Perhaps nowhere are the political implications of the family bond given greater scope during this period than in Thomas Paine's remarkably influential treatise supporting American independence, *Common Sense*. Paine makes both implicit and explicit connections between the integrity of the home and of the nation, juxtaposing the selfish private interest of a British monarchy with the honorable, socially responsible interests of Colonial families and arguing for political affiliation based on shared investments, both economic and emotional.[25]

The third section of the treatise, "Thoughts on the Present State of American Affairs," opens with the first allusion to the pamphlet's title:

> In the following pages I offer nothing more than simple facts, plain arguments, and common sense; and have no other preliminaries to settle with

the reader, than that he will divest himself of prejudice and prepossession, and suffer his reason and his feelings to determine for themselves; that he will put *on*, or rather that he will not put *off*, the true character of a man, and generously enlarge his views beyond the present day.[26]

In his recourse to "plain arguments" and "simple facts," Paine suggests that one need not be a member of the educated elite to possess the kind of sensibility that apprehends a danger to one's interests.[27] The phrase "common sense" reinforces this idea, alluding as it does to a system of moral philosophy predicated on the assumption of a common human nature.[28] Whether that common human sense be located in reason, as it is in Locke's philosophy, or in feeling, as it is in Hutcheson's, the implication remains that there exists a natural, universal "character of man" to which Paine may appeal. This "true character" will lead men in a common cause of separation from England, a cause that subsumes both reason and feeling under the greater rubric of nature, whose "weeping voice" echoes the "blood of the slain" to cry, " 'TIS TIME TO PART" (83).

The connection between nature and blood in this quotation reveals the paradox inherent in the concept of common sense as both universal and exclusionary. While the reference to blood reinforces the idea of commonality by reducing it to its most fundamental element, the specificity of the blood referred to—that of the "slain"—denotes natural but selective ties of kinship. Thus, for Paine, the shedding of blood on the battlefield at Lexington marks the decisive moment in Anglo-American affairs: after this battle, a "new era of politics" arises, one that reconceives the relationship between Britain and America as economically and not sentimentally based. Paine asserts that Britain's motive in protecting America from foreign invaders was always "*interest* not *attachment*": "She did not protect us from *our enemies* on *our account*, but from *her enemies* on *her own account*." To cling to the notion that England is America's "parent country," then, only heaps "more shame upon [England's] conduct," for "[e]ven brutes do not devour their young, nor savages make war upon their families" (81). By debunking the myth of a filial and thus reciprocal relationship between Britain and America, Paine redraws the boundaries between "foreign" and "domestic," between those interested parties who are allies, those who are enemies, and those who are family. Britain may have been the first and may become the second, but it never was the third. As further evidence, Paine refers readers to simple geography: "Even the distance at which the Almighty hath placed England and America, is a strong and natural proof, that the authority of the one, over the other, was never the design of Heaven" (83).

The physical distance between the two continents allows Paine to articulate the battle at Lexington in terms of an invasion rather than a civil war and thus to further encourage a geographic narrowing of obligation. The fact that it is *American* property that is threatened in the ongoing conflict provides tangible evidence of national difference. Such evidence must result in a change of sentiments, regardless of one's previous political position:

> But if you say, you can still pass the violations over, then I ask, Hath your house been burnt? Hath your property been destroyed before your face? Are your wife and children destitute of a bed to lie on, or bread to live on? Have you lost a parent or a child by their hands, and yourself the ruined and wretched survivor? *If you have not, then are you not a judge of those who have. But if you have, and can still shake hands with the murderers, then are you unworthy the name of husband, father, friend, or lover*, and whatever may be your rank or title in life, you have the heart of a coward, and the spirit of a sycophant. (85, emphasis mine)

In a provocative union of interest and attachment, Paine equates the economic loss of one's house with the emotional devastation of loss of family. Such loss must be felt by those whose homes have been destroyed; those who have not experienced this loss, however, are forced to sympathize or be silent.

Paine's rhetoric proposes sympathy as the basis of democratic society: one must be able to put oneself in the other person's shoes in order to judge adequately that other's actions. At the same time, Paine delineates a hierarchy of suffering whereby a man's personal losses place him beyond such judgment. According to Paine's law of sympathy, no one may judge the responses catalyzed by suffering unless he himself has experienced such pain. Affective response becomes the measure of a man, in fact.[29] For Paine goes on to say that his purpose in putting the matter in such personal terms is not to "[provoke] revenge," but to "awaken" readers from their "fatal and unmanly slumbers." To this end, Paine is compelled to examine current events in the light of "those feelings and affections which nature justifies, and without which, we should be incapable of discharging the social duties of life" (85). Paine thus affirms that proper socialization begins at home and that to deny or suppress these familial feelings constitutes a breach not only of one's relative identities as "husband, father, friend, or lover" but also of one's essential identity and "character of a man."

In the midst of arguing the *difference* between economics and sentimentalism, then, Paine employs the rhetoric of filial loyalty in order to explain and justify the colonists' desire to protect (or expand) their economic interests. Such loyalty extends even to future generations: "As parents, we can have no joy, knowing that *this government* is not sufficiently lasting to ensure any thing which we may bequeath to posterity . . . as we are running the next generation into debt, we ought to do the work of it" (84). The British "family of kings" is to be superseded by the authentic American family, whose economic ties are legitimated by the sentimental attachments those ties inspire. "Nature hath deserted the connection" between England and America, writes Paine, "and Art cannot supply her place." Rather than continue with a *fiction* of the family, therefore, "let us come to a final separation, and not leave the next generation to be cutting throats, under the violated unmeaning names of parent and child" (86).

In the decade after *Common Sense* was published, the first American fiction of the family made its mark on the imaginations of American readers. *The Power of Sympathy* continues Paine's campaign for domestic attachment, offering as it does a national "domestic" literature that brings the issue of attachment to a dramatic conclusion. On the surface, William Hill Brown's novel gives us a moral cautionary tale in which, in Brown's own words, "the dangerous consequences of seduction are exposed, and the advantages of female education set forth and recommended."[30] The father's seduction and abandonment of a young woman become the story of corruption and deceit whose impression cannot be wiped clean from the slate of either personal or national history. What becomes clear in the course of reading Brown's tale, however, is the novel's complicity in sentimental arrangements of influence. *The Power of Sympathy* focuses on the emotional and psychological dynamics between individual characters and then attempts to recreate that powerful dynamic in the reading experience. The "power of sympathy" thus denotes more than the natural sentiments blood kinship calls forth: it alludes to the pedagogical model by which sentimental literature claims its own authority over the hearts and bodies of its readers.

The Erotics of Common Sense: *The Power of Sympathy*

Paine's revolutionary pamphlet demonstrates the ways in which sympathy may be used to undo previously accepted obligations even as it creates or reinforces others. This ability was in fact one of the most serious charges leveled against the early sentimental novel. Contemporary critics of the early novel believed that, regardless of the author's intentions, the power of sympathetic attachment might provoke uncontrolled and unreasoned responses on the part of readers.[31] In Brown's novel of seduction, the unpredictability of influence is itself made the central focus of the narrative. In effect, *The Power of Sympathy*, *or The Triumph of Nature* eroticizes the concept of common sense, revealing the power of Nature to be not only sentimental but sexual as well. Such a revelation calls into question the reader's own responses to the story—his or her ability to resist narrative seduction.[32] It also challenges the kind of family dynamic espoused by Paine and others: in Brown's narrative, familial bonding becomes the forbidden impulse one must resist. While it is true that Brown's novel fails to adequately theorize its own assumptions and conclusions regarding sentimental influence, this failure only serves to underscore critics' concerns over the kinds of models being offered to the public. As itself a model of American sentimental literature, *The Power of Sympathy* represents the complex and often involuntary mechanisms at work in negotiating external and internal authority, mechanisms that sympathy itself simultaneously exposes and imposes.

The main line of Brown's story involves a wealthy young man and a financially dependent woman, Harrington and Harriot, who meet, are drawn to each other, and fall in love. The hero eventually opts for marriage to, rather than seduction of, the apparently orphaned woman he loves, only to find out before their wedding day that they are half-brother and sister. Not an orphan at all, Harriot is the senior Harrington's illegitimate daughter, the result of his earlier seduction of an impressionable and unconnected young woman. The revelation of their sibling relationship dampens the lovers' spirits but does nothing to dry up their desire. By the end of the novel, scandal is abroad, families are torn apart, and three out of the four principal players are dead. Harriot, unable to overcome either her passion for her brother or the social restrictions of her culture, succumbs to depression and dies, while Harrington, in a rather conventional turn of revolutionary ardor, claims his "independence" through suicide.

Mr. Harrington's seduction of Harriot's mother, Maria, provides the discernible cause for the tragedy that follows. Supporting this reading is the subplot of Brown's novel in which a father's refusal to forgive his daughter's "incestuous" relationship with her brother-in-law leads to her suicide.[33] Both plots demonstrate that the consequences of paternal error are not to be taken lightly. But the threat to individual liberty goes beyond mere human frailty. For instance, when Mr. Harrington discovers that his two children are engaged, he immediately rejects reason's ability to explain the event: "But how shall we be able—how shall we pretend to investigate the great springs by which we are actuated or account for the operation of sympathy. My son . . . has accidentally seen her and, to complete the triumph of nature, has loved her" (102). In its eighteenth-century context, sympathy connotes identification: not feeling for a person from a distance, but feeling *with* or *alongside* of a person. According to Brown's novel, such a blurring of ego boundaries is Nature (including and subsuming human nature) in full force. At first the younger Harrington tries to deny this fact by claiming that, had he known Harriot was his sister, he would have loved her as such. But in the next letter to his friend Worthy he asks if it were possible for him *ever* to live with Harriot in this world, answering, "Ah no! it never would *here*—it *never* would. I will fly to the place where she is gone. Our love will there be refined—it will be freed from all criminality" (118). Harrington envisions his love being freed not from passion but from the censure that passion invites; the "natural," then, describes a force that overrules convention. Nature itself is finally offered as the author of Harrington and Harriot's misfortune, calling into question the power of human reason and resolution ever to overcome the power of sympathy.

Brown's emphasis on the power of filial sympathy subordinates free will to kinship, or the "voice of blood."[34] In the late eighteenth-century debate between heredity and humanism, *The Power of Sympathy* vacillates between older notions of destiny and contemporary republican standards of moral culpability. This appears in a modified form in nineteenth-century novels as well, but in these narratives the "brother" and "sister" are invariably not related by blood. Sibling attraction thus reflects an ideal rather than a taboo. In the reconstructed family, attraction is based on emotional rather than genetic familiarity: the hero and heroine have grown up together and have a common background. The fact that they are not physically related to each other makes their attachment both satisfying and suitable. Harriot and Harrington, by contrast, have not grown up together. They do not even lay eyes on each other until they are of marrying age, and, when they do meet, the attraction is instant and irrevocable: neither can modify personal feeling to the demands of the situation. At a time when the rhetoric of liberty, rights, and independence still echoes in the ears of most Americans, *The Power of Sympathy* speaks for the "voice of blood," a voice that carries with it an implicit critique of the promise of freedom. It suggests that, because we cannot choose to whom we are related, we can't choose whom we love. We are destined to be attracted to those with whom we share a common parentage.

The relationship between Harrington and Harriot represents the fantasy of complete identification that must be terminated because it has no place in this world. But, despite the outcome, it is the fantasy that drives the plot and finally effects the reader's "education," lessons that can only be taught by and through the operations of sympathy. The epistemological problem posed by sympathy is addressed by Adam Smith, who in *The Theory of Moral Sentiments* asserts that "our senses will never inform us of what [another] suffers. They never did, and never can, carry us beyond our own person." In what could pass for an endorsement of the power of fiction, Smith adds that "it is by the imagination only that we can form any conception of what are [another person's] sensations"; it is by the imagination only, in other words, that we experience sympathy. The power of sympathy notwithstanding, it is clear that, for Smith, even the imagination cannot make what is another's completely our own, for it can only "[represent] to us what would be our own [sensations], if we were in his case. It is the impressions of our own senses only, not those of his, which our imaginations copy" (8).[35]

As if this secondary sense of alienation were not enough, Smith theorizes a primary alienation from *oneself*, the result of a kind of "mirror of sympathy," in David Marshall's words, whereby initial sufferers become "spectators to [their] spectators and thereby spectators to [themselves]."[36] Putting himself in the position of the observer, the sufferer acts as observer to himself, becoming at once both spectator and spectacle. This sense of alienation is for Smith the greatest affliction, just as the strongest desire is not a relief *from* pain but *for* a "more complete sympathy. [The sufferer] longs for that relief which nothing can afford him but the entire concord of the affections of the spectators with his own" (22). Of course, this is exactly what the experience of sympathy has taught him he cannot have.

For Smith, sympathetic identification is a relational dynamic. Total identification with the other person might extinguish sympathy altogether since sympathy operates by a simultaneous awareness of separateness and inclination to overcome it.[37] Therefore Harrington and Harriot, though connected down to the roots of their names, cannot be read as gendered halves of a single being. Their distinct identities and physical kinship work together and against each other to keep perspectives (and passions) constantly in flux. This is perhaps made clearest in Harriot's final letter to Harrington, in which she wrestles with their relative positions:

> Allied by birth, and in mind, and similar in age—and in thought still more intimately connected—the sympathy which bound our souls together at first sight is less extraordinary. Shall we any longer wonder at its irresistible impulse? Shall we strive to oppose the *link of nature* that draws us to each other? When I reflect on this, I relapse into weakness and tenderness and become a prey to warring passions. I view you in two distinct characters: if I indulge the idea of one, the other becomes annihilated; and I vainly imagine I have my choice of a brother or—(112).

As sympathy makes the sufferer aware of her own predicament through the eyes of the other, thus doubling her subject position, so it forces Harriot here to double her perception of the other with whom she identifies. But not only does she read Harrington as both brother and lover, she multiplies her experience as spectator as well—she must read her own pain through the eyes of one who feels the same pain himself and who calls up *her* sympathy even in the act of imagining his. Suffering is thus compounded rather than alleviated by the double mirroring of sympathy that causes each character to experience the tragedy twofold.

From Smith's analysis it would appear that sympathy doesn't just fail to bridge the gap between psyches, it forces recognition of that gap in the very attempt to traverse it. Harrington and Harriot thus become victims of a desire heretofore unexpressed because unknown until the moment its potential fulfillment faces them in each other. Once aware of their desire, Harrington and Harriot are unable or unwilling to return to their previous condition as autonomous beings. And it is in this that the story's true rebellion lies. Threatening to eschew social and moral strictures in order to embrace her ideal attachment, Harriot declares, "I see the danger and do not wish to shun it, because to avoid it is to forget it" (111). Although Harriot's death is inevitable—a novel predicated on "exposing vice" cannot countenance incest—it also short-circuits the obligatory conversion of erotic into fraternal sympathy, a conversion Harriot sees as tantamount to "forgetting" sympathy itself. In a like spirit, Harrington announces his decision to take his life despite the social censure it may incur: "As to the world . . . I despise its opinion. *Independency of spirits* is my motto—I think for myself" (121). Given the attachment that prompts his decision, this is an ironic declaration indeed. What these examples suggest is that sympathy results not in a loss of self but in a dynamic interchange between senses of self and other.

A similar dynamic is played out between characters and readers as well. Applying his theory of sympathy to the reading experience, Smith observes that through "imagination we become the very person whose actions are represented to us: we transport ourselves in fancy to the scenes of those distant and forgotten adventures" (75).[38] This sympathetic process of identification is just the method by which Brown's pedagogy is put into practice.[39] Since the novel of seduction works by negative example, readers must be willing to put themselves in the character's position in order to experience the full effects of the punishment meted out. What happens, then, when the desire to identify leads the reader astray? How are the effects of sympathy to be discarded once the impulse has been indulged? Although Harrington and Harriot are not finally joined in *earthly* union at the end of the novel, the high drama and emotional intensity with which their separation and eventual deaths are expressed serves to idealize their attachment rather than critique it. Their deaths therefore do less to register a moral warning with readers than to secure the fantasy of a "complete sympathy" that Smith both imagined and discounted. Put another way, the lure of sympathetic identification is reproduced rather than annulled in the experience of reading their story. This might not appear so disturbing if the outcome weren't so tragic or if Brown's novel did not contain within it a striking example of just how seductively influential narrative models can be.

The portrayal of a father's sexual transgression and its unfortunate consequences in *The Power of Sympathy* makes tangible the problem of paternal influence in postrevolutionary politics. It also serves as a catalyst for the translation of paternal into narrative authority: Mr. Harrington's failure as moral exemplum to his children becomes the exemplum of the novel. As Fliegelman observes more generally, "Literature could play the exemplary role parents were obliged, but often failed, to fill. It could educate as well as corrupt."[40] What remains in question is just how clearly the line is drawn between education and corruption. If the power of sympathy cannot be contained within the novel's plot, there is little reason to assume that its readers, swayed by the sympathetic impulse, will be any more circumspect. *The Power of Sympathy* illustrates this conclusion in the final pages of its story.

   After learning of Harriot's death, Harrington resolves to join her where their love "will be freed from all criminality." His choice of suicide is not prompted solely by his love for Harriot, however; it is also informed by the narrative he has been reading just before his death. When Worthy finds his friend's body, on the table beside Harrington lies—perhaps predictably—a copy of Goethe's *The Sorrows of Young Werther*.[41] That Harrington felt himself a kindred spirit to Goethe's hero is evidenced by the language and reasoning of Harrington's last letter, which closely follows Werther's own justification for suicide. Werther takes his life for the sake of a woman he can never possess, for in death, reasons Werther, lies the fulfillment of his dream: "From this moment you are wholly mine: I go to my Father, to thy Father, I shall carry my sorrows to the feet of his throne and he will give me comfort until you arrive. Then will I fly to meet you, I will embrace you, and remain with you forever in the presence of the Almighty."[42] In like spirit, Harrington's final letter asserts that surely the "Eternal Father" will "let the tears of sorrow blot out [Harrington's] guilt from the book of [God's] wrath." In their lives, he and Harriot "loved, but were unhappy—in death they sleep undivided" (127–128).

Just as the congruity of language and idea between Harrington's and Werther's last letters indicate a sympathetic connection between the two, so the juxtaposition of Harrington's body and Goethe's novel epitomizes the intimate relation between reader and text. In the final moments before his death, Harrington becomes a model reader, reading himself into the narrative and making the story his own. His suicide attests not only to the power of sympathy but the power of fiction as well. As if to underscore the point, after his death Harrington serves as a sight for sympathetic eyes to observe and interpret: "Great numbers crowded to see the body of poor Harrington; they were impressed with various emotions, for their sympathizing sorrow could not be concealed" (128). Although the spectators acknowledge the young man's error, they attribute Harrington's intemperate action to his "genius," which inflamed his "violent passions" and "too nice sensibility." In the end they cannot condemn him, for, knowing his history, they know that he was the "dupe of nature, and the sacrifice of seduction" (128).

As Werther serves as a model for Harrington, so the fictional readers of Harrington's body and story serve as a possible model for sentimental readers. While the onlookers' "sympathizing sorrow" grants them humanity, their critical distance and judgment afford them a safe position outside of the emotional fray. Yet the latter condition undercuts the former, since, by the terms in which we have been examining it, sympathy requires identification with the sufferer. As Marshall points out, "If the spectators withhold sympathy, they remain spectators. If they grant sympathy—if they enter into the sentiments of the person they are beholding, if they become in some measure the same person as him, identify themselves with him through a transfer of persons and characters—then they stop being spectators."[43] The very scene in which the reader reads the spectators viewing Harrington's body bespeaks the spectacle that Harrington has become. If sympathy is to do its office, the reader must resist identifying with the onlookers, must resist becoming a spectator to the theatricality of this final scene. To fail to do so is to turn the hero into nothing but a corpse. It is also to have failed in the final lessons of sympathy, lessons that teach that the extent to which one is willing to be a spectator is the extent to which one must imagine oneself a spectacle. When read in this light, the novel's attempts to mitigate the effects of sympathetic identification, both in the early lectures on novel reading and in the final scene of judgment, appears disingenuous, as does the final line of the poem that concludes Brown's novel: "May you never love as these have loved" is a wish made in vain on behalf of eighteenth-century readers. According to the lessons of sentimental education, they already have.

The Man Within the Breast

Ironically, it is as parental substitute that *The Power of Sympathy* reveals the difficulty of transcending familial models: by authorizing its own sympathetic identification between reader and protagonist(s), Brown's novel reproduces the attachment first authored by the father. As my examination of Common Sense philosophy has shown, this sympathetic attachment forms the basis of sentimental politics. In an ideal republic, government functions as an extension of the people's desires. The question of whether or not autonomy can ever be achieved—whether the son, or the nation, can ever outgrow the father's influence—is rendered moot once the subject's private voice is perceived as speaking the same language as the public voice of authority.

This negotiation of public and private authority, of community and individual rights and privileges, lies behind the metaphor I have been examining. "Fatherhood," for all its negative as well as positive connotations, implies a bond of the blood. Yet, as Paine has argued, more important even than biological ties is the emotional investment that legitimates them. This is substantiated in the novel by Harriot, who, never having been able to claim kin with her own father, attempts to convert into a father that person for whom she feels the greatest affinity: "Come, O Harrington! be a friend, a protector, a brother—be him on whom I could never yet call by the tender, the endearing title of *parent*. . . . I will be dutiful and affectionate to you, and you shalt be unto me as a father" (112). In a final effort to construct a family, Harriot participates in the sentimentalization of authority to which common sense has led her. In doing so, however, she reenacts the drama she is seeking to revise. By conflating the junior and senior Harringtons, Harriot eroticizes the father through the would-be lover who represents him. For Harriot, as for the novel of which she is a part, there is no solution to the dilemma of domesticated desire: the very attempt to turn the forbidden into the familiar leads back to incest.

In keeping with the age, *The Power of Sympathy* strives to personalize authority—to bring it back home, as it were. As the novel ultimately reveals, however, what constitutes domestic space is a matter of perspective. Shifting boundaries between the familial, the political, and the individual body confuse the very categories they are meant to protect and bring paternalism and eroticism together under one roof. This confirms as well the relational dynamic inherent in constructing categories of identity. Again, Smith's spectacular theory of morality helps illustrate this point. Claiming that through the mirror of sympathy, through "the eyes of other people," we can "scrutinize the propriety of our own conduct," Smith turns the individual into his own judge, his own internal and, by extension, his own external monitor, housed in a single psyche. Smith's "man within the breast"—that "ideal spectator" and "arbiter of conscience"—effectively renounces the need for an external authority even as it underscores the relational matrix at the center of identity.[44]

The Power of Sympathy not only depicts such a matrix, it attempts to generate it. According to Smith, the "lesson of self command" is learned through mediated experience. Literature, and sentimental literature in particular, provides such mediation, allowing the reader to examine him- or herself and, in the reading experience, to take authority to heart. After this fashion, Harrington, in a last letter before his death, claims he can read the end of his life in the work before him: "I just opened a book, and these are the words that I read: 'The time of my fading is near, and the blast that shall scatter my leaves. Tomorrow shall the traveller come, he that saw me in my beauty shall come; his eyes will search the field, but they will not find me.' These words pierce me to the quick—they are a dismal prospect of my approaching fate" (124). We are to conclude from Harrington's interpretation of this event that literature does not coerce the reader into an unwanted act but confirms to the reader what the heart already knows. It is a subtle difference, but a significant one. The work of the sentimental novel of seduction is to educate the heart, but, when the work is done, one can rarely distinguish between the operations of the heart and the operations of influence. But, then, this is where seduction truly begins.

3

Seductive Education and the Virtues of the Republic

Midway through a protracted debate on the merits of narrative education, William Hill Brown's *The Power of Sympathy, or The Triumph of Nature* offers the following pithy comment by a discerning mother: "I conclude from your reasoning," said Mrs. Holmes, "and it is besides, my own opinion that many fine girls have been ruined by reading novels" (46). Implicit in her remark is the idea that all novels are not created equal. This was certainly the view of many critics troubled about the negative influence literary works might exert over their readers, but it was also the concern of novelists themselves. Such novelists went to great lengths to ensure that readers learned to discriminate between those dangerous romances that filled young women with fanciful notions about the future and their own "realistic" tales offering women valuable insights into the characters of men. Lessons of the first kind were considered seductive; lessons of the second were called education. The distinction between the harmful and the edifying is not necessarily an easy one to draw: in general, supporters of the early novel believed that the function of art—including fiction—was not to suppress but to arouse readers' emotions, because through their emotions an audience would be awakened to truths that logic alone could not impart.[1] The difference between education and seduction lay not in pedagogical practice, nor even in affective response, but in practical consequence—that is, how the organization of emotional stimuli caused an individual to *act*. Seduction could be distinguished from education only after the fact, depending on whether the protagonist—or reader—was led aright or astray (a determination itself subject to interpretation). Given these circumstances, it is no wonder that an author like Brown felt the need to include in the preface, the frontispiece, and even the body of his novel dedications to and examples of the "advantages of female education" and the "dangerous consequences of seduction." His success at anticipating and encoding reader response could well be all that distinguished his tuition from the lessons that had ruined many a fine girl.

Sentimental frameworks reinforce the congruity between education and seduction. The evocation of feeling becomes its own instrument of discipline, as readers' sympathies are employed in the service of modifying readers' behavior. As Brown's reference to "female education" indicates, sentimental pedagogy is gender-inflected. While the typical gentleman was schooled in situational discourse that allowed him to view the verbal arts as a means to an end, women and the middling and lower classes were specifically taught to accept their positions and to internalize rather than manipulate the information given them. The difference between these pedagogical premises can be said to reflect not only the difference between men and women, or the upper and lower classes, but the difference between performers of language and responders to it, that is, between seducers and seduced. Although educational experiences were necessarily different for women than for men, the designation of a specifically "female" education is somewhat misleading. For, in the novel of seduction, "female education" signifies the coding of the reader—whether female or male—as feminine and therefore as an appropriately affective respondent to the novel's rhetorical designs.

This chapter looks at some of the ways in which constructions of gender, marriage, patriotism, and especially education "seduce" audiences into intimate relationship with patriarchal authority after the Revolution. My readings suggest that sentimental literature and politics encourage a heteroerotic construction of the body politic, whereby both ideal readers and citizens are imagined as suggestible women—specifically, as the wives and daughters of a democratic paternalism. Articulating the popular connection between female and national bodies, John Adams compared the American people to a seducible young woman, tempted by the trappings of wealth and the promise of freedom: "Democracy is Lovelace, and the people are Clarissa." In Adams's Federalist view, democracy was itself the vehicle of seduction, and the republican Fathers the people's only means of securing liberty. Jefferson, by contrast, saw democracy and republicanism as conjoined in one sure system of fair and impartial representation. But he, too, imagined such representation as built upon a family model. For Jefferson, those individuals not otherwise considered citizens—those who could not vote—were given a voice and an interest in national affairs by a patriarchal system of democractic representation. Thus, although the Federalist and Democrat-Republican parties viewed democracy differently—one as seductive evil and the other as liberal champion—each agreed that the method of combating or instituting democracy was through a politics of paternalism.

Somewhat paradoxically, the overarching framework for early republican's politics of paternalism is marriage. As Tony Tanner has argued, narratives of personal private love often lay the ideological groundwork for stabilizing public political relations.[2] In the republican period, marriage stands as the political and ideological symbol of virtue and unity in a culture potentially coming apart at the seams. As Joseph Boone notes, marriage represents both an ideological tool and a symbol of the ways in which ideology operates. "Ideological structures work to create the appearance of a unitary, coherent worldview by eliding the multiple social contradictions . . . that would challenge their dominance and power," writes Boone; "as the construct of experience through which the individual perceives the world, ideology . . . tightens its grip on its subjects by representing its system of beliefs and ideas as *natural*, as necessary."[3] In the postrevolutionary period, marriage represents one of the foremost of these natural systems. "In the republic envisioned by American writers," observes historian Jan Lewis, "citizens were to be bound together not by patriarchy's duty or liberalism's self-interest, but by affection, and it was, they believed, marriage, more than any other institution that trained citizens in this virtue."[4] What becomes clear in the readings that follow is how marriage and paternalism intersect: in American fiction, husbands and fathers become inextricably connected, resulting in an ethos of seductive paternalism that characterizes republican culture.

If marriage and virtue represent the ideal in social relations, seduction, as the antithesis of both, constitutes a breach of republican ethics and the subversion of national identity. Yet what remains unspoken in this equation is the extent to which the seduction model informs republican politics. Although the postrevolutionary era is replete with novels of seduction, seduction is evoked in order to *contrast* with the ideal union that the presence of seduction threatens to undo. Critics from the eighteenth through the twentieth centuries have been invested in just this enterprise of differentiation. Rather than look at the differences between seduction and marriage, however, I propose we examine how intimately related the two actually are. In order to understand more fully the effects of sentimental literature, we must first acknowledge the ways in which seductive practices inform domestic models. When we do so, we see that Adams's allusion to *Clarissa* not only confirms the potentially fatal effects of poor political choices but perfectly exemplifies sentimental literature's role in republican education: the novel of seduction expresses and informs the ways in which "the people" are taught to think about themselves, their choices, and their futures. Signifying as it does the fluid boundaries between coercion and consent, or free will and influence, seduction offers the ideal metaphor for wedding republican discipline with the liberal belief in personal independence. While ostensibly representing the perversion of republican virtue, "seduction" actually signifies the sentimental operations by which patriarchal politics gains access to the national body.

Conventional Rebellions

As the previous chapter argued, "fatherhood" had become a contested site of power in seventeenth- and eighteenth-century Anglo politics. The question for postrevolutionary America was how to redeem the image of the "father"— the educated Anglo male—while preserving liberal and revolutionary ideals of equality and independence. One answer was to locate those ideals in the very figure who threatened to compromise them. Mason Weems's *The Life of Washington* (1800) participates in the reconstruction of patriarchal authority by offering a paternal figure whose life is made to represent the renunciation of English history and the inauguration of a new American epic. George Washington represents the quintessential American: a gentleman farmer with the will of a revolutionary hero and the heart to become the "father" of his country. The significance of fatherhood is made clear throughout the narrative. Weems's apocryphal accounts of Washington's boyhood—his fab- ricated but now legendary anecdote of George's chopping down the cherry tree, for instance—stress the crucial role Washington's father played in the son's formation as a moral man and citizen. Moreover, Weems represents Washington's service to his country, in military and political arenas, as a mat- ter of paternal instinct devoted to "carefully guarding and preserving the union."[5] Washington's altruism and sense of honor earned him the love of soldiers and citizens alike, so that his voice "sounded in their ear as the voice of a father" (119). In this popular account of the nation's honeymoon period, Weems makes clear that the model American is not a radical out to overturn the principles of just authority but a conservative committed to reestablishing them. There will be no need to rebel against *this* father.

What is perhaps most compelling about Weems's biography is the private life he invents for this very public figure. Although his readers have heard the elegant orations, claims Weems, they have seen "nothing of Washington below *the clouds*—nothing of Washington the *dutiful son*—the affectionate

brother—the cheerful school-boy," etc. (3). Weems subscribes to the sentimental politics of the time, which subordinates the public image to the
authenticity of the private self—the "real" self—that either bears out the image
or belies it:

> It is not then in the glare of *public*, but in the shade of *private life*, that we
> are to look for the man. Private life is always *real* life. Behind the curtain,
> where the eyes of the million are not upon him, and where a man can have
> no motive but *inclination*, no excitement but *honest nature*, there he will
> always be sure to act *himself*; consequently, if he act greatly, he must be great
> indeed. Hence it has been justly said, that, "our *private deeds*, if *noble*, are
> noblest of our lives." (2)

Weems's construction of Washington's private virtues both confirms his wor-
thiness to be a public leader and satisfies readerly expectations for intimate
details in the rendering of literary character. Moreover, Weems's emphasis on
Washington's private deeds allows him to market his book as a model of the
democratic character as well as the democracy *of* character. He brings
Washington down to earth, where children of succeeding generations will be
able to reach and emulate him: "Give us his *private virtues*! In *these*, every
youth is interested, because in these every youth may become a Washington"
(5). Washington, "*Columbia's first* and *greatest Son*" (4), is exceptional, but
only in the way that *all* Americans may be exceptional, if only they would follow his humble example.

The *Life of Washington* represents a pattern in American literature whereby
acts of rebellion or revolution against the norm become the means by which
social standards are reestablished. Harrington, the protagonist of *The Power of
Sympathy*, provides another example of this phenomenon. Harrington's claim
that "*Independency of spirits* is my motto—I think for myself" clearly identifies
him as a democratic son of liberty. While his death nullifies the threat that his
autonomy poses, it also crystallizes his reputation as an independent spirit: he
has committed suicide in the tradition of romantic rebellion. However, as we
have seen, Harrington's susceptibility to literary influence—reading Goethe's
Werther before his death—actually undercuts the power and originality of his
final act in its indebtedness to an earlier model. In addition, although Goethe's
unconventional life allied him with social and sexual immorality in the minds
of most Anglo-American readers, Werther's romantic tragedy, which Brown
both alludes to and appropriates, was already a literary convention by this time.
Harrington's "Independency of spirits" must therefore be qualified, if not
made ironic, by his participation in a model already familiar to eighteenth-
century readers. As if Harrington's suicide were not sufficiently overdeter-

mined, Brown's final twist on the irony is to convert Harrington's act of ultimate independence into an opportunity for educating readers on their interpersonal responsibilities.[6]

Early American cautionary fiction typically features rebellious protagonists
whose abrogation of certain social codes reflects the revolutionary spirit of the
times. Readers' vicarious participation in these rebellions accounts for the cautionary tale's reputation as dangerously seductive.[7] At the same time, the dis-
mantling of an ostensibly outmoded patriarchal structure takes place coevally
with the establishment of a distinctly "American" character and nation; the latter circumstance requires that subversive impulses — themselves denoting
American freethinking — be contained in narrative plots that teach readers the
value of good citizenship. Thus one could say that while patriarchal authority
is superficially reinscribed into middle-class culture through the literary representation of free will, its position is crystallized through the representation
of free will as fatal.

What I am suggesting is that rebellion, exemplified in such unconventional
acts as seduction, infidelity, and incest, becomes itself a crucial part of the
American literary convention. The typical American novel of seduction follows a line of British literature devoted to the instruction of young people,
especially women, in proper manners and morals. Its most famous predeces-
sors, Samuel Richardson's *Pamela* (1740–1741) and *Clarissa* (1747–1748), set
the stage for investigating the moral implications of sensibility and the minute
particulars of both women's and men's psychological states. Although
Richardson's heroines are virtually innocent of wrongdoing, many seduction
stories feature protagonists who are complicit in their own destruction. The
result is a tale truly about seduction rather than coercion, abduction, or rape.
Along with *The Power of Sympathy*, works such as *Charlotte Temple* (1794),
The Coquette (1797), "Amelia" (1787), and *Wieland* (1798) foreground situations wherein the characters' own emotions or senses lead them astray. Read
along the lines of conventional education, these characters suffer the consequences of their own weaknesses; read in the spirit of seductive subversion,
they die from the strength of their passions.[8]

In the American seduction novel, personal autonomy is constantly challenged by the literary conventions designed to represent it. It is a concept alternately validated and undermined as not only physical but psychic boundaries
are assailed, penetrated, and reconfigured by influential sources who seek to
redefine the subject and what it stands for. While American protagonists may
appear all the more revolutionary for their sins, they rarely succeed in altering
the status quo; more often than not they are made to capitulate to it. As

Foucault would argue, the "authentic" self is shown not so much in contrast to convention as constructed by it. Protagonists ranging from Eliza Wharton to Hester Prynne to Edna Pontellier begin by weighing the primacy of their individual selves and desires against the mundane and conventional sentiments of their peers; they end by sacrificing their rebellious souls to forces greater than themselves.

The extent to which even twentieth-century literary critics contribute to translating scenes of seduction into forms of "female education" becomes apparent in a well-known essay by Sacvan Bercovitch on *The Scarlet Letter*. In "Hawthorne's A-Morality of Compromise," Bercovitch explains why the most rebellious heroine in American literature, Hester Prynne, must return to America at the end of the story to take up her letter. Hester relinquishes the privilege of self-construction (something Hawthorne never believed in anyway) in order to become, in Bercovitch's words, "an agent of social cohesion and continuity."[9] This, according to Bercovitch, is the pedagogical plan of Hawthorne's novel—to instruct readers in the art of "liberal consensus": "It is the office of *The Scarlet Letter* to teach us why this romantic heroine, who had turned being compromised into a source of uncompromising resistance, *must* now make compromise the work of culture" (346). How is this accomplished? It is achieved in true sentimental style, by dressing influence in the guise of interpretation:

> The silence surrounding Hester's final conversion to the letter is clearly deliberate on Hawthorne's part. It mystifies Hester's choice by forcing us to represent it through the act of interpretation. Having given us ample directives about how to understand the ways in which the letter had not done its office, Hawthorne now depends on us to recognize—freely and voluntarily, for his method depends on his seeming *not* to impose meaning (as in his remark that "the scarlet letter had not done its office")—the need for Hester's return. (356)

Although Bercovitch uses different terms, he is describing consensus arrived at through seductive measures, whereby readers are discouraged from distinguishing the difference between the author's politics—or will—and their own.

While Bercovitch recognizes Hawthorne's model as one that owes a debt to the "ambiguity universalized in the Declaration of Independence: 'We hold these truths to be *self*-evident,' " he insists that the problematics of such silencing mechanisms are necessary to "guide us toward accommodation" (356, 357). In fact, Bercovitch attempts to create his own consensus by conscripting not only nineteenth-century readers of literature but also twentieth century readers of literary criticism to the "self-evident" reading of Hester's reversal: "*My* purpose is to explain *our* complicity in Hester's return by exploring the historical ground and substance of her heroism of compromise" (346, emphasis mine). Hester's feminist rebellion, one that prompts Hawthorne to declare, "The scarlet letter had not done its office," allows Hawthorne to critique the conventions of Puritan (and antebellum) society while ultimately making stronger its claims once Hester is reintegrated into the community. If readers are sympathetic to Hester, as Bercovitch points out, they will be reintegrated as well. What is left out of this reading are the implications of a seductive education that buries not only its device but its disadvantages as well. What Bercovitch terms Hester's "choice" is qualified by her own, and Hawthorne's, inability to justify it. Choice, most clearly represented by Hester's internal revolution, is surrendered in the name of compromise, consensus and convention.

Joel Barlow's *Advice to the Privileged Orders in the Several States of Europe* (1792), as Gordon Wood reminds us, suggests that what separates the free from the oppressed is a "habit of thinking." When the majority of men believe that some are born to rule while others are born to follow, their government reflects this belief. What is deemed "natural," as Wood observes, is "*cultural nature*":

> It was custom, mental familiarity, culture, not force, that supported social gradations and distinctions, and even tyranny itself. . . . In the final analysis, concluded Barlow, it was the Americans' habit of thinking "*that all men are equal in their rights*" which had created their Revolution and sustained their freedom.[10]

Barlow's analysis suggests that revolution itself is a convention written into the script of early American culture, raising issues and questions about what is "natural" in political, familial, and social relationships. One could argue that what separated the oppressed from the free was equally a *habit of reading*.[11] And the lessons of early American literature do not always reflect the democratic optimism that Barlow identifies as constitutive of revolutionary American culture. Though early novels tend to validate the significance of human attachments—the feelings and affections that integrate one into a community, even if it is only a community of two—they also show the cost of those attachments to be the freedom to choose and the power to control them. The *habit of feeling*, as well as of thinking or reading, may impede as easily as facilitate one's journey to freedom.

The Art of Seduction: *The Crimes of Love* and *Wieland*

The eighteenth-century novel of seduction capitalizes on a cultural paradox, namely, the fetishization of "female innocence" that is itself held responsible for the woman's predicament. One proposed solution to the dilemma is the representation of patriarchy—in the form of government, husbands, and even pedagogical narratives—as protector of the innocent. But what happens when patriarchy itself becomes "corrupted"? When the protection offered turns seductive and potentially contaminating?[12] These questions reflect anxieties over the relationships between authority, intimacy, and influence: how, for instance, is one to distinguish between the seducer's and the author's craft? Moreover, what differentiates the father's from the seducer's loving persuasion?

Seduction fiction's influence was pervasive throughout the North Atlantic in the eighteenth century. One of the key figures both exploring and popularizing the genre was the Marquis de Sade. De Sade's *The Crimes of Love* (1800) makes explicit many of the implicit assumptions of standard seduction tales, and therefore serves as a useful counterpoint to this discussion. Writing in the wake of his own country's revolution, de Sade openly acknowledged the need for morality in the novel but criticized the facile way in which many novelists introduced morality into their tales. In *Reflections on the Novel* (*Idée sur les romans*), published as a preface to *Crimes de L'Amour*, de Sade offers his theories on the art of novel writing, the most essential requirement for which is the novelist's "knowledge of the human heart." The novelist is "the child of Nature, [and] she has created him to be her painter; if he does not become his mother's lover the moment she gives birth to him, let him never write, for we shall never read him."[13] According to de Sade, "knowledge of the human heart" does not stem from an education in social etiquette but from comprehending and faithfully representing one's own nature, however inglorious that nature may appear:

> 'Tis therefore Nature that must be seized when one labors in the field of fiction, 'tis the heart of man, the most remarkable of her works, and in no wise virtue, however becoming, because virtue, however necessary it may be, is yet but one of the many facets of this amazing heart, whereof the profound study is so necessary to the novelist, and the novel, the faithful mirror of this heart, must perforce explore its every fold. (172–173)

For de Sade, as for many American novelists writing at this time, Nature stands in opposition to conventional morality and to those "virtues" of which society approves. Unlike most American writers, however, de Sade views the faithful representation of Nature as an education in itself.

De Sade's fundamental distaste for the hypocritical conventions and moral codes of Western society manifests itself in his aberrant and sexually perverse stories about physical and psychological domination. Touted by Aldous Huxley as "the one completely consistent and thorough-going revolutionary of history,"[14] de Sade delves unflinchingly into the human psyche, teasing out motivation and desire while bringing us into contact with various unfortunates, ranging from the unlucky to the deranged. Two of the novellas included in *The Crimes of Love* follow the conventions of the typical cautionary tale while offering an ironic critique of its moral lessons. In "Florville and Courval," for instance, the protagonist becomes caught in a web of illicit relationships that are revealed only at the last moment when Florville, now an "object of horror," discovers that she has unwittingly married her father, been seduced by her brother, killed her nephew, and indirectly caused her mother's death. In this story, de Sade takes the seduction tale to its most absurd end, casting all blood relationships in the light of fateful bonds meant to fetter the individual to ignominious acts born of her unrealized connections to other persons. His concluding moral then puts a tragic twist on the seduction novel's conventional exhortation to live a virtuous life by suggesting that no such life is ever possible:

> [Each of the characters] is peacefully finishing a sad and oppressive life which was given to him only to convince him, as well as those who will read this tragic story, that it is only in the darkness of the tomb that man can find the calm which the wickedness of his fellow man, the disorder of his passions, and, above all, the decrees of his fate, will always refuse to him on this earth. (208)

The glib assertions of eighteenth-century didactic literature are here transposed to acknowledge the impotence of human will in the face of those forces that revolve around and within the individual. In de Sade's fiction, fate takes the shape of the individual's passion: one's desires enact one's fate. As in *The Power of Sympathy*, Nature is decreed the author of those passions which are "natural" by virtue of the fact that they are located within the individual. Nature and fate, two external forces once denoting the individual's subordinate status in the metaphysical chain of being, are now personalized, constructing and constructed by the individual's desires, which are themselves out of the individual's control. The seduction novel's attempts at "female education," lessons that presuppose an individual's ability to change, are undermined by the inevitable victory of those elements that made the lessons necessary in the first place.

De Sade's *Crimes of Love* puts erotic tension squarely within the family. His novella entitled "Eugenie de Franval" exploits the relationship between education and seduction through the story of a father, the "artful" (de l'art) Franval, who raises his daughter to become his mistress. The narrator is no less artful than the father: the frame of the tale opens with the quintessential line of seduction, one designed to assure readers of the narrative's pedagogical purpose. The narrator then goes on to titillate readers with a promise of the story's scandal and abuse:

> To instruct man and correct his morals: that is our only purpose in writing this story. We hope that reading it will make one keenly aware of the peril that always dogs the steps of those who stop at nothing in satisfying their desires. . . . We ask to be forgiven for the monstrous details of the abominable crime we shall be forced to describe: it is not possible to make others detest such wrongdoing if one does not have the courage to lay it bare. (3)

Although these sentiments will strike the reader as disingenuous, it is precisely this tension between what one says and what one means—or what one thinks one should want and what one desires—that drives the plot. Franval's daughter, Eugenie, embodies the riddle that cannot be solved: deemed "the horror and the wonder of nature," de Sade's ingenue inspires the incestuous desire that will subsequently become the ruling passion of *her* life as well. Her innocent nature first targets her for manipulation and then renders her unable to resist it. Yet "wonder" and "horror" refer not only to what Eugenie is and becomes, but to what she represents for readers: the desire for innocence whose very attainment will destroy it.

The narrator leads his readers into a plot whose conflicts reproduce the readers' own relationship to illicit stories. After Eugenie is born, Franval insists on overseeing his daughter's education. He separates her from her religiously minded mother and avoids giving her any knowledge of religious or moral principles, since, as he puts it, "such fantastic nonsense" would only "trouble the serenity of her life and would not add any truth to her mind or any beauty to her body" (8). When she is older, he instills in Eugenie his own views on morality. But since Franval's goal was "not merely to strengthen her mind, his lectures seldom ended without inflaming her heart." Eventually, he "corrupted [his daughter] so skillfully, made himself so useful to her education and her pleasures, and so ardently anticipated everything that might be agreeable to her, that in the midst of the most brilliant company she found no one as charming as her father" (11–12). Eugenie's education becomes a method of seduction, so that by her fourteenth year, Eugenie's desires are indistinguishable from her father's.

The intimate connection I am arguing between education and seduction can actually be traced linguistically. The root of both words is the Latin for "to lead": *dūcere*. *Sedūcere* is "to lead aside, or mislead"; *ēdūcere* is "to lead in the way of life, or to rear (a child)."[15] Educating is akin to parenting, and parenting to authoring a child's life. Franval alludes to this himself by proclaiming his affinity with Pygmalion (23).[16] More than this, however, the linguistic root of the words suggests that the difference between to lead and to mislead is not definitive but relative. Franval argues this very point with the clergyman, Clervil, when the latter comes to confront Franval with his crime.

In the intellectual debate between these two classically educated men, de Sade pits the philosophy of anarchy against the nationalism of Western morality. When Clervil argues that it is impossible to be happy in crime, Franval replies with the words of an artist as well as a radical: "Happiness is . . . the work of the imagination. It's a way of being moved which depends solely on our way of seeing and feeling" (41). If a man doesn't subscribe to the limits imposed on him by his fellow men, he can create his own moral code and thus his own happiness. Clervil concedes the somewhat arbitrary foundation of moral standards, citing the "banks of the Ganges" as a place where incest is permitted, but he goes on to invoke the authority of convention to check a man's actions: "If there is no universal conscience for man, there is at least a national one relating to the existence we've received from nature, and in which her hand has written our duties in letters that we cannot erase without danger" (43). Clervil equates national with natural laws and warns that in transgressing such laws, Franval not only risks public censure but also the very authority of influence by which he wields his power over Eugenie: "You're forcing your daughter to despise her most precious duties, you're making her hate the woman who carried her in her womb; and without realizing it, you're preparing the weapons she may use against you . . . if some day her hand makes an attempt on your life, you yourself will have sharpened the dagger" (44). Speaking as the conscience of society, Clervil assures Franval that in flouting the moral law of the land he negates authority—and parental rights—altogether. His daughter will ultimately lose more freedom than she gains and be consigned to the meaningless existence to which complete autonomy always dooms the unrepentant criminal.

Clervil's words prove prophetic. Franval convinces Eugenie to kill her mother so that father and daughter may be free. But after she does, she is struck by a fit of conscience and dies atop her mother's body. Franval, returning to the castle and encountering Clervil there, is forced to listen while the narrative, thrust like a "dagger into [his] heart by degrees" (77), slowly saps him of his will to live. He hears Clervil's somewhat self-satisfied report of how his daughter was finally "returned to nature" (78) and, in an act of remorse, Franval commits suicide. His dying words return us to the story's moral frame: "Tell those I leave behind of my deplorable end and of my crimes; tell them that thus must die a poor slave of his passions who has been vile enough to stifle the voice of duty and nature" (82).

The irony, of course, is that it is convention and not rebellion that kills Eugenie and her father: both suffer the nominally "natural" remorse that turns pleasure into pain and both die from the experience. In a work that has made the social construction of natural feeling a central issue, "nature" is suddenly cast as the embodiment of social order and the avenging force through which that order is restored. De Sade's ironic reversals help to reveal a fundamental contradiction in American romantic philosophy and literature: the celebration of nature's "triumph" over socialization, including nature's affirmation of individual affective power, and the evocation of nature as the secular incarnation of God's social order. The representation of nature in "Eugenie de Franval" takes on the appearance of "deus ex machina," allowing wary readers to recognize the artifice behind any attempts to create an allied natural-social order. Such artifice is, of course, the province of the author—the god behind the "god from a machine." In a work of fiction it is the storyteller who has the authority to shape events, as well as readers' expectations and interpretations of those events. Thus Clervil, demanding that Franval listen to his story "as a reparation for [Franval's] crimes," verbally tortures the reprobate into a state of contrition that ends with Franval's death. In this highly improbable and inconsistent ending, what is clear is that it is Franval's *repentance*, rather than his sin, that is unnatural. In de Sade's view, moral education is the perversion, as subjects strive to conform to conventional standards of reading and repenting. Seduction is the work of the author who must lead the reader. Whether that leading be astray or not is a matter of opinion and depends as much on a reader's willingness to confront and accept his own desires as on the author's ability to manipulate them.

One of the most well-known early American authors, Charles Brockden Brown, offers a slightly different perspective on the dangers of naturalizing the social order. As in "Eugenie de Franval," fathers and seducers are difficult to differentiate in Brown's work: in *Wieland, or The Transformation* (1798), for instance, Brown never makes clear whether the origin of Wieland's mania is God, the ultimate father figure, or Carwin, the ventriloquist and known seducer. But Brown seems uninterested in debating the difference; rather, Brown presents seduction—whatever its origin—as an epistemological dilemma that registers national consequences. Unlike other seduction novels, *Wieland* goes beyond the analogical implications of a woman's threatened virtue to the greater danger that such a loss signifies. The story of Clara and Carwin, Mrs. Stuart (Louisa Conway's mother), and Maxwell, prove localized instances of a more extensive drama: the rise and fall of romantic education.

What readers are supposed to learn from Brown's self-proclaimed exemplary "American Tale" has been a matter of critical debate, but that Brown indeed has a pedagogical purpose is evidenced from the first to the last page of Clara Wieland's story. Clara opens her epistolary narrative by expressing her desire to "contribute what little [she] can to the benefit of mankind" by communicating to the world "the duty of avoiding deceit."[17] In a novel that highlights the fatal effects of verbal artifice—illustrated through plots of seduction, hallucination, and ventriloquism—one might expect deceit to be associated with the villains of the tale. But in her final remarks, Clara suggests that deception does not always come from sources outside the familiar body:

> I leave you to moralize on this tale. That virtue should become the victim of treachery is, no doubt, a mournful consideration: but it will not escape your notice, that the evils of which Carwin and Maxwell were the authors, owed their existence to the errors of the sufferers. . . . If Wieland had framed juster notions of moral duty, and of the divine attributes; or if I had been gifted with ordinary equanimity or foresight, the double-tongued deceiver would have been baffled and repelled. (244)

The novel's concluding lesson makes clear that the real danger is *self*-deception. Even Clara the rationalist has given credence to bodiless voices that were but the verbal traces of an illusion; she admits to an initial attraction to Carwin that had no intellectual foundation and she mistakes her friend Pleyel's fraternal interest in her as romantic. Her brother Wieland also makes the mistake of putting his faith in the insubstantial and nonverifiable: believing that God has demanded his family as a sacrifice, Wieland murders them. Later, in an attempt to recall Wieland to himself, Clara declares that it is "not heaven or hell, but thy senses [that] have misled thee to commit these acts" (230). Whether the voice had an external cause, Carwin's ventriloquism, or an internal one, hallucination or wish fulfillment, is never explained, and the omission is significant. Deceptions outside the body mirror deceptions within it. The characters' physical senses deceived them, but their minds much more so, because, according to Brown, they should have known better than to trust those senses. The lesson readers learn is not only that one cannot trust strangers, but that one cannot trust oneself.

Read in its literary as well as political context, *Wieland* serves as a cautionary tale directed at the future; it raises such questions as how authority will be constructed after the fact of revolution and what kind of education will reestablish domestic order. For Brown, the key lies in eschewing individual sense for a *consensus* of opinion. Consensus arises in part from common education: a normalized perception of the world is essential to the process of socialization, which is itself a prerequisite to consensus. In the late eighteenth century, standard education included instruction in Christian dogma as well as in the fundamentals of verbal communication (reading, writing, spelling, grammar, etc.). Wieland's error in judgment can be traced back to his father's own imperfect religious education. Brought up without religious training, Wieland's father one day comes across a book on the doctrine of a dissenting Christian sect, the Camissards, and he eagerly devours its teachings. Its allusions to the Bible lead Wieland to study that book as well, but all its teachings are "viewed through a medium which the writings of the Camissard apostle had suggested." The result is that the elder Wieland's "education" becomes a travesty, unsynthesized and assimilated without benefit of proper context:

> [Wieland's] constructions of the text were hasty, and formed on a narrow scale. One action and one precept were not employed to illustrate and restrict the meaning of another. Hence arose a thousand scruples to which he had hitherto been a stranger. He imagined himself beset by the snares of a spiritual foe, and that his security lay in ceaseless watchfulness and prayer. (9)

He compounds his mistake of studying in private by worshipping in private as well: "[Wieland] allied himself with no sect, because he perfectly agreed with none. Social worship is that by which they are all distinguished; but this article found no place in his creed. . . . According to him devotion was not only a silent office, but must be performed alone" (11). Eventually he falls ill under the weight of a "command" he feels has been laid upon him, but which he has "delayed to perform." He refuses all efforts at communication or guidance. He dies alone in a mysterious accident inside the temple he had built for his deity.

Wieland inherits his father's propensity for religious reflection, but the "mind of the son was enriched by science, and embellished with literature" (23). Wieland turns his father's temple into an arena of activity for his family and friends, a place where "the social affections were accustomed to expand, and the tear of delicious sympathy to be shed" (24). Even so, Wieland's private community proves a poor substitute for the larger one. As Clara herself admits,

Our education had been modelled by no religious standard. We were left to the guidance of our own understanding, and the casual impressions which society might make upon us. My friend's temper, as well as my own exempted us from much anxiety on this account. It must not be supposed that we were without religion, but with us it was the product of lively feelings, excited by reflection on our own happiness, and by the grandeur of external nature. We sought not a basis for our faith, in the weighing of proofs, and the dissection of creeds. (22)

The family circle and the philosophy it produces is described in almost solipsistic terms. Isolation and innocence are the dangerous states that education and experience must ameliorate. Of course, these conditions also have national significance. The perversion of filial love, exemplified in Wieland's murder of his family, signifies that threats to American society may lie not in foreign bodies but in its own. However, the answer for Brown is not to dismantle the "family" but to expand it. Dissenting doctrines must give way to traditional ones, and one must test one's private lessons against the knowledge of the more experienced. In the long run, for Brown, the private societies that herald the freedom of a liberal culture may ultimately signal its undoing.

Like most American novels of seduction, *Wieland* is invested in teaching readers to read—their circumstances, their acquaintances, their relations, and themselves—more judiciously. The way to begin one's lessons is by reading novels like Brown's. But, as Michael Warner argues, in the republican period novel reading was not presented as a private experience but as a public or political act. Such at least was the claim of authors who knew that antifictional sentiments lay in the fear that "fiction would detach readers' sentiments from the social world of the polity, substituting a private drama of fancy."[18] Through the character of Wieland, Brown writes the threat of private fancy into the heart of his story, thereby negating the model of individual interpretation. *Wieland* seeks to reform Enlightenment constructions of knowledge by turning common sense into fantasy and by demonstrating that what readers rely on for truth not only may but probably will deceive them. To what then does one look for truth? According to Brown, to the voice of the author—that "moral painter" whose art is neither "selfish nor temporary" but who exhibits his "subject in its most instructive and memorable forms."[19] For Brown, as for de Sade, the author is an artist who "paints" the human heart. The seducer's arts are thus superseded by the art of the novelist, whose own method of influence distinguishes him from the seducer chiefly by position: i.e., in the novel of seduction, the author has the last word.

"Female Education" and Its Discontents

Read on one level, susceptibility to influence represents a threat to national security; on another, less superficial level, however, suggestibility represents one of the most valuable and well-guarded assets of a patriarchal culture. A conversation from de Sade's "Eugenie de Franval" provides a perfect case in point. When Clervil accuses Franval of coercing Eugenie into turning down a suitable marriage partner, Franval replies with his usual equanimity: "I've never hidden the world from her. . . . I offered myself and left her free to choose. She didn't hesitate: she said she could find happiness only with me" (45). Franval's denial of Clervil's charge reflects a more fundamental refusal to appreciate the ways in which influence compromises autonomy. In Franval's mind, freedom, equated with the capacity to choose, remains unmediated by that loving influence that I have been arguing gives freedom its illusion. The "freethinking" Franval thus reveals here is his affiliation with conventional patriarchal structures of education. What constitutes his radical status is not so much his method of education as his justification of that method: that is, Franval articulates the fundamental patriarchal fantasy of keeping daughters close to home. In addition, Franval's contention that Eugenie has been left "free to choose" puts the burden of decision—and reponsibility—squarely on the woman he has influenced. Eugenie's inability to resist her father's seductive lessons—her seducibility, in short—reinforces readers' perceptions that, left to their own desires, young women will always make the wrong choice.

Thus the benefits of patriarchy are reestablished in the readerly imagination in part through two figures of benign authority: the protective father and the loving husband. Each serves a function in preserving the virtue of the republican home, but the conflation of their roles and responsibilities produces an ethos of seductive paternalism whereby the positions of fathers and lovers become confused and intertwined. The seduction novel exploits such confusion, evincing the ceaseless modulation of masculine identities and exploring its effects on female character(s). One of these effects is the construction of women as constitutionally unable to make rational choices. Ostensibly crippled in mind by the emotional overload of their hearts, women become the targets of sentimental lessons designed to arouse and intensify their "natural" sympathies. "Female education" becomes a question of influence, persuasion, and the manipulation of those senses that supposedly disabled women in the first place. In other words, women are to be *seduced* into proper action.

Theories of and anxieties over female desire and irrationality have a long and imaginative history. Though treacherous combatants in the emotional and sexual war against men, women were considered helpless when it came to contests with their own emotions.[20] Woman's physiological and psychological makeup supposedly led her to fits of irrationality, jealousy, even hysteria, which were themselves regularly attributed to the woman's sympathetic susceptibility—her tendency to overidentify.[21] Anthony Benezet's *Some Necessary Remarks on the Education of Children* (1778) emphasizes the need to monitor young girls' education, because *their* natures in particular require it:

> It is an established and universally received maxim, that the future sentiments and actions and characters of men are considerably influenced by their earliest education; and, if we consider the superior susceptibility of women, and that exquisite sensibility, which so wonderfully dispose them to receive all impressions—and, infact, have made so many of that sex, in different periods, and in various circumstances, martyrs to love, to friendship and devotion, it is reasonable to conclude that, if they are defective in any rational attainments, it is for want of a judicious and timely cultivation. (5)

A woman's highly impressionable nature leaves her open to any man wishing to make his mark, causing her desires to become indistinguishable from his.[22]

In marriage, wandering female desire may find a home in a venue where sympathetic identification—even overidentification—has its sociopolitical benefits. Charles Francis Adams, editing his grandparents' correspondence in *Familiar Letters of John Adams and His Wife Abigail Adams, During the Revolution* (1876), bases the volume's significance on just this kind of emotional contribution made by women to the War of Independence. Although many have written the "history of action" superficially associated with Revolution, observes Adams, few have written the "history of feeling" that undergirds it. His *Memoir* of Abigail Adams, included as a preface to the succeeding correspondence, attempts to recover the private sympathies foundational to social and political transformations. According to Adams, Abigail Adams serves as an "exemplar" of women's political participation in the American Revolution by virtue of both her sentimental influence on and her patriotic sacrifice for husband and family. As Adams has it, the trials of the Revolution were especially difficult for women because of their inability to distinguish real from imaginary danger; they therefore suffered doubly from the exigencies of war:

> The trial Mrs. Adams was called to undergo from the fears of those immediately around her was one in addition to that caused by her own apprehen-

sions; a trial, it may be remarked, of no ordinary nature, since it demands the exercise of a presence of mind and accuracy of judgment in distinguishing the false from the true, that falls to the lot of few even of the stronger sex. It is the tendency of women in general to suffer quite as much from anxiety occasioned by the activity of the imagination, as if it was, in every instance, founded upon reasonable cause. (xix).[23]

Left in charge of their family's protection, women like Abigail Adams played a part equal (if not equivalent) to their husbands' during the war. Nevertheless, Charles Adams's references to women's lack of reason identify his tribute to female heroism as itself embedded in certain cultural assumptions that presuppose any battle with reality to be heroic for women.[24]

Married women and mothers, though themselves often unable to distinguish "false from true," had at least a suitable outlet for their overactive imaginations. Single women, on the other hand, were a different story. In his *Memoir*, Adams lamented the "defective nature of female education before the Revolution" that rendered women passive responders to, rather than writers of, their own stories.[25] Philosopher-educators in the postrevolutionary period took their own special interest in "female education" and its potential benefits to the republic. One of those benefits was the transformation of women into wives and mothers. Although what is meant by the term *female education* varies from writer to writer, very few social critics advocated giving women an *intellectual* education; such would unfit women for, in John Bennett's words, "their original destination to be the companions and comforters of men."[26] To this end, the Reverend Enoch Hitchcock warned in 1790 that education for women should be fashioned in such a way that women do not take into marriage "expectations" that are above the "drudgery of learning the necessary part of domestic duties." And in 1791 Caleb Bingham encouraged education for women that would "enable them to become amiable sisters, virtuous children, and, in the event, to assume characters [as mothers] more interesting to the public, and more endearing to themselves." In general, most social critics and politicians were not interested in teaching women how to rise above their stations but in how best to fit into them with the least amount of effort or disturbance. Such a goal carried an implicit, and often explicit, political component: "In a free country, under a republican form of government, industry is the only sure road to wealth; and economy the only sure means of preserving it. . . . [Thus] we see the necessity of educating females in a manner suited to the genius of the government."[27] Paradoxically, it is the *freedom* of their country that necessitates giving women a "peculiar and suitable education," for a free society requires especially virtuous and responsible citizens. More than this, however, well-taught wives and mothers ensure the freedom of their men to go out and make the family's fortune without worrying about what the women are doing at home.

As Cathy Davidson has pointed out, in the postrevolutionary period, "there was education and then there was female education—a different concept entirely."[28] A notable exception to the rule of separatist philosophers, however, is Judith Sargent Murray. In her articles "On the Equality of the Sexes" (1790), "On the Domestic Education of Children" (1790), and "Desultory Thoughts" (1784), Murray makes practical often otherwise vague principles of female education. Murray was one of the few writers in America to argue the intellectual equality of men and women, an equality obscured by the upbringing of girls that teaches them to appreciate nothing but the outer form. In "Desultory Thoughts," Murray emphasizes the need for women to cultivate a healthy self-respect: "You must learn 'to reverence yourself,' that is, your intellectual existance [sic]; you must join my efforts, in endeavouring to adorn your mind, for, it is from the proper furnishing of that, you will become indeed a valuable person." It is a woman's education—in reading, writing, history, and literature—that will keep flatterers and seducers at bay and keep women themselves from becoming simply decorative objects, "hung up as a pleasing picture among the paintings of some spacious hall."[29]

As if to make literal Murray's connection between education and discernment, warnings against seducers are written into even children's rudimentary lessons on the English language. *Cobb's Spelling Book, Being a Just Standard for Pronouncing the English Language* (1829), for example, concludes its "Easy Reading Lessons" with a chapter entitled "An Address to Youthful Females," which begins,

> Listen, fair daughter of innocence, to the instructions of prudence, and let the precepts of truth sink deep into thy heart. . . . It is a melancholy truth, that *man* too often prostitutes his boasted faculties to the destruction of female happiness. How necessary, then, to fortify your minds against the attacks of vile seducers! Blemishes in female characters seldom are effaced. Not so with man. He tarnishes his name and brightens it again.[30]

Rules of conduct and morality constitute the essential grammar of female character; these rules are to become second nature, as routine as proper spelling or pronunciation. More than this, however, the causal relationship between literacy and self-regard emphasizes the associative link between deciphering human and literary characters, an association on which, by 1829, early American authors and publishers had already long been trading.

The Authority of Representation: *Charlotte Temple*

Eighteenth-century seduction novels offer their own full-length "easy reading lessons" for feminine audiences, displaying and inculcating sympathetic attachments that will put narrative lessons (in)to effect. Women are not only construed as the target of the sentimental market, they become the central figures in these stories of seduction. One explanation for this has already been suggested: women's bodies and minds signified spaces that were singularly penetrable, thus constituting women as the logical emblems of a postrevolutionary culture's engagement with issues of influence and autonomy. Literary protagonists simultaneously evoking and expressing sympathy model an ideal readership for the literary market, one based on an economy of affective exchange.

The model of affective exchange informs political as well as literary structures. Both structures rely on modes of representation to engage the subject in acts of identification that affirm, simultaneously, personal and communal authority. As Christopher Newfield observes, in representative democracy a citizen "finds freedom in consenting to laws that he can claim were legislated, if not by him directly, then by others in his name."[31] Political representation has its premise in the flexible boundaries of subjectivity. Such a notion complicates traditional historical analyses, and even much eighteenth-century republican rhetoric, which posits disinterested benevolence as singularly fundamental to republican virtue. Popular sentimental ideology reveals republican virtue to be inseparable from the sympathetic mechanism that compels one to view others in light of one's own intellectual and affective position. The abstract concept of the Public Good shows itself grounded in the particulars of private desire, and civic disinterestedness in terms of the *self*-interest that underwrites it.

In *The Letters of the Republic*, Michael Warner contends that representation works via a "negative relation of private subject to the state and to the public discourse."[32] Personal or private desire is subsumed in the greater authority of the Public Good, which is itself an intangible concept fashioned from the material arts of a rising print culture. Citing the Constitution's "We, the People" as prime example, Warner persuasively argues that the success of representational polity hinges on the assurance that "the people" never be named, never be less than the whole, never, in effect, become personal. Disinterested republican virtue, embedded in the principle of public interest over private views or ends, finds its "voice" in the printed text that represents all men but is embodied by none.[33]

It is Warner's privileging of republican disinterestedness over liberalism that allows him to emphasize the generalized, impersonal, and public persona of "the People" in late eighteenth-century American culture. I suggest that representation works toward both republican *and* liberal ends, an idea we see most clearly presented in sentimental literature. Early fiction supports the republican cause of female education but effects this education through liberal strategies designed to conflate private and public authority and interest. Contrary to Warner's claim that the representation of letters denotes the depersonalization of authority for the greater glory of Union, sentimental literature confirms (and then often exploits) individual autonomy, authority, and desire through readers' sympathetic identification with the protagonist who represents them. Individuals are singularly affected in order to create a consensus of sensibility whereby the public is served through the modification of private desire, yet private liberty is affirmed by the attention to personal feeling.

At its most effective, sentimental representation obscures the distinctions between fiction and reality, heroine and reader, so that readers feel personally invested in the story's events. Susanna Rowson's purported "Tale of Truth," the seduction novel *Charlotte Temple* (1794), exemplifies sentimental representation at its best.[34] *Charlotte Temple* tells the story of a young woman at an English boarding school who is persuaded by a handsome soldier to leave home and family to cross the sea with him to America. The lover, Montraville, eventually abandons Charlotte and she, unmarried and alone, dies after giving birth to a baby girl. In her preface to the novel, Rowson requests that her "fair readers" consider the tale "not merely the effusion of Fancy, but as a reality" (5). Her readers apparently acceded to her request. A best-selling novel for over a century and boasting over two hundred editions by 1964, *Charlotte Temple* is arguably the most popular novel in American literary history.[35] Its popularity is directly proportional to its power of representation: as Davidson points out, despite the lack of verifiable evidence, "for Rowson's readers Charlotte was real" (xv).[36] Thus Davidson records that, following Montraville's example in the last pages of the novel, thousands of sympathetic readers made a pilgrimage to Charlotte Temple's New York "grave," marked by a headstone that bore her name. As late as 1903 a gentleman whose office overlooked the cemetery testified to the faithful mourners who offered their tribute in the form of tears:

> When I was a boy the story of Charlotte Temple was familiar in the household of every New Yorker. The first tears I ever saw in the eyes of a grown person were shed for her. In that churchyard are graves of heroes, philosophers, and martyrs, whose names are familiar to the youngest scholar, and whose memory is dear to the wisest and best. Their graves, tho marked by

imposing monuments, win but a glance of curiosity, while the turf over Charlotte Temple is kept fresh by falling tears.[37]

As this witness would have it, "heroes and martyrs"—historical figures representing culture's most cherished values—are overshadowed by the image of a fallen but repentant young woman who brings those values down to earth where readers from all walks and classes of life could vicariously possess them. It is clear that the "reality" of Rowson's fictional character is proven not by historical record but by affective response. Charlotte's personhood is continually reconstituted by the emotions of those who sympathize with her plight. Such sympathies may be exploited, manufactured, even mass-marketed, but readers nonetheless experience them as personal and, in that sense, real.

Rowson's achievement is to make particular for readers the otherwise generalized strictures of female education. This is in effect the hermeneutic exercise of the eighteenth- and nineteenth-century Anglo-American novel—to inscribe the law of the narrative onto individual hearts.[38] In terms of American culture, liberalism intersects with republicanism through the process of sympathetic identification, in which lessons in virtue are registered not as imposition but as instinct. Since the perception of natural instinct is often shaped through artificial means, one finds Rowson's novel replete with narrative intrusions designed to direct reader response as well as to forestall potential criticism. With chapters entitled "Teach me to feel another's woe, / To hide the fault I see, / That mercy I to others show / That mercy show to me," and "Which People Void of Feeling Need Not Read," Rowson separates the sympathetically redeemed from the unaffected, the literate from the untutored and emotionally stunted. Judging by the narrator's moments of direct address, men and middle-aged women typically fall into the latter category:

> It may be asked by those, who, in a work of this kind, love to cavil at every trifling omission, whether Charlotte did not possess any valuable of which she could have disposed. . . . [She did not]. . . . I hope, Sir, your prejudices are now removed in regard to the probability of my story? Oh they are. Well then, with your leave, I will proceed (106).

> Now, my dear sober matron (if a sober matron should deign to turn over these pages, before she trusts them to the eye of a darling daughter), let me intreat you not to put on a grave face, and throw down the book in a passion and declare 'tis enough to turn the heads of half the girls in England. (28)

The author goes beyond the creation of a sympathetic protagonist to the creation of an ideal sympathetic reader as well. Married women and men are not in themselves antipathetic; they simply represent readers who cannot adequately identify with the main character. Thus, when Rowson's narrator declares, "to my dear girls . . . only am I writing," she is not addressing young women exclusively but any reader affected by the novel who is thereby constituted a "dear girl."

What this suggests is that seduction novels not only imagine but also construct their readership in ways that make them particularly susceptible to the novel's rhetorical designs. Exploring the relationship between reader and text in the twentieth century, Janice Radway focuses on the historical subjectivity of women readers by trying to account for the "patterns or regularities" in women's responses to romance fiction. "Similar readings are produced," writes Radway, "because similarly located readers learn a similar set of reading strategies and interpretive codes that they bring to bear upon the texts they encounter."[38] But where do readers learn these strategies and codes? I would argue that, in the case of sentimental fiction, the novels themselves attempt to teach readers how to read. Through the formulaic repetition of certain plots, direct authorial address, and heightened affective manipulation, seduction novels attempt to put individual readers in a similar frame of mind, thereby minimizing the risk of deviant interpretations while perpetuating a market for their own kind of story.[40]

In these respects, Rowson's novel proves a highly successful work of fiction, for *Charlotte Temple* appealed to readers from diverse backgrounds and situations. Although the novel was, as Davidson notes, "specifically targeted for working-class readers"—factory girls vulnerable to the sexual as well as economic exploitation of well-educated and well-connected young men—in terms of sales, *Charlotte Temple* was popular with "both sexes and all classes." Actual consumers included mothers, fathers, new brides and their husbands, sisters, brothers, grandmothers, and grandsons. Quotes Davidson, "Writing in 1870, Elias Nason observed [*Charlotte Temple*] in 'the study of the divine and . . . the workshop of the mechanic,' in the 'parlor of the accomplished lady and the bedchamber of her waiting-maid.' "[41] What unites these readers is their mutual characterization by publisher, author, and novel as respondents to rather than performers of language. Of course, inherent in the seduction is the capacity to make readers feel that their responses are equivalent to actions and thus that they themselves are performers of *feeling*. The correspondence between affect and effect is beautifully exemplified in the pilgrimage of readers to Charlotte Temple's grave: by making this journey, readers act out as well as on their sympathetic feelings, so that text, headstone, and pilgrimage all transcend their status as empty signifiers to become once more meaningful through the emotions they signify.

The construction of readers as feminine, and the corresponding manipulation of "feminine" suggestibility intrinsic to the novel, becomes even clearer once we recognize the ways in which the seduction novel aligns itself with the classically educated gentleman-seducer it is attempting to denounce. Schooled in history and rhetoric, the typical upper-class male had the advantage of understanding both his own historical context and the significance of context in everyday discourse: "The gentry understood rhetoric not as the communication of definitive truth but as situational discourse aimed at persuading a clearly defined implied reader or auditor of the present worth of a present proposition for that particular audience."[42] Put another way—J. L. Austin's way—a gentleman views language as "performative" rather than "constantive."[43] Citing Austin for a similar purpose, Shoshana Felman argues that whereas the victim sees language as "an instrument for the transmission of *truth*" the seducer is "not susceptible to truth or falsity, but rather, very exactly, to felicity or infelicity, to success or failure."[44] In the seduction novel, the gentleman-seducer depends on his verbal skills to break down the woman's resistance. The novel itself does much the same thing. Each acts with intent—not to inform or to educate in and about context but to "modify the situation." In other words, to alter the woman's behavior.

Like the seducer it works simultaneously to undermine and emulate, the seduction novel exploits the suggestibility of its feminized audience by a performance of language designed to achieve a particular response.[45] In *Charlotte Temple*, the narrator secures readers through explicit and implicit moments of identification: "In affairs of love, a young heart is never in more danger than when attempted by a handsome young soldier. . . . When beauty of person, elegance of manner, and an easy method of paying compliments, are united to the scarlet coat, smart cockade, and military sash, ah! well-a-day for the poor girl who gazes on him." Following this sympathetic gesture on behalf of young women, the narrator changes tack to assume the father's jealous part: "When I think on the miseries that must rend the heart of a doating [sic] parent, when he sees the darling of his age at first seduced from his protection, and afterwards abandoned . . . my bosom glows with honest indignation, and I wish for power to extirpate those monsters of seduction from the earth" (28–29). The narrator's ability to take on a variety of different subject positions in these moments of sympathy establishes the free-floating nature of affective response: sympathetic identification may transcend conventional limitations such as age, experience, even gender. However, sympathy has a disciplinary function as well, one that blurs the distinction between theatricality and authenticity. For, in order to fulfill its pedagogical function, the novel of seduction must outperform the performer; it must win over its readers with the definitive show of sincerity. Only if the novel succeeds in this impersonation, this intimate and individualized representation of affection, will acts of seduction be translated into female education.[46]

"This Man Will Seduce Me Into Matrimony": *The Coquette*

The seduction novel's female education comes not only in the form of a warning against the verbal manipulations of classically educated and well-connected young men but in both implicit and explicit testaments to the benefits of marriage. In a somewhat tautological frame, marriage signified women's only protection from the consequences of a patriarchal system marriage itself embodied, though neutralized through its philosophy of domestic affection. Marriage as both metaphor and social institution was to epitomize the union of civil and domestic governments so central to the political imagination. In the loving partnership between husband and wife, citizens could envision their individual relationships to larger communities. As one writer for the magazine the *Royal American* put it, the "happy state" of marriage "collects a man's views to a proper center" and "calls in his wandering affections"; through the intimacy of his "little circle . . . man feels a growing attachment to human nature and love to his country." Another writer of the same period endorsed marriage as society's only real mainstay against the corruption of America's growing prosperity:

> It has been observed, that the more cities increase in wealth and the luxuries of life, the less the inhabitants are disposed to obey the laws of Reason, Nature and Heaven, by entering into that *social union* which the beneficent Creator instituted for the Happiness of Man . . . without this virtuous union, there cannot be prosperity and happiness in a community, or among individuals.[47]

In the revolutionary and postrevolutionary periods, marriage represented the ultimate in voluntary contracts; a growing belief in affectionate marriages— ones formed by choice rather than arrangement—corresponded to and even symbolized contemporary political theories of government based on individual consent.

As political authority is reconceived in terms of a republican vision of voluntary obligation to which all citizens are bound, the result is a more liberal, humanistic, and egalitarian notion of government than Americans had ever known. Yet, while social contract theory was instrumental in reconciling individual and community needs, it also served to obscure the power relations inherent in postrevolutionary systems of government, both political and personal. The emphasis on consent as a precondition for government transformed relations between "free and equal" individuals, but it clouded the issue for those who could claim neither legal nor economic independence.

Thus Stephanie Coontz observes that despite the attempt to minimize class difference by emphasizing the common denominator of family life, two glaring inconsistencies in republican politics stood out. One was the continued spread of slavery; the other was the fact that male liberty was purchased at the price of female autonomy. The exclusion of slaves and women from the pursuit of economic or political liberty posed "a major challenge to republican ideology, especially to its conception of the links between public and private life." The result of this irreconcilable contradiction, according to Coontz, was a sea change in the way gender, class, and racial differences were conceptualized, including a "rejection of the social necessity to *impose inequality* and insistence on the *natural* bases of *differences* in role and position."[48] In other words, what began as a problem for republican politics—the inclusion of the disenfranchised into the liberal promise of liberty and property—later became the basis on which white male privilege perpetuated and even expanded its authority.

The point here is not that marital union failed to live up to its ideal, but that it represented that ideal in a particularly seductive, if generally unacknowledged, way. While Carole Pateman rightly contends that political theorists can represent the victory of contractualism over paternalism only because they "are silent about the sexual or conjugal aspect of patriarchy,"[49] I would argue that what appears a discrepancy in republican politics turns out to be practically foundational to it. The transformation of what Pateman terms "patriarchal" into "masculine" right constitutes one of the ways in which authority is made familiar. The old model of patriarchy, associated with coercive and arbitrary rule, is supplanted by a domesticated version of male prerogative, represented as the champion of all Americans'—*especially* women's—rights. In the seductive paternalism of this period, patriarchy is not repudiated but reconceived: as republican rhetoric presents it, the problem is not filial allegiance but allegiance to an authority that does not have the family's best interests at heart.[50]

Republican marriage exemplifies the perfect balance between personal fulfillment and collective commitment; its associations with personal choice, economic independence, and mutual affection underscore the importance of private life. On the other hand, marriage stands as a figure for social relations, representing as it does the "republic in miniature . . . chaste, disinterested, and free from the exercise of arbitrary power."[51] In effect, marriage reveals one of the ways in which private relations serve as a public model while simultaneously making what is public, or political, appear more natural and intimate. Specifically, republican marriage contributes to the domestication of authority by embodying a patriarchal structure and representing it as benign. Partisan conflicts and allegiances are thus subsumed in a vision of domestic union in which, as Jan Lewis puts it, "The husband and the wife are one, and the husband is the one."[52]

As a story about a young woman's reluctance to marry, and her eventual seduction as a result of this fact, Hannah Foster's *The Coquette* (1797) underscores the fine distinction thought to separate licit from illicit unions. The novel itself is to function as a method of discrimination; consciously or unconsciously, however, it brings us deeper into the heart of the problem. Based on a factual incident reported in local newspapers, Foster's novel provides a fictional history of Elizabeth Whitman, a thirty-seven-year-old educated and unmarried woman who died in childbirth at the Bell Tavern in Danvers, Massachussetts in 1788. By the time of Foster's novel, Whitman's story had already been referenced in William Hill Brown's *The Power of Sympathy* (1789), where it was declared an "emphatical illustration of the truth" that a "young lady who has imbibed her ideas of the world from desultory reading . . . falls a sacrifice to her credulity" (45). More to the point, in an editor's note that articulates almost verbatim the pronouncement of a report in the *Massachusetts Centinel*, Brown avers that Whitman's reading practices led her to become "vain and coquetish [*sic*]" and to reject "several offers of marriage in expectation of receiving one more agreeable to her fanciful idea" (46). According to these official views, Whitman's feminine susceptibility led her to "imbibe" the dangerous fancies of "novels and romances" and, ultimately, to take on the role of a female seducer.

That Whitman's reading was believed to have compromised her essential qualities as a woman is evidenced by the term most frequently applied to her: the term *coquette* is linguistically rooted in the Old French word for *cock*.[53] Official interpretations of Whitman's character thus introduce issues of transvestism and transsexuality to the seduction tale. Such "gender trouble" signifies broad-based anxieties concerning social and narrative indeterminacy as well as their potential effects on one other. To the extent that she can adequately be read, Whitman appears a woman committed to keeping her options open. Rather than interpreting her actions as the inevitable consequence of unrealistic expectations, we may read them as a sign of her resistance to being summed up in a totalizing and domesticated narrative. To avoid this particular end, a woman might present herself as virtually "unreadable"—a *coquette* who personifies the indeterminate because overdetermined subject of both sexual and narrative possibility. Considered in this light, the causal relation between Whitman's reading habits and her character also becomes clearer: for critics, both Whitman and the novel signify the impossibility of total semiotic control.

Given assumptions about the relationship between reading and influence that inform interpretations of Whitman's story, *The Coquette, as* novel, cannot escape the self-reflexivity of its pedagogical position. The problems of social, sexual, and narrative indeterminacy intersect in Foster's novel, making it an appropriate text for exploring the ways in which literary representation works to construct, reinforce, and/or destabilize women's position in early national culture. The epistolary frame of the novel, as well as the lack of narrative intrusions or prefatory remarks, contribute to lending Whitman's literary double, Eliza Wharton, a degree of autonomy unusual in tales of this kind. Unlike Rowson, Foster does not direct reader response through authorial or narrative address; readers are made sympathetic to Eliza's position by their familiarity with her writing style, her patterns of speech, and her ability to articulate, precisely and well, her intellectual and emotional conflicts. Foster's ability to "flesh out" conventionally melodramatic and didactic representations of female education results in various hermeneutic gaps between authoritative readings of Whitman's identity and desire and the desires that Eliza is allowed to, in a sense, express for herself. Eliza's "version" of the story, while coded from the outset as a tale of seduction, still manages to call official interpretations into question. As it does, female education comes under scrutiny as well.

As *The Coquette* opens, Eliza Wharton has just been "extricated" from the "shackles" of an arranged marriage and a patriarchal family by the death of both her fiancé and her father. She is then faced for the first time with choices. Although she prefers to indulge in her "liberty," at least temporarily, Eliza is immediately besieged by two contrasting suitors. One is a sober clergyman and the other a dashing rake. As Carroll Smith-Rosenberg points out, these two characters embody republicanism's safest and most dangerous figures, respectively:

> The reverend Mr. Boyer, as a minister, represents simultaneously the authoritative voice of social norms and the hard-working, honest, professional middle class. . . . The second suitor, Major Sanford, is a rake, corrupt and deceitful. He assumes the airs of the very wealthy and the distinction of a military title—both highly suspect within either classical or commercial-

republican ideology. Worse yet, having wasted his fortune, he pretends to a station he has no right to claim.[54]

The correct choice is clear to Eliza's mother and friends but hardly clear to Eliza herself. To choose between a man with whom, she says, she has nothing in common, and another whose libertine habits represent a threat to a stable home life, is for Eliza no choice at all. She therefore declares that, until she finds a man in whom "the graces and virtues are . . . united," she will "continue to subscribe [her] name Eliza Wharton."[55] What the title of the novel indicates, however, is that this is not an option.

In her analysis of The Coquette, Smith-Rosenberg positions the discourse of sensational seduction fiction alongside republican political rhetoric to investigate the changing terms of republican virtue, independence, and liberty. To a polity suspicious of such concepts as "individualism," "egotism," and "freedom" (all of which concepts Eliza claims to support), Eliza's hesitation to marry signals a dangerous state of mind. But it is not only her liberal values that threaten to undermine republican prudence and obligation, it is her identity as a woman as well. Eliza wishes to claim for herself the fruits of republican rebellion, namely, the right to link virtue with independence. Yet, throughout the novel, Eliza's attempts to defer marriage are characterized by others as unwomanly; she is denounced as a "rake" by Boyer's friend, and even Sanford himself (rake though he is) employs the language of combat in his vows to "avenge [his] sex, by retaliating the mischiefs, [this coquette] meditates against us" (18). Eliza's desire for independence is read by other characters as a desire for male privilege; consequently, she suffers the epithets, censure, and recriminations traditionally reserved for the male seducer in the tale.

In retrospect, Eliza's "choice" between Boyer and Sanford proves to be an illusion, for Sanford was never the (marrying) man he pretended to be. But, in his pursuit of Eliza, Sanford manages to ruin her chances of marrying the minister as well. When Boyer one day discovers the two of them closeted in intimate conference, he withdraws his proposal and leaves town. Having beaten Boyer, Sanford then marries a wealthy woman in order to gain her estate. In her despair, Eliza writes to Boyer to ask his forgiveness and to request another meeting, but Boyer smugly replies that he has found a more worthy woman to marry. In an attempt to retrieve, as Eliza puts it, both his proposal and her character, Eliza was willing to acquiesce in Boyer's judgment of her. When Sanford returns a year or two later and renews his addresses (now clearly for an illicit purpose), Eliza, resigned to a future with no prospects, succumbs to his importunities and eventually dies in childbirth as a result of their affair.

Although seduction fiction rarely makes explicit the illicit behavior that drives its plots, such behavior nevertheless comprises the basis of the novel's moral message (as well as its popular appeal). Seduction plots testify to the existence of secret acts and desires that lie beneath the surface of everyday living. Private egos constitute both the foundation of and potential threat to democratic society, for individual choice may at any time unravel the tightly knit garment of republican union. In order to neutralize the effects of private desire, seduction novels make desire public, as is evidenced by the novelization of Whitman's history. The woman's body becomes a metaphor of publication; it brings to light those secret desires once suspected but hidden from view. Read in this way, pregnancy can be said to reestablish the protagonist's sexual and social position in the world at large. In *The Coquette*, the protagonist's gender status is reestablished as well, for Eliza's pregnancy marks her in such a way as to resolve the gender ambiguity associated with her coquettry. Her story fulfills its pedagogical mission by rendering Eliza—and the historical figure she signifies—once again decipherable as both gendered and literary subject.

What I am suggesting is that, while ostensibly denoting the tragedy of the novel, Eliza's seduction paradoxically *redeems* her as "woman." It presents her as ultimately suggestible and, therefore, as essentially female. It follows, then, that after her rejection by Boyer, Eliza relinquishes all claims to language, action, and independence, exemplifying instead her susceptibility to influence—both Boyer's *and* Sanford's. Having internalized the social censure that Boyer's judgment represents, Eliza's letters dwindle to a handful in the last quarter of the novel. When she does write, we find that her affair with Sanford has rendered her virtually inarticulate: "My Honored And Dear Mama, In what words, in what language shall I address you? What shall I say on a subject which *deprives me of the power of expression*? Would to God I had been totally deprived of that power before so fatal a subject required its exertion!" (153, emphasis mine). All Eliza can truly say is that, up to this point, the fundamentals of female education, "precept and example, counsel and advice, instruction and admonition" (153), were not properly taken to heart. And although Eliza can now testify to her conversion, it is a conversion whose authenticity can only be substantiated by her death: "Be assured, that affection and gratitude will be the last sentiments, which expire in the breast of [this] repenting . . . Eliza Wharton" (155).

By the end of the novel, Eliza is tranformed from a woman who writes her own story to one who is conscripted by it. The term *coquette*, once signifying the mastery of language and the privilege of the actor, now denotes a woman sentenced to the word others use against her. Eliza Wharton, in effect, becomes pure text, bound from first to last by a title instead of a name and, on the final page, by the reproduction of a headstone that recapitulates both her history and her character:

> This Humble Stone,
> In Memory of
> ELIZA WHARTON,
> Is Inscribed By Her Weeping Friends,
> To Whom She Endeared Herself By Uncommon
> Tenderness and Affection . . .
> Let Candor Throw a Veil Over Her Frailties,
> For Great Was Her Charity To Others.
> She Sustained the Last
> Painful Scene, Far From Every Friend . . .
> And the Tears of Strangers Watered Her
> Grave. (169)

This final textual summation verifies Eliza's redemption not only as a spiritual but also as a narrative model. Since Eliza's end is prefigured from the beginning, her power to evoke sympathy becomes the last measure of her agency. Both Eliza's seduction and her repentance allow her to become an object of pity rather than resentment and thus to serve as an example to others. No longer pursuing her own course or thinking for herself, Eliza may receive the tears worthy of a sentimental heroine.

Exactly who constitutes the true seducer and what the true seduction remain central questions posed by *The Coquette*. Although Eliza herself does not, *The Coquette* as text resists codification; "female education" becomes overdetermined to the extent that, in the final analysis, it is unclear whether Eliza, Elizabeth, or the readers of cautionary tales are the victims of seduction. Foster's novel complicates facile connections between female education and marriage, exposing ideological flaws in the construction of a sentimental culture that tries to assert the reality of self-determination while simultaneously yoking it to standard norms of behavior. Eliza, read sympathetically or not, represents the impossibility of such a union. Confessing midway through the novel her fears that Boyer will "seduce [her] into matrimony," Eliza articulates the relationship between seduction and female education. Her turn of phrase also confirms her perception—at least at this point in the novel—that influence compromises choice. Such a revelation is in fact what the seduction novel is designed to obscure; in order for seduction to be successful, it must be represented as something other than what it is. Influence is therefore represented as choice and choice is represented as fatal.

In this respect, *The Coquette* may be said to represent the whole seduction oeuvre. While the personalizing of heroines contributes to liberal ideas of individual autonomy and authority, it has the concomitant effect of making larger social problems appear personally idiosyncratic. That is, by and large, seduction novels do not attribute the problem of seduction to the political flaws of republican society but to the personal flaws of each particular heroine. These personal flaws must in turn prove fatal, for only if she dies will readers be able to imagine the heroine as having (had) other options. Considered in broader terms, *The Coquette* reminds us that the belief in self-determination, one of the most persistent of American liberal ideals, must be continually undercut in order to prove that it still exists. To see choice—and woman's choice in particular—through to the end, unmediated by the effects of seduction, is to come face-to-face with the limits of free will. And, in a democratic society, this is the story that cannot be told.

The ostensible public function of seduction novels is to engage the audience so successfully that what is written on the page will be transcribed onto readers' impressionable hearts. An objective correlative to such a concept appears in the prevalence of iconic testimonials—headstones and monuments—that conclude seduction stories, which testify to the sublimation of desire that perfects female character and education. In the anonymously authored "Amelia, or the Faithless Briton," the story ends with the protagonist's father erecting a monument "in commemoration of [his daughter's] fate." Though heartbroken, he consoles himself with the idea that "whatever may be the sufferings of virtue HERE, its portion must be happiness HEREAFTER" (42). Likewise, *The Coquette* concludes with a friend's reassuring words to Eliza's mother that, though the daughter's desires were never destined to be fulfilled in this world, they will be in another: "I hope, madam, that . . . [the inscription of her headstone] . . . may alleviate your grief; and while they leave the pleasing remembrance of her virtues, add the supporting persuasion, that your Eliza is happy" (169). These narrative monuments to dead desire signify that bodily weakness has finally been transcended. The woman's sensibility is preserved, while her susceptibility—her penetrability—is forever neutralized, turned to stone.

Of course, from an economic standpoint, there exists a logical flaw in the sentimental goal, for a truly successful education will render the seduction novel's lessons obsolete.[56] But, as previous critics have claimed, literary history—and the literary marketplace—is constituted by a constantly shifting "horizon of expectations."[57] With regard to sentimental fiction, such a shift takes place in the early to mid-nineteenth century with the introduction of a revised version of the "woman's story," represented by the domestic novel.[58] The domestic novel proves the logical extension of the seduction story's "education," as protagonists learn through various forms of religious and literary instruction to "compose" themselves. In the domestic story, self-possessed middle-class heroines no longer have to die to embody the transcendence of desire, for now it is written into the script of their lives.

4

Changing the Subject: Domestic Fictions of Self-Possession

I have been arguing that sentimental strategies inform American revolutionary and early national politics and that sympathetic identification supplies a key element in the sentimental construction of both personal and political unions. As a sentimental genre, seduction fiction sought to dramatize cultural connections between filial sympathy and sociopolitical allegiance through pedagogical narratives centering on the power of emotional response. Emotional response is crucial to the novel's methodology as well, as readers' sympathies are employed in the service of modifying readers' behavior. One could say then that "seduction" signifies not only what the story is about but what it does: while warning young women to avoid the seducer's verbal arts, the seduction novel attempts to snare the reader in its own.

Thus, while ostensibly representing a threat to national unity and "republican virtue," seduction and incest actually epitomize the political and narrative strategies popularly constructing American identity. Inasmuch as it reflects a culture preoccupied with loving familiar, rather than foreign, subjects, incest becomes the central metaphor in these narratives of national union. Interestingly enough, what we see in the nineteenth-century "domestic" novel is not a rejection of incest and seduction but a perfecting of these concepts. Loving what is familiar becomes the ideal in these texts, as virtual incest—the love between surrogate brothers and sisters, fathers and daughters—takes the place of biological incest.[1] Domestic novels are thus aptly named, both for their reference to the household sphere represented in these stories and for the *domestication of desire* that has all along been the aim of sentimental literature. The conflation of social and familial ties, and the resultant eroticization of kinship relations, is not only legitimated but idealized in this version: marriage is now shown as the "natural" teleology of a preexisting familial love.

Incest as a cultural ideal is reinforced by the Christianizing of sentimental narratives. In the wake of America's Second Great Awakening, these novels introduce the concept of conversion into the woman's story. Whereas the protagonist was once susceptible to both positive and negative influence (itself a relative distinction), now her psyche is first penetrated by the ideal Father. As befits the goal of conversion, God's divine will ultimately becomes indistinguishable from the heroine's own. With unlimited access to the Father within, domestic security is assured and individual will is shown to be aligned with a heavenly power structure. Ironically, though excluded from the rights of citizenship herself, the woman comes to symbolize the perfect liberal individual in antebellum culture, self-mastered and seemingly in control of her domestic future.

This last point does *not* suggest, as other critics have claimed, that the domestic subject is essentially autonomous. In arguing that feminine suggestibility represents an ideal reading subjectivity (for both male *and* female readers), I have attempted to demonstrate the relational dynamic inherent in the construction of both individual and political identities. The trope of conversion highlights this point, for, in gaining control of her own emotions, the heroine must first see herself in relation to a disciplinary father figure. Rather than fashioning either a completely independent or a submissive individual, then, domestic literature reaffirms the revolutionary practice of its seductive predecessor: it brings together republican and liberal concerns — the rights of the community and the rights of the individual — under one overarching frame of familial Love.

Domestic Reformations

In her path-breaking study of the politics of the English novel, *Desire and Domestic Fiction*, Nancy Armstrong contends that the "modern individual was first and foremost a woman."[2] Crediting eighteenth-century domestic literature with helping to shape the attitudes and imaginations of England's future middle class, Armstrong shows how the domestic ideal, and the woman who represented it, brought into being "a concept of the household on which socially hostile groups felt they could all agree." Attentive to "the subtlest difference in status," conduct books, and the novels patterned after them, provided a model of domestic refinement that could be "realized in any and all respectable households," not just those of the upper class. The result was the creation of a "fiction of horizontal affiliations that only a century later could be said to have materialized as an economic reality" (69). By virtue of their nonpartisan status—i.e., their exclusion from political and economic spheres of action—women became the forerunners of middle-class hegemony. The image of the ideal woman culled from domestic manuals represents a distinctly modern conception of the self as independent of the material conditions producing it, able to "transform itself without transforming the social and economic configuration in opposition to which it is constructed" (94–95).

Domestic literature offers a paradigm of self-production whereby the written word serves as both the means by which subjectivity is apprehended and a metaphor for the many ways the self can be shaped. In Armstrong's story of self-production, however, the subject is encrypted by the books that represent her. Individualism becomes synonymous with autonomy, a self-sustaining state produced by the rhetorical operations of domestic narratives. Yet, if sentimental literature attempts to teach us anything, it is that psychological boundaries are permeable and that "selfhood" is a distinctly relational construct. Autonomy thus becomes an often sought but ever elusive epistemological condition. In American sentimental fiction—seduction as well as domestic stories—the concept of self-possession is complicated not only by the manipulative narrative techniques that attempt to produce it but also by the examples of corporate identity ubiquitous within the tale. Such examples help reconcile the basic conflict between personal autonomy and external authority by destabilizing the frameworks supporting each of these ideological positions.

Armstrong's equation of conduct books and domestic novels further obscures the sentimental principles by which domestic fiction operates. The difference between conduct literature and the novels they inspire lies in the latter's self-conscious attempts to employ strategies of identification to construct its ideal reader. Although, as Nina Baym points out, early novels were often thought to foster "self-love and a tendency to self-assertion" that might undermine social feeling, sentimental fiction works on a different premise altogether, one that imagines self-interest as fundamental to the development of social relations.[3] The sympathetic bond between familiars—whether parents and children, husbands and wives, or readers and characters—becomes a catalyst for the less personal altruism that will eventually bind all citizens together. The reception of Susan Warner's female bildungsroman, *The Wide, Wide World* (1850), offers an excellent example of the sociopolitical significance of sentimental feeling. Warner's novel traces the history of a young girl who, once orphaned, must find her own way in the world. Acclaimed one of the two "national" novels of its decade,[4] *The Wide Wide World* is singled out by one reviewer specifically for its ability to foster sympathetic family feeling: "The interest [in this novel] . . . lies in the most life-like picture of the character and fate of a little girl . . . *such as any of our daughters may be.* . . . We care for all else only as this little piece of tender, budding womanhood is affected or influenced."[5] Warner's novel gains status as a national icon by virtue of its popularity: in representing what the majority of American people desire to read, the novel is to represent, by extension, what the American people value. As the above review indicates, what the American people value is not simply a young girl's faith and perseverance but the *familiar feelings* she evokes. In other words, readers value the sympathetic attachment that makes another's experience feel as if it were their own. [6]

What I am essentially arguing for here is a new model of social relations in early national and antebellum culture, one that acknowledges permeability as a defining psychological category in the nineteenth-century American mindset.[7] The model can be extended to the political realm as well: as I have already shown, the concept of mutable domestic boundaries has its roots in the eighteenth century, when the clash of colonialism and nationalism became popularly represented in America through redefinitions of the parent-child relationship. In the years following America's War of Independence, the question of "American" identity grew increasingly complicated as Americans recognized their reliance on foreign markets and powers for their own national prosperity. Clearly American "independence" did not mean autonomy but rather the right to balance domestic integrity with international cooperation.

Although by the first decade of the nineteenth century there was no doubt that free trade played an essential part in the United States' intention to "figure on the face of the earth, and in the annals of the world,"[8] dealings with foreign governments were nonetheless viewed with suspicion.[9] One can read distrust of foreign interference, along with a desire to reestablish ideological boundaries, as contributing to the valorization of the "domestic" that distinguished itself from common, and seemingly corrupt, commercial interactions. After all, Jefferson's agrarian vision of small independent landowners did not die out in the nineteenth century but rather moved westward. In its own way, the frontier, with its "endlessly retreating vision of innocence," provided an imaginative alternative to the cramped quarters of urban trade society.[10] Urban culture in turn, settling in to an increasingly commercial and industrial way of life, manufactured its own model of innocence through a romanticized view of a separate and private sphere.[11] Although American autonomy proved more of an ideal than a reality, the dream did not altogether disappear. On the contrary, for the middle classes, this vision simply worked itself into a smaller frame of reference, a domestic vision not so easily manipulated by external forces.

Of course, despite these correspondences between political and literary preoccupations with national identity, we have no reliable way to chart the direct or indirect influence between sociopolitical happenings and domestic ideology. Nor would domestic fiction lend itself to such an endeavor. Domestic fiction does not reflect the actual events of its time; in fact, more often than not it attempts to improve upon them. My intention, therefore, is not to make a case for the ways in which sentimental fiction illuminates the mental or social activities of its readership but to address some of the ways we might rethink and complicate the concept of domesticity itself. As Mary Ryan has observed, the standard historical hypothesis concerning the nineteenth-century family "contended that large extended households were decimated into small, 'isolated, nuclear families' by the process of industrialization." The modern family thereafter became typified by greater affective interaction and a "remoteness from society, politics, and production."[12] Scholars of domestic fiction have tended to perpetuate this paradigm, alternately criticizing or celebrating domestic ideology's renunciation of the marketplace.[13] Although most domestic novels do in fact critique, implicitly and explicitly, various displays of "market" mentality (including the *marriage* market), they do so not as a way of isolating the domestic sphere from the world at large but as a way of advocating a more liberal view of domestic relations. The most popular sentimental novels of the nineteenth century—*The Wide, Wide World*, *Uncle Tom's Cabin*, and *The Lamplighter*—redraw the boundaries of the American family to make central the socially and politically marginalized. To effect such a change, these novels actually abstract concepts of home, family, and self from their physical and biological moorings, thereby legitimizing the incestuous alliances of earlier seduction stories. In effect, domestic novels divorce sentiment from blood and recast family feeling from a stumbling block into a cornerstone of sentimental union.

The Conversion to Love: *A New-England Tale*

What Nina Baym terms the "reconsituted family" of American domestic literature owes its imaginative framework, at least in part, to a rising evangelicalism that pervades nineteenth-century sentimental culture.[14] Popular domestic stories reconceive the family along the lines of a Christian paradigm that supplants an Old Testament model of exceptionalism based on heredity—as exemplified in the Jews as God's "chosen people"—with one based on the heart. The emphasis on spiritual over biological kinship is consistent with a New Testament ethos that sees filial relations as determined by faith rather than blood. In the evangelical Christian scheme, family ties are represented as both voluntary and inherently reproducible: i.e., what matters is not the family into which the individual is born but the one into which the individual *grows*.

The Christian story of salvation intersects with the story of psychological development, the bildungsroman, so prevalent in nineteenth-century Anglo and European literature. Unlike the eighteenth-century seduction novel, which depicts the problems attending young women at a particularly vulnerable moment in their romantic history, domestic novels trace the development of the woman's psyche over a period of years.[15] These nineteenth-century stories aim to model for readers the psychological transformation that readers themselves are to internalize and emulate. Conversion thus typically serves as the central trope of these narratives. Arising as it does in the midst of America's Second Great Awakening, the domestic novel foregrounds the importance of feeling—and filial feeling specifically—in discovering and sustaining spiritual truths. Mothers, in particular, become the representatives of these truths. In the 1820s and 1830, women were viewed as the vehicles through which husbands and children came to God, supplanting the professional minister in the role of imparting moral and spiritual guidance. "The accounts in the mother's magazines seldom recognized ministerial interference in the conversion of children," writes Mary Ryan; "In 1833 the editor of *Mother's Magazine* put it directly: 'The church has had her seasons of refreshing and her turn of decay; but here in the circle of mothers, it is felt that the Holy Spirit condescends to *dwell*. It seems his blessed rest.'"[16]

Despite the Christian doctrine that children come to know God through the parent's example and instruction, domestic stories tend to feature heroines who have lost the security of their homes and are thrown into the "wide, wide world." In the course of the narrative they learn to reconstruct those familial bonds by relying first on the bond that cannot be broken: the bond between God and his child. Reminiscent of the early sentimental genre, parents are represented as the catalyzing force in shaping a child's world view; yet the parent's (now typically the mother's) ultimate aim is to give her child the tools for letting the earthly parent go. By encouraging reliance on a Parent who never errs and never dies, mothers equip their children in the virtue of self-sufficiency, teaching them to take to heart the love and authority that, through conversion, will become indistinguishable from their own desire.

Published in 1822, Catharine Sedgwick's *A New-England Tale* represents the first in a long line of domestic novels that would convert the threat of influence into a sanctifying force.[17] The plight of the young protagonist, Jane Elton, typifies the position of many domestic heroines: at the age of thirteen, Jane finds herself orphaned and, due to her father's unethical and inept business practices, she discovers herself penniless as well. Jane's mother, although ineffectual in her attempts to reform her husband's character, could boast one significant achievement before she died: she had "watched over the expanding character of her child with Christian fidelity" (33).[18] Having been "gently led in the bands of love," Jane has acquired a "habit of self-command" (24) that serves her well in the trying years ahead. Raised on her mother's Methodist principles, Jane has also acquired a belief in the individual's ability to reform the world around and within her.[19]

A New-England Tale bears the stamp of a rising middle-class evangelicalism with its emphasis on the redeeming influence of affective feeling. Jane's internalization of her mother's faith, as opposed to her father's unregulated and unprincipled financial interests, exemplifies this new dimension in parent-child relations. Even so, for Sedgwick, as for most domestic novelists, it was not one's *gender* but one's *capacity for sympathy* that determined one's fitness as a role model. In this, middle-class mothers were thought to have the natural advantage, for in both giving birth to and becoming the primary caretakers of their children, mothers experienced daily the power of sympathetic attachment. Sympathy proves the golden rule of Sedgwick's domesticity; it is the standard against which all strictures of education are to be measured. It is also the point upon which sentimental fiction turns. For, in converting the hapless protagonist of seduction fiction into a new and virtuous heroine, Sedgwick attempts to reform the role of sympathy itself—to teach by *positive* rather than by negative example.

A New-England Tale condemns the cautionary form of Puritan theology that teaches children to despise their own natures, for such doctrines inevitably teach children to despise others as well. This idea is most forcefully examined in the context of the family to which Jane is sent. Since Jane's youth and poverty necessitate that she be raised by one of her relatives, she is taken in by her aunt, Mrs. Wilson, who runs a school for the "discipline of christian character." A selfish and mean-spirited apologian to original sin, Mrs. Wilson attempts to efface the principles of love on which Jane was raised and to put in their place a theology of debt: "You must remember, child, that I am at liberty to turn you away at any time, whereas, as you will always be in debt to me, you can never be at liberty to go when you choose. . . . my word must be your law" (37). Mrs. Wilson evinces a brand of Christian discipline that smacks of the marketplace, where all acts of charity have their price. In bringing up her own children by the "letter" rather than the "spirit" of the law, she withholds from them not only love but any hope of a productive and moral life: " 'The kingdom of grace is very different from the kingdom of nature,' [claimed] Mrs. Wilson. 'The natural man can do nothing towards his own salvation. Every act he performs, and every prayer he offers, but provokes more and more the wrath of the Almighty' " (148). Here God takes on the qualities of a cosmic loan-shark—at once disdainful of meager contributions yet inexorable in his demand that the debt be repaid.

Like Sedgwick's second novel, *Redwood* (1824), and her most famous novel, *Hope Leslie* (1827), *A New-England Tale* juxtaposes the tolerance of a liberal religious education against the narrow-minded and judgmental teachings of Calvinist theology.[20] For Sedgwick, the latter's doctrine of natural depravity represents an outmoded and destructive model of social and spiritual relations. This is driven home by the hardened characters and unhappy fates of Mrs. Wilson's children. Writing to his mother from prison after his indictment for robbery, Mrs. Wilson's oldest child, David, speaks to the outrage of a tyrannical theology that leaves one no hope for redemption and no responsibility for its loss:

> You, it was, that taught me, when I scarcely knew my right hand from my left, that there was no difference between doing right and doing wrong, in the sight of the God you worship; you taught me, that I could do nothing acceptable to him. If you taught me truly, I have only acted out the nature totally depraved, (your own words,) that he gave to me, and I am not to blame for it. . . . If you have taught me falsely, I was not to blame; the peril be on your own soul. My mind was a blank, and you put your own impressions on it; God (if there be a God) reward you according to your deeds! (155).

In contrast to his mother's essentialist philosophy, David articulates the prevailing view that character is formed *after* birth—not by God but by the parents who represent Him. Never having been taught to value himself, David in turn never learns to value others. In keeping with the goals of sentimental pedagogy, sympathy is represented as *learned* behavior with far-reaching social consequences.

David's rejection of his mother's mode of education is on a broader level a rejection of the cautionary tale itself. According to the new domestic model, by impressing on children an image of what they should *not* become, cautionary fiction ultimately *produces* the actions it seeks to condemn. By contrast, A *New-England Tale* exemplifies love's power to (re)form individual feeling and thereby the individual's experience of the world. Sympathy is reformed as well in this model; rather than signifying the "voice of blood" to which Nature draws its unwitting victims, sympathetic attachment betokens a complementarity of interests and values to which reciprocal feelings give proof. Put another way, love is perfect sympathy: a mutual, freely consenting surrender of self-interest in the interest of the beloved.

The absence of such feeling is what leads Jane to break off her engagement with her first suitor, Edward Erskine. Erskine is the first to defend Jane against her aunt's unjust treatment, but his true character eventually surfaces and Jane discovers him to be undisciplined, anti-religious, and mercenary. Although Erskine protests that Jane "owe[s]" him her love (126) and so "ought to be blind" to his faults (125), Jane adverts to the lack of affinity between them: "Oh, Edward! . . . Examine your heart as I have examined mine, and you will find that the tie is dissolved that bound us; there can be no enduring love without sympathy; our feelings, our pursuits, our plans, our inclinations, are all diverse." When Erskine assures her that he will be "as plastic as wax, in [her] hands," Jane dissents: "No, Edward; I have tried my power over you, and found it wanting" (129). Like her mother before her, Jane discovers religious conviction ineffective against a fully formed commercial mentality. The fact that her love cannot reform him only underscores for Jane the incompatibility of their sentiments.

Erskine's vision of the domestic sphere—the frame of his reference and responsibility—is too limited in its scope, and his emotions prove equally restrictive. In essence, Erskine's feelings are *too personal*. Rather than functioning as an affective catalyst to disinterested benevolence, Erskine's love for Jane remains doggedly fixed, rooted in the object of his affections. While he is overly possessive of her, he is insensible to the unjust treatment of others.[21] Put in sentimental terms, Erskine suffers from a failure of the imagination that would allow him to see beyond himself and his immediate family to conceive the family of humanity. For Sedgwick, such a conceptual leap is only possible through the psychologically reorganizing power of religion.

Erskine's lack of faith leads Jane's childhood maid and fellow Methodist, Mary, to question Jane's initial engagement to him. After all, reasons Mary, "I know, you [Jane] think there is nothing binds hearts together like religion—that bond endures where there is neither marrying nor giving in marriage" (109). The fact that Mary gives priority to spiritual over earthly attachments is meant in part to reflect her views on the transcendental qualities of perfect sympathy. It is also, however, a comment on marriage as an imperfect and man-made institution. By alluding to Jesus's declaration that in heaven there is neither "marrying nor giving in marriage,"[22] Mary reminds Jane that in another and *better* age marriage will be superfluous. Jane eventually comes to the same conclusion. In her last interview with Erskine, she tells him she has realized "that religion alone can produce unity of spirit; alone can resist the cares, the disappointments, the tempests of life; that it is the only indissoluble bond. . . . I have felt that my most sacred pleasures and hopes must be solitary" (130). These lines suggest that it is not Erskine's selfish tendencies alone that have caused Jane to reevaluate her commitment to him, but her growing conviction that human relationships in general are insufficient to support a true and lasting union.

As Jane articulates it, affiliations of the flesh make poor substitutes for the spiritual bond that cannot be broken. No man is therefore required to produce the "unity of spirit" that she aims to achieve. The "indissoluble bond" of religion is shown to be essentially *self*-generated. As Jane's reference to her "solitary" pleasures indicates, her principal attachment is to the religion of her own heart; it is in communion with herself that she attains the "unity" she seeks. Therefore, although Jane does marry in the end, her marriage is not meant to confer on her a wholeness she would otherwise lack. Rather, in marrying the Quaker Robert Lloyd, Jane marries a man akin to herself. His own religious sympathy confirms their compatibility; in addition, it initiates a triangulation of desire wherein religion mediates romantic attachment. In other words, love proves a *doubling* rather than a *merging* of sympathies. Such a representation of romantic love prevents heterosexual bonding from becoming too exclusive: in this model, the power of sympathy evinces a centripetal rather than a centrifugal force, moving desire out into the world where it can have a socially beneficial impact.

The conflicts attending heterosexual relationships first made apparent in sentimental seduction fiction are alleviated here by the redirection of sympathy. In the earlier stories, models of affinity worked to obscure as much as to illuminate the hierarchical structure inherent in conjugal relationships. As if taking a lesson from its literary predecessor, *A New-England Tale* carefully distinguishes perfect sympathy from the merely human emotions that exist to emulate it. Religion becomes the unseen affective force that completes heterosexual union by detaching it from its predominantly physical conditions. As a result, familial attachment becomes the romantic ideal.

By liberating romantic love from its material (i.e., sexual and biological) base, Sedgwick's domestic tale is able to idealize the seduction novel's correlation between filial and conjugal attachment and thus to perfect the philosophy of seductive paternalism. The conclusion of Jane's story—with her marriage to Robert Lloyd—helps illustrate this point. A man eleven years Jane's senior and with a daughter of his own, Lloyd initially represents a father figure for the thirteen-year-old Jane. His purchase of the bankrupt Elton estate at the beginning of the novel gives material shape and direction to the filial sympathies with which Sedgwick later invests him: "[Lloyd] had loved Jane first as a child, and then as a sister; and of late he had thought if he could love another woman, as a wife, it would be Jane Elton" (108). This curious blend of paternal, fraternal, and romantic feeling is not meant to challenge Lloyd's fitness as a potential lover. On the contrary, Lloyd's filial sentiments are invoked to *substantiate* rather than controvert his suitability as Jane's future husband. His desire to "imitate the Parent of the universe" becomes a gloss on his symbolic, though more earthly, role: Lloyd represents the (kind of) father Jane never had. In subordinating secular to spiritual unions, A *New-England Tale* does not reject filial attachment but romanticizes it. Even in this domesticated version of the sentimental tale, fathers still make the best lovers.

A *New-England Tale* inverts the terms of filial sympathy made popular by eighteenth-century stories: whereas biological ties once evoked the sympathy they could not control, shared sympathies are now meant to confirm that one has found a home. And like the concept of the family, "home" has been dissociated from its physical setting. Ironically, true domestic values are not located in the conventional household but in those spaces, and in those characters, existing on the fringes of mainstream society. John of the Mountain, the itinerant vagrant, Crazy Bet, the seduced and abandoned Mary Oakley, and the comunitarian, Robert Lloyd, represent, as Jane does, the disenfranchised—those who must build a family from the company of loved ones. It is their very exclusion from the dominant social group that identifies them as a model community. Yet, despite this shift in priorities, Sedgwick manages to wed spiritual with material forms of domestic value by the end of her story. After all, as owner of the Elton estate, Lloyd is able to offer Jane more than a *symbolic* recovery of family life. In marrying him, Jane recovers her childhood home as well.

Corporate Individualism: *The Lamplighter*

Written more than forty years after A *New-England Tale*, *The Lamplighter* (1854) constitutes one of the last and most popular of the domestic novels. It also reveals the extent to which literary depictions of Christian individualism have facilitated the reconstruction of paternal authority in the intervening years. Whereas Sedgwick's novel assumes from the outset its heroine's "habit of self-command," *The Lamplighter* traces the psychological mechanisms by which passionate individuals achieve their self-possession. What the novel's investigation reveals is, paradoxically, a relational model of selfhood that undergirds nineteenth-century notions of independence. Through the trope of conversion, *The Lamplighter* links self-determination to sympathetic mediation: in order to be reformed, the heroine must first learn to see herself as she would be viewed through the eyes of an all-seeing Father. She must then go on to internalize that perspective. Adam Smith's "man within the breast," that eighteenth-century model of mediated subjectivity, takes on renewed significance in a story in which, to use Smith's words, "the lesson of self command" is achieved by an *alienation* from one's normal emotional and psychological frames of reference and, thus, from one's habitual responses. Put another way, *The Lamplighter* is a story about an individual who is taken possession of by the ultimate father figure and finds her "self" in the process.

As the novel opens, the reader is introduced to the eight-year-old protagonist, Gertrude Flint, sitting on a city sidewalk amidst the grimy snow. She is "scantily clad, in garments of the poorest description" and bears the signs of emotional as well as physical neglect. As the narrator quite candidly points out, there is nothing about the child that would recommend her to the casual observer. She is "thin and sharp," with a sallow complexion, and though she has "fine, dark eyes," they are "so unnaturally large . . . in contrast to her thin, puny face, that they only increased the peculiarity of it, without enhancing its beauty."[23] Her mother died five years earlier while a boarder at a house owned by Nan Grant, and Gerty has been kept on in order to do the owner's bidding. After Gerty is cast out of Nan's house and onto the streets, she is taken home by the kindly but poor lamplighter, Trueman Flint. In his modest home, she experiences her first feelings of security and love. "True" makes tangible the Love that comes from an unseen source: the humble man who lights the lamps becomes for Gerty the embodiment of the Father who lights the stars. Living with her adopted father and his neighbors, the Sullivans, Gerty learns what family means. Through them she finds a way out not only of a dark and cheerless world but of her own dark heart as well.

Although Gerty discovers a new source of security, her loyalty remains discriminate; familial attachment does not initiate a sympathy for humankind but for those who treat her like family. With the unadulterated honesty of a child, Gerty freely admits her feelings of hatred and revenge. In fact, she takes great pleasure in indulging in them. Her real problem, we are told, is that she has never been loved. She has therefore never known the bonds of affection that cement social relationships or that enable a child to convert passionate instinct into a willful self-control. It is Emily Graham, a beautiful young blind woman, who first initiates Gerty's transformation through religious instruction. Part of that instruction involves replacing Gerty's "eye for an eye" philosophy of justice with a psychology of mercy. In a conversation that illuminates for readers the necessity of uprooting "natural" instincts in the greater interest of social bonding, Gerty tells Emily that she won't return to school because she hates the girls who tease and demean her. Emily responds by citing the golden rule of Christianity:

> "Gerty," said Emily, solemnly, "didn't you tell me, the other day, that you were a naughty child, but that you wished to be good, and would try?"
>
> "Yes," said Gerty.
>
> "If you wish to become good and be forgiven, you must forgive others."
>
> Gerty said nothing.
>
> "Do you not wish God to forgive and love you?"
>
> "God, that lives in heaven,—that made the stars?" said Gerty.
>
> "Yes."
>
> "Will he love me, and let me some time go to heaven?"
>
> "Yes, if you try to be good, and love everybody."
>
> "Miss Emily," said Gerty, after a moment's pause, "I can't do it,—so I s'pose I can't go."
>
> Just at this moment a tear fell upon Gerty's forehead. She looked thoughtfully up in Emily's face, then said,
>
> "Dear Miss Emily, are you going?"
>
> "I am trying to."
>
> "I should like to go with you," said Gerty, shaking her head meditatively.
>
> Still Emily did not speak. She left the child to the working of her own thoughts. (62)[24]

Emily's construction of mercy—the idea that one must forgive in order to be forgiven—makes explicit the sympathetic relationship that exists between victim and oppressor. Emily in effect demands that Gerty identify with her assailants—to see herself as part of a universal company of sinners. To do this, she must learn to look outside of herself and to view her actions as another would view them. Specifically, Gerty must imagine how she is perceived by One who is Himself sinless yet merciful. According to Emily, only by identifying with *His* mercy will Gerty experience her own. Gerty is thus asked to enter into a process of double identification: she must simultaneously acknowledge her kinship with those she hates and psychologically transcend that kinship in order to model the Father whose mercy will redeem her.

The Lamplighter exemplifies sentimental fiction's self-conscious modeling of sympathetic identification by linking the heroine's change of heart to story-telling. Through narratives, characters learn to sympathize with one another and to unite in emotional kinship. Thus Gerty, who has cried many times for herself, first cries on someone else's behalf when she hears the story of Emily's blindness (54). True, we are told, hears Gerty's sad tale of abuse many times over, "but never *without crying*" (33). And in a climactic moment early in the novel, Gerty becomes transfixed by her own story when she hears it narrated in True's own words; it represents an irrevocable moment of bonding between them:

> True was so excited and animated by his subject, that he did not notice what the sexton had observed, but did not choose to interrupt. Gerty had risen from her bed and was standing beside True, her eyes fixed upon his face, breathless with the interest she felt in his words. She touched his shoulder; he looked round, saw her, and stretched out his arms. She sprang into them, buried her face in his bosom, and, bursting into a paroxysm of joyful tears, gasped out the words, "Shall I stay with you always?"
> "Yes, just as long as I live," said True, "you shall be my child." (22)

In keeping with the principles of sentimental pedagogy, stories become vehicles through which individuals are made familiar to each other, breaking down barriers between disparate experiences and personalities in a drama of filial love. Moreover, in hearing her history told by True, Gerty not only experiences an emotional connection with him, she learns to see herself through his eyes. Thus begins the process of first perceiving and then internalizing the loving parent's perspective. Although it is some years before Gerty will manage the self-control for which she later becomes known and admired, her conversion has its roots in a desire to please the father who has taught her the value of her *self*.

Though the road to heaven may be paved with familial sympathy, human attachments alone are not enough to transform a proud spirit into a sympathetic soul. As Emily says, there is but one power strong enough to "quell and subdue earthly pride and passion; the power of Christian humility, engrafted into the heart,—the humility of *principle*, of *conscience*,—the only power to which native pride ever will pay homage" (73). For the next few years, Emily will devote herself to teaching Gerty Christian humility. As Cummins's novel presents it, conscience, or one's sense of right and wrong, is not innate but acquired; it is "engrafted" into the heart. Although originally existing outside the body, once taken to heart conscience has the power to transform the body into a model of self-possession. "In teaching her the spirit of her Divine Master," the narrator tells us, "Emily was making [Gerty] powerful to do and to suffer, to bear and to forbear, when, depending on herself, she should be left to her own guidance alone" (73). Like Smith's "impartial spectator," conscience performs a self-disciplinary function. It works to alienate us from our "native pride" that we might view our actions through the eyes of others: "We endeavor to examine our own conduct as we imagine any other fair and impartial spectator would examine it," writes Smith. "If, upon placing ourselves in his situation, we thoroughly enter into all the passions and motives which influenced it, we approve of it. . . . If otherwise, we enter into his disapprobation, and condemn it."[25] Conjoined as it is with a Christian ethos in *The Lamplighter*, conscience becomes not only externalized but *personalized*; the "man within the breast" becomes indistinguishable from the loving and omniscient Father whom Gerty sees as both independent of and intrinsic to herself.

The success of Emily's tutelage is proven in a trial that, some years before, would have ended in the child's wrath. One day, while ostensibly tidying up Gertrude's room, Mrs. Ellis, jealous of the attention paid to Gertrude, throws out all the momentos of Gerty's past life—gifts from True and from Willie Sullivan, Gerty's brotherly confidant. When Gerty discovers the betrayal, she enters into a contest with her own emotions:

> Once or twice she lifted her head, and seemed on the point of rising and going to face her enemy. But each time something came across her mind and detained her. It was not fear;—O no! Gertrude was not afraid of anybody. It must have been some stronger motive than that. Whatever it might be, it was something that had, on the whole, a soothing influence; for, after every fresh struggle, she grew calmer, and presently, rising, seated herself in a chair by the window. (117)

In the end, a "wonderful composure stole into Gertrude's heart," announcing the beginnings of a new and different strength: "She had conquered; she had achieved the greatest of earth's victories, a victory over herself" (117). Gertrude has just turned thirteen at this point in the novel. Puberty becomes associated with—even intercepted by—a "soothing influence" that redirects her desire. This influence is the affective trace of "Him who is strength to the weak and comfort to the sorrowing," the "Father of spirits" to whom Gertrude submits herself (164). The potentially devastating effects of male manipulation—so central a mechanism of the seduction plot—is supplanted by an image of the all-seeing Father who ushers the child into womanhood.

Gertrude exhibits now a correspondence between private and public selves that is the mark of a true heroine. Where the young Gerty once hid in corners, behind doors, and behind furniture, the mature Gertrude can enter public spaces with the same self-assurance as if she were in private:

> As she came in alone, and unexpected by the greater part of the company, all eyes were turned upon her. Contrary to the expectation of Belle and Kitty, who were watching her with curiousity, she manifested neither embarrassment nor awkwardness; but, glancing leisurely at the various groups, until she recognized Mrs. Jeremy, crossed the large saloon with characteristic grace, and as much ease and self-possession as if she were the only person present. (197)

Gertrude's ability to appear the same in public as in private puts to rest the anxieties over women's hidden physical and emotional spaces so prevalent in seduction stories. The problem of privacy, and of the emotional susceptibility that gives rise to illicit private acts, is alleviated by the condition of transparency—the woman's capacity to withstand both external and internal scrutiny. Ironically, *self*-discipline is shown forged from the bonds of filial devotion, and privacy made perfect through the incorporation of paternal influence.

Through her identification with the spiritual Father, Gertrude achieves a self-possession that is both consistent with and independent of public forms of control. It is a condition conducive to capitalist as well as evangelical constructions of liberal individualism. As C. B. MacPherson has argued, capitalist ideas inform both the conception and the structure of American liberal democracy.[26] Gillian Brown summarizes MacPherson's conclusions by identifying the "possessive" nature of liberal individualism: "According to this concept of self evolving from the seventeenth century, every man has property in himself and thus the right to manage himself, his labor, and his property as he wishes. . . . This is a market society's construction of self, a self aligned with market relations such as exchange value, alienability, circulation, and competition."[27] Liberal democracy's development alongside a capitalist market economy results in a view of the (male) individual's right to property as both personal and exclusive: "The very concept of property is reduced to that of *private* property," MacPherson asserts, "an individual's right to use to the exclusion of others."[28] The domestic novel, with its flawed but resourceful heroine, draws on the principle of possessive individualism to assert woman's independence through *spiritual* liberation. By extending the limits of the body to include the sanctifying presence of paternal influence, *The Lamplighter* effec-

tively weds capitalist and religious values, envisioning a self that is at once private—"self-possessed"—and corporate.

The marriage of capitalist and Christian philosophy can be seen in the
ways in which *The Lamplighter* aligns material property with the intangible
sentiments that give such property meaning. Thus houses become symbols in
the novel not only of material security but also of the domestic values an individual must internalize before such treasures can be possessed. A memorable
example appears early on in the novel, when Gerty and Willie Sullivan stand
outside the window of a beautiful home meant to epitomize the domestic
dream. The vision brings home to Gerty the material luxuries from which she
is excluded:

> It was now quite dark, so that persons in a light room could not see anyone
> out of doors; but Willie and Gerty had so much the better chance to look in.
> It was indeed a fine mansion, evidently the home of wealth. A clear coal-fire,
> and a bright lamp in the centre of the room, shed abroad their cheerful
> blaze. Rich carpets, deeply-tinted curtains, pictures in gilded frames, and
> huge mirrors, reflecting the whole on every side, gave Gerty her first impres-
> sions of a luxurious life. (45)

The Lamplighter is filled with such descriptive details of the affluent life, a life
that Gerty will later discover is hers by rightful inheritance but that comes to
her only after she has learned to live without it. Confronted with this image of
domestic bliss, Willie vows to work hard and grow rich in order to buy his family a fine house when he is older, but his self-made-man philosophy is subsequently put to work in building *character* as well as a bank account. After many
years of working in a business trade in India, far from the watchful eyes of family and friends, Willie is tempted to indulge in the debauched lifestyle of
many of his associates; guided by the spirit of his departed mother, however,
Willie is able to resist the impulse. His desire to make a life for himself
through hard work is translated from material terms to the terms of sensibility:
he makes himself a man of integrity—constant in his affections and sensitive
to the needs of others. While the novel suggests that the inner man is more
important than the outer one, the internal and the external are never truly separated. Gerty and Willie's success at mastering their personal flaws results in
an earthly reward of financial security, one that confirms rather than competes
with the sentimental value of self-possession.

Like *A New-England Tale*, *The Lamplighter* ultimately reconciles material
with affective forms of domesticity by returning the heroine to familiar
ground. Whereas Jane Elton regains the childhood home from which she

was originally expelled, by the end of *The Lamplighter* Gerty is reunited with her blood kin. Befriended by a man others believe to be a suitor, Gerty discovers the stranger is actually her father. To add to the drama, the man turns out to be Emily's stepbrother and long-lost love as well. While such coincidences may appear a simple—and incredible—plot contrivance, the reconvergence of family relations at the end of the novel actually affirms the power of affinity at the core of sentimental narratives. Moreover, the return of the biological father gives a material structure to the free-floating familial feelings that have been driving the plot. What has long been established in spirit—that is, the kindred connection between Gerty and Emily—is now made legal when Emily marries Gerty's father. Gerty and Willie, too, who have been brought up as brother and sister, cement their familial attachment by marrying each other. While *The Lamplighter* offers a new basis on which to define the family, the natural justice of the characters' affective arrangements is proven by the return of the father who can give those feelings social and legal validity.

Lawrence Stone has argued that two key characteristics of the modern family are "intensified affective bonding of the nuclear core at the expense of neighbors and kin" and a "strong sense of individual autonomy and the right to personal freedom in the pursuit of happiness."[29] *The Lamplighter* brings these oftentimes conflicting impulses together in a heroine whose self-possession reinforces familial bonds. The potentially fatal effects of intensive bonding are annulled by the redistribution of filial ties—turning "neighbors" into family. Independence is reinforced rather than undermined by familial allegiance, as the heroine's self-possession is achieved through her internalizing of paternal influence—both True's and God's. *The Lamplighter* thus represents an achievement in modern domestic drama: it offers a vision of domestic unity in which independence leads one back to the family.

Reimagining the Familiar Body: *Uncle Tom's Cabin*

The idea of familial attachment as the basis of social organization and national identity structures both seduction and domestic narratives for nearly a hundred years after the inception of the American democratic republic. As both *A New-England Tale* and *The Lamplighter* demonstrate, by abstracting the concept of family ties, patriarchal power becomes more *invasive* as well as pervasive. The conversion of sympathy from dangerous to conventional feeling ultimately legitimizes incestuous familial bonding by detaching it from the material base that renders incest taboo. But redefining the family according to what one has in common with others has distinctly political implications. It aligns sympathy—and the influence that arises from sympathy—with a recognition of likeness, thereby equating democracy with similarity. In Harriet Beecher Stowe's *Uncle Tom's Cabin* (1852), the incendiary politics of race becomes domesticated through just such an equation. Stowe's novel perpetuates a tradition of constructing sympathy as a narcissistic model of projection and rejection: claiming that individuals are all alike under the skin, *Uncle Tom's Cabin* makes diversity virtually unrepresentable, reinforcing the idea of humanity as dependent upon familiarity.

One of the key strategies Stowe employs for creating a democratic readership is the subordination of physical difference to psychological and emotional sameness. Thus, despite its subject matter—the dehumanizing effects of slavery—*Uncle Tom's Cabin* is not about literal bodies; rather, it is about the feelings and perceptions that come to stand for bodies—both the individual body and the body politic. According to Shirley Samuels, it is around the issue of the body that much of the critical controversy surrounding sentimental works like *Uncle Tom's Cabin* revolves. These controversies

> involve a debate between a *dismissal* of the sentimental move outside or beyond the boundaries of a gendered or racialized body—a move seen as a *betrayal* of the specific embodiment figured—and, alternately, a celebration of the emancipatory strategies of a sentimentality that *rescues* subjects from the unfortunate essentializing that the fact of having a body entails.[30]

My own reading of the novel seeks neither to dismiss nor to celebrate the transcendental strategies of liberation so personally and politically problematic; instead, it attempts to identify and elaborate on the sympathetic mechanisms that make such strategies meaningful. Stowe's novel exemplifies the particular methods by which fictional characters are brought to life for readers, becoming embodied through a sympathetic identification that substantiates the reader's own, and by extension the character's, reality. By relying on representations of filial feeling to engender identification, however, *Uncle Tom's Cabin* reveals its contribution to an affinitive politics wherein sympathy is made contingent upon similarity: that is, upon one's ability to perceive others as related to oneself. Ironically, in order to effect the political union she envisions for her readers, Stowe must first elide the personal differences that constitute individuality.

In the chapter entitled "In Which It Appears That a Senator Is But a Man," Senator Bird and his wife debate the ethics of the Fugitive Slave Law that forbids aid to escaped slaves on their way to the Northern states and Canada.[31] The senator has voted for the law, and his wife is appalled:

"I put it to you, John,—would *you* now turn away a poor, shivering, hungry creature from your door, because he was a runaway? *Would* you now? . . .

"Of course, it would be a very painful duty," began Mr. Bird, in a moderate tone.

"Duty, John! don't use that word! You know it isn't a duty—it can't be a duty! If folks want to keep their slaves from running away, let 'em treat 'em well,—that's my doctrine. If I had slaves (as I hope I never shall have), I'd risk their wanting to run away from me, or you either, John. I tell you folks don't run away when they are happy; and when they do run, poor creatures! they suffer enough with cold and hunger and fear, without everybody's turning against them; and, law or no law, I never will, so help me God!"

"Mary! Mary! My dear, let me reason with you."

"I hate reasoning, John,—especially reasoning on such subjects. There's a way you political folks have of coming round and round a plain right thing; and you don't believe in it yourselves, when it comes to practice. I know *you* well enough, John. You don't believe it's right any more than I do; and you wouldn't do it any sooner than I." (144–145)

Mary Bird's resolution to break the "shameful, wicked, abominable law . . . the first time [she gets] a chance" (144), signifies her challenge to a political structure that has no way to take *her*—a woman's—interests and emotions into account. The fact that the senator—acting on every level as his wife's representative—may vote against his wife's conscience highlights the necessity of bringing sympathetic feeling back into some kind of normative line. For Mrs. Bird, politics, or the "coming round and round a plain right thing," has proven itself at odds with common sense—that universal human feeling whose truths are made self-evident to each individual via his or her own emotional responses. Her contention that "folks don't run away when they are happy" serves to underscore the affective foundation on which she sees human action based. Right feeling becomes a law unto itself, superior to the legal injunctions that blindly ignore what the heart deems moral by instinct. Read in this light, one could say that rather than denouncing the present political system Mary Bird (and Stowe through her) seeks to broaden its representative capacity. Mrs. Bird's claim to "know" her husband—that is, to know how he feels and how he would act—is a claim to her own power of representation. Her words reflect her desire to bring the senator quite literally back to his senses as well as her belief in the importance of aligning those senses along a common axis.

As Stowe's chapter goes on to demonstrate, in order for individuals to find their common ground, abstract principles must first be rooted in the sympathetic affections that alone render individuals intelligible to one another. This point becomes clear in the moments immediately following Mr. and Mrs.

Bird's exchange. During the couple's debate, Mrs. Bird is called away to attend a commotion in the kitchen; shortly thereafter she asks her husband to join her, and the narrator describes the scene from his perspective:

> [Mr. Bird] laid down his paper, and went into the kitchen, and started, quite amazed at the sight that presented itself: —A young and slender woman, with garments torn and frozen, with one shoe gone, and the stocking torn away from the cut and bleeding foot, was laid back in a deadly swoon upon two chairs. There was the impress of the despised race on her face, yet none could help feeling its mournful and pathetic beauty, while its stony sharpness, its cold, fixed, deathly aspect, struck a solemn chill over him. He drew his breath short, and stood in silence. His wife, and their only colored domestic, old Aunt Dinah, were busily engaged in restorative measures; while old Cudjoe had got the boy on his knee, and was busy pulling off his shoes and stockings, and chafing his little cold feet (146).

The passage refers to the arrival of Eliza and her young son, Harry, two slaves who have fled the Shelby plantation after Eliza learns that Harry is to be sold. Faced with this living image of human suffering, Mr. Bird is forced to bring reason and feeling, head and heart, together, and to acknowledge the failure of his imagination in adequately representing the concept of slavery. As the narrator ironically observes, "What a situation, now, for a patriotic senator, that had been all the week before spurring up the legislation of his native state to pass more stringent resolutions against escaping fugitives, their harborers and abettors!" But then, before this unexpected vision, the senator's "idea of a fugitive was only an idea of the letters that spell the word. . . . The magic of the real presence of distress,—the imploring human eye, the frail, trembling human hand, the despairing appeal of helpless agony,—these he had never tried" (155–156). The senator's conversion from rhetorical agent to affective respondent is engendered by the living embodiment of abstract concepts—words that come to life. This, in essence, is the heart of Stowe's sentimental project: to make real for readers what have heretofore been letters on a page. The senator's representative function takes on narratological significance as he becomes invested with the qualities and experiences of an ideal reader, a position with which Stowe's readers are themselves to identify: i.e., as external readers become witnesses to the senator's awakening of sympathy, they experience, through him, the "magic" of the living word.

Uncle Tom's Cabin offers here a glimpse of the methodological crux of sentimental fiction, where acts of sympathetic identification are performed for, in order to be reproduced in, the sympathetic reader. While the mediating function of sentimental literature might appear only able to approximate "true" acts of sympathy, by engaging the reader in imaginative flights of fancy, this is not the case. Rather, the cultural and political work of Stowe's novel rests on the dynamic process of sympathy that attempts to break down barriers between real and fictive bodies—between, as the narrator says, the "idea of the letters" and the "idea of the fugitive" those letters signify. In either case, as Stowe's repetition makes clear, it is the idea that matters.

Karen Sanchez-Eppler has claimed that sentimental fiction relies on the body as the privileged site of communication.[32] In the bodily act of weeping, "the feelings in the story are made tangibly present in the flesh of the reader," signifying the successful transmission of meaning between reader and text. With regard to slave narratives in particular, Sanchez-Eppler writes that tears signify "the power of sentiment to change the condition of the human body, or *at least, read symbolically,* to alter how that condition is perceived."[33] I would argue that it is exactly the reader's *perception* of conditions, rather than the material conditions themselves, that is at issue in sentimental fiction. Sentimental narratives eschew the need to concretize fictional bodies by relying on another strategy altogether, one that converts all bodies into representations, subjecting them to interpretive—and affective—mediation. In other words, sentimental fiction suggests that, in order to be read at all, the material body *must* be read symbolically. Although the body serves as a vehicle for the transmission of the signs of feeling, it is feeling itself that constitutes the individual. More often than not, the autonomous body represents an obstacle to sympathy, denoting as it does the physical limits of sentimental union. By evoking and circulating feeling, sentimental fiction strives to move beyond the material limits of both the body and the page to participate in the representation of selfhood.

This is not simply to say that feelings matter more than bodies; it is rather to suggest that in terms of the sympathetic mechanisms by which sentimental fiction operates both the physical and the fictional body must always be read as projections of the sympathetic reader. For sentimental writers, literature serves as an extension of the mediating function of the human imagination. As we have seen, sympathy itself depends upon such mediation. For example, Adam Smith claims that it is by the "impressions of our own senses" that we imagine what others feel: "We enter as it were into [the other's] body, and become in some measure the same person with him."[34] In this model, one's senses become the context for another's authenticity: e.g., by imagining what he would feel in their position, Eliza and Harry become as real to the senator as he is to himself. Stowe's seemingly paradoxical phrasing of the senator's vision—that in confronting the fugitives he is witness to "the *magic* of the *real* presence of distress"—becomes clearer when considered in this light, for "*magic*" refers not to supernatural agency, per se, but to the imaginative power that defines subjectivity.

One of the things this suggests is that reading cannot be divorced from "real life," because the reading experience replicates what goes on between individuals every day: sentimental literature, with its emphasis on identification, engages readers in imaginative acts of sympathy broadly acknowledged to underwrite all human relations. Sentimental works do not differentiate between real and fictional characters for the simple reason that, based on the principles of sympathy, other people become real to us through our projected sentiments, not by their objective presence in the world. The obligatory claim to "truth," so important a convention of the sentimental genre, takes on new signficance in this regard. The attempt to demonstrate a novel's veracity—as evidenced in the prefaces of American novels from the late eighteenth to the late nineteenth century—speaks less to the novel's plot than it does to the novel's purpose: i.e., in a successful sentimental novel, real and fictive bodies are perceived as virtually interchangeable. The sentimental logic of sympathy reverses twentieth-century pragmatic logic, wherein the individual is understood to have feelings for others because they are real; rather, in the sentimental paradigm, others (including characters) are made real by the feelings with which the individual invests them. This, in part, accounts for why readers find Stowe's politics so seductive and yet so disturbing. In a novel ostensibly concerned with the emancipation of human bodies, bodies are treated as primarily affective rather than material.

By representing bodies in this way, *Uncle Tom's Cabin* aligns itself with a tradition of sentimentalism that sees social change as accomplished by teaching individuals to read other people as extensions of themselves. As if to make plain this impulse, Senator Bird responds to the plight of the two fugitives by dressing them in the clothes of his wife and son. He asks his wife if Eliza "couldn't wear one of [her] gowns . . . by any letting down, or such matter" (147). Likewise, Harry is given a bundle of clothes once belonging to the Birds' youngest son, Henry, who has recently passed away. It is in fact Harry's appearance in the "lost boy's well-known cap" that triggers the senator's aforementioned sympathetic reverie—his self-conscious recognition of the difference between words and real presence. The external similarities between the sons—their names, their ages, and their apparel—are meant to overshadow what is for Stowe their most superficial difference: the color of their skin. The love Senator Bird bears his dead son becomes identified with the living boy who now wears his clothes, signaling, at one and the same time, the transcendence of bodily difference and the successful conversion of lifeless letters into flesh and blood. That it is the senator's *own* flesh and blood with whom Harry is identified is in part accounted for by Stowe's Christian vision, one wherein all people, regardless of race, class, age, or gender, are seen as members of the family of God. It is also, however, indicative of the peculiarly egocentric nature of sympathetic identification. That is, the senator's desire to dress Eliza and Harry in familiar clothing indicates the particular way in which sympathetic feeling is to be evoked and exploited—by making others appear related to oneself. Rather than teaching readers to appreciate difference, sentimental lessons reinforce for readers the idea that recognition relies on likeness—that one is bound to love whatever or whomever appears most like one's own.

The construction of sympathy in relation to familiar objects is, as Philip Fisher argues, one of the principal ways in which sentimental novels seek to extend human rights to the disenfranchised and underprivileged.[35] According to Fisher, the family stands as the "only social model" for imagining "relations between non-equal members of a society, relations based on dramatically different and unequal contributions to the group and equally dramatically different and incomparable needs." No other unit "provides for helplessness, whether in childhood or old age, or for the temporary helplessness of illness."[36] Yet, while the family model challenges the assumption of human rights based on economic contribution, it intensifies the psychological link between humanity and homogeneity. The sympathetic power evoked by Harry's donning of the dead son's cap is emblematic of sympathy's homogenizing function. At its most effective, sympathetic identification converts the foreign into the familiar by exploiting feelings and associations to which readers can easily relate. Sentimental fiction's pedagogical function is a matter of constructing such relations. Common sense shows itself aligned with certain feelings that readers are taught to see as natural to themselves and therefore intrinsic to humanity. Whatever character(istic)s cannot be made to conform to the family image must remain excluded from sympathy, while those that are included must be represented in such a way that they prove familiar and thus identifiable.

The political implications of filial attachment take on renewed significance at the end of the chapter in which the effects of sympathy are shown to have made the senator more than a patriot and thus part of a collective; they have made him a man. As such, he is now in Stowe's view truly qualified for public service. In response to the senator's change of heart, Stowe's narrator ironically concludes that "as our poor senator was not stone or steel,—as he was a man, and a downright noble-hearted one, too,—he was, as everybody must see, in a sad case for his patriotism" (156). The facetious observation of the senator's "fall" from patriotism into manhood is meant to reinforce the necessity of grounding political principle in personal feeling. To do otherwise is to reveal oneself as either hard-hearted or hypocritical. Stowe then goes on to include her imagined readers in the ever widening circle of sympathy through rhetorical maneuvers fashioned to divide the unfeeling from the humane:

> You need not exult over [the senator], good brother of the Southern States, for we have some inklings that many of you, under similar circumstances, would not do much better. We have reason to know, in Kentucky, as in Mississippi, are noble and generous hearts, to whom never was tale of suffering told in vain. Ah, good brother! is it fair for you to expect of us services which your own brave, honorable heart would not allow you to render, were you in our place? (156)

By the use of the first-person plural, the narrator acknowledges her own identification with the senator, and she constructs her readers as similarly sympathetic. To the extent that her readers are able to identify with her depiction, they are allowed to partake in the senator's manhood, his humanity, and his rehabilitated patriotism.

Written to a nation of readers on the brink of war, *Uncle Tom's Cabin* exploits the experience of filial attachment to create and sustain the idea of an American democratic family. By equating sympathy with familiarity, however, Stowe's novel reveals the sentimental necessity of sacrificing democratic difference to the cause of union. Although Fisher contends that sentimentalism is democratic in that it "experiments with the extension of full and complete humanity from which it has been socially withheld,"[37] we must see that sentimental literature's reliance on the concept of familial attachment to evoke sympathy counters democratic principles and ultimately constructs the framework for future "identity politics." Insofar as democracy implies the representation of individual difference, sentimental politics reveals itself to be a politics of affinity rather than of democracy. Individual material differences are elided through models of sympathy that teach readers to view other "selves" as projections of their own and to care for others in proportion to how convincingly those others can be shown as related to oneself.

In using *Uncle Tom's Cabin* as an exemplary sentimental text, I have focused on a chapter in which the relationship between masculine and political agency is undermined by showing the extent to which a politics divorced from feeling proves not only impotent but un-American. The importance of womanly feeling in connection with democratic politics is reinforced throughout the novel by Stowe's consistent associations between motherhood and aboli- tion—what is for Stowe the tangible acting out of democratic equality. This is made most explicit at the conclusion of her novel, when Stowe exhorts the "mothers of America" to put their filial sympathies to political work: "And you, mothers of America, —you who have learned, by the cradles of your own chil- dren, to love and feel for all mankind, —by the sacred love you bear your child . . . I beseech you, pity the mother who has all your affections, and not one legal right to protect, guide, or educate, the child of her bosom!" (623). Mothers represent for Stowe both ideal readers and ideal Americans: through their attachment to their children, mothers exemplify the sympathetic identi- fication necessary to bridge the distance between distinct personalities and experiences, between humanity and inhumanity, between reality and fiction. As the following chapter shows, however, mothers represent as well the affec- tive vehicles through which the seductive nature of sympathetic identification may make its way into the heart of the sentimental domestic story.

5

Mothers of Seduction

As Jane Tompkins has argued, *Uncle Tom's Cabin* depicts women wielding a sentimental power that stereotypically masculine men can only dream about.[1] Women achieve sentimental power primarily through structures of identification: brought up to be Christians, wives, and mothers, women are trained to imagine themselves as psychically inhabited by another being. The novel then gains its *political* urgency by demonstrating that men need to access this power as well. In effect, men need to become more "feminine" if political choices are ever to become more humane and thus more American. Yet, despite the satisfying coherence of Stowe's model, what many domestic novels illustrate, however unself-consciously, are the devastating consequences of maternal influence. In this chapter, I examine the seductive effects of maternal power and the ways in which the mother-daughter bond epitomizes the problem of achieving independence through filial identification. Nina Baym has argued that the shift in popular storylines from seduction to domesticity is "a crucial event in woman's fiction, and perhaps in woman's psyche as well."[2] According to Baym, domestic authors rejected the eighteenth-century story of seduction, where the heroine inevitably would fall "victim in her first contest and never recover" (26). The following readings suggest, however, that seduction plots were not overcome but rather sublimated into subtler, conventionally safer, yet ultimately more sinister forms. The fiction of transformation—the domestic novel's conversion of feminine suggestibility from a corruptible to a redeeming attribute—collapses in the dangerous dynamic between mother and daughter.

In keeping with the American obsession with filial identification, the eighteenth-century woman's story of betrayal and misreading, ostensibly expurgated from the nineteenth-century plot, is reintroduced in the domestic novel through the figure of the mother. In the narrative legacy handed down from mother to daughter lies the history of seduction long ago made familiar to readers of sentimental fiction. By positing the maternal as the womanly ideal, the domestic novel proves at odds with itself; it offers a mother both against and by whom the daughter is to fashion herself. As recounted within the daughter's story, the mother's history not only reenacts her own victimization, it implicates her daughter in the seduction. Having "naturally" identified with her mother in the story, the heroine is then unable to differentiate between her mother's history and her own. In light of this pattern, Jane Tompkins's reference to American culture's favorite story as "the story of salvation through motherly love"[3] is given an ironic twist. For "motherly love" as an internalized force and a narrative model threatens to lock the daughter in a new cycle of appropriation. A more skeptical reading of nineteenth-century fiction thus complicates the domestic ideology of maternal love and the idea of a cooperative network of female relations.[4] It suggests the need to read American sentimental fiction and politics in a new way: not simply as a story of psychic (and thus potentially political) liberation, but as its mirror image, where both heroines and readers alike are not freed from but limited to the depth of their own reflections.

The Lessons of Womanhood

When Gabriella Lynn, the heroine of Caroline Lee Hentz's *Ernest Linwood*, gazes into the mirror and sees for the first time a beautiful woman there, she feels a sense of triumph, of power, and of destiny. However, as she herself goes on to say, "The moment of triumph was brief. A pale shadow seemed to flit behind me and dim the bright image reflected in the mirror. It wore the sad, yet lovely lineaments of my departed mother."[5] Gabriella's vision of her mother in this scene highlights a central tension in the novel—and in many nineteenth-century domestic novels—the daughter's physical and emotional tie to the figure whom she most closely resembles and yet whose fate she fears. Since Gabriella's birth, she and her mother, Rosalie, have lived alone on the outskirts of town, Rosalie suffering the effects of her seduction into an apparently bigamous marriage, Gabriella attempting to fill the emotional void in her mother's life left by the father's absence. The two have become bound together in relative isolation, and Gabriella has come to learn firsthand the emotional, physical, and financial costs of disappointed love. It is no wonder then that as Gabriella looks in the mirror she sees the figure of her mother cast its shadow over the brightening future; she intuits that her entrance into womanhood, for all its glory and influence, is also an opening up to the disappointment and disillusionment that surrounded her mother's life.

Gabriella's tuition in the lessons of womanhood is afforded by the visible example of her mother's isolation and, perhaps more important, by Rosalie's written record of her mysterious and unhappy past, which she bequeaths to Gabriella on her deathbed. "My Mother's History," as Gabriella terms it in her narrative, tells the story of passionate but misguided love to a duplicitous man whose own sordid past blights any hope for their future happiness. According to Rosalie, her history is meant as both an explanation and a warning to Gabriella, to be read at that time when Gabriella's own heart "awakens to love." But as the novel illustrates, this is exactly when a warning comes too late. Rosalie's history proves ultimately designed to foretell her daughter's future rather than divert it: since it is woman's "destiny" to love, Gabriella is doomed to repeat the past in her own unique way. And she does this, in fact, by falling hopelessly in love with the intensely moody Ernest Linwood, an emotional tyrant whose jealousy soon turns Gabriella's dream of domestic bliss into a nightmare. The product of these intense attachments is Gabriella's autobiography, and the connection between mother and daughter narratives is only too clear in this case. Gabriella's written record of her own "heart's history"—the novel we presently read—not only includes the mother's story of seduction and betrayal but becomes its own version of the story, leaving the reader to question whether any attempt on the daughter's part to write her own story can ever result in anything but a resurrection of the past.

This anxiety over preestablished modes of writing can be viewed in a larger context as well, where similar but individualized subgenres intersect in a growing literary market. The relationship between "mother" and "daughter" texts of the late eighteenth and mid nineteenth centuries provides a grid onto which we can map changing and somewhat contradictory cultural attitudes about women. In framing the relationship between the seduction and domestic novel in terms of the mother-daughter relationship, I mean to emphasize not only the actual historical connection between women writers and their cultural descendants but also the literary relationship between successive subgenres that legislate the character of the woman, the nature of her attachments, her role in the community, and her destiny in light of these things.

Domestic fiction, when viewed in light of seduction fiction at all, has been read as a new and improved version of the eighteenth-century story. In it, the victimized woman and the threat of appropriation is ostensibly laid to rest. Motherhood is heralded as the ideal, and daughters aspire to self-sufficient vulnerability and moral steadfastness. While one can view the shift in plot from woman as victim to woman as moral warrior to be progressive, the threat to woman's independence is far from eradicated. The protagonist of domestic fiction, on the whole, remains a woman divided.

One of the sources of ambivalence in domestic fiction is its tendency to glorify "maternal" values even as it locates the source of pain and weakness in the mother's character. What the daughter-heroine cannot explicitly acknowledge, the narrative consistently makes clear: the heroine's mother is a failure as a model for successful romance. In fact, the mother comes to represent those aspects of failed femininity against which the domestic heroine is constructed. As Baym points out, the domestic heroine is fashioned in opposition to two types of femininity: "the 'belle,' who lived for excitement and the admiration of the ballroom," and "the passive woman—incompetent, ignorant, cowed, emotionally and intellectually undeveloped." Such types are considered by domestic writers to be anachronistic. And, Baym notes, the heroine's mother is often just such a type.

Yet it is not merely within the confines of the domestic plot that the daughter attempts to assert her individuality. For what Baym does not acknowledge in her analysis is that one can find the prototypes for these two aspects of the failed feminine in the two most popular seduction novels of the early national period: Susanna Rowson's *Charlotte Temple* and Hannah Webster Foster's *The Coquette*. Although bestsellers in their own day, neither novel confined itself to its own historical period but in fact spilled over into the nineteenth-century literary market amidst the growing popularity of the new domestic fiction. *The Coquette* reached the height of its popularity between 1824 and 1828, when it was reprinted eight times, while *Charlotte Temple* boasted over two hundred editions by 1905. Susanna Rowson's domestic sequel to *Charlotte Temple*, *Charlotte's Daughter*, was published posthumously in 1828, marking a literary intersection of "mother"-"daughter" texts in the mid-nineteenth century.[6] Domestic writers were not simply writing against abstract types of womanhood but against particular models of femininity that had once cornered and still continued to infiltrate the literary market. Thus, while the specter of the mother's story may have conjured up anxieties concerning literary competition, it threatened to perpetuate disturbing images of women and their futures. Its presence in the culture forced domestic writers to question whether women could be different—write themselves differently—than their mothers did and, if so, to question how it was to be done in the shadow of a related paradigm.

In writing themselves into a new tradition, domestic authors experienced anxiety not only over their bold intrusion into a patriarchal culture[7] but over their inheritance of a literary and imaginative space that had not been fully deserted by the mother as well. Such an image is wonderfully figured in a novel like *Ernest Linwood* in which the mother's story, Rosalie's "heart's history," literally appropriates the "space" of the daughter's autobiography for several chapters in order to tell its own story. Nor is *Ernest Linwood* an anomaly in the domestic tradition: popular novels ranging from the 1824 edition of Catharine Sedgwick's *Redwood* to Susan Warner's *The Wide, Wide World* foreground the mother's history, which mirrors the seduction story in its portrayal of femininity and the problems of passion. The intrusion of the mother's story into the daughter's narrative signals a return of what has been repressed in the domesticated version of the woman's story. And it is a lesson that reflects on its own textual nature. The mother often dies early in the domestic novel, and in her place is left a text—a Bible, a letter, a "history"—that functions as a substitute for the mother and her wisdom. This text testifies to the sacrificial and, more often than not, painful nature of "true womanhood"; it serves also to reify, and to universalize, the traits associated with womanhood that the daughter inherits—and not simply inherits, but internalizes; for the daughter is to inscribe her mother's precepts upon her heart. By the mid nineteenth century, associations between mother and text render them practically interchangeable: not only does the domestic novel feature the mother-as-text, it itself becomes an example of the text-as-mother, with the daughter figure now performing the mother's leading role.

Literate and Literary Daughters: *The Wide, Wide World*

The relation between mothers, texts, and the disciplinary function of novels is addressed by Richard Brodhead, who explores the shift in mid-nineteenth-century America from corporal punishment to less visible and yet apparently more effective forms of discipline.[8] In his Foucauldian model of disciplinary intimacy, or "discipline through love," as Brodhead terms it, authority is required to "put on a human face." Once made personal, external authority becomes associated with the affective feelings the person in authority evokes. In the final stage, authority leaves the particularized body altogether to "inhere in a disciplinary *function* that can be performed by anonymous, interchangeable personnel."[9]

According to Brodhead, parents, and specifically mothers, become first the embodiment and then the representation of corrective love. By "enmeshing the child in strong bonds of love," the parent introduces its charge "to its imperatives and norms. . . . What the parent-figure believes in comes across [to the child] indistinguishably from his love, so that the child imbibes what the parent stands for in a moral sense along with the parent's physical intimacy and affection."[10] Lydia Sigourney's *Letters to Mothers* (1839) supports Brodhead's claim. As she represents it, the mother's particular responsibility is to infiltrate the child's heart that will remain long after the mother is gone:

> [The mother] should keep her hold on his affections, and encourage him to confide to her, without reserve, his intentions and his hopes, his errors and his enjoyments. Thus maintaining her pre-eminence in the sanctuary of his mind, her image will be as a tutelary seraph, not seeming to bear rule, yet spreading perpetually the wings of purity and peace over its beloved shrine, and keeping guard for God.[11]

That the reponsibility for the child's moral growth resides mainly in and with the mother in the nineteenth century is a well-documented fact, a result in great part of the separation of male and female spheres into marketplace and domestic realms of action and authority. The prevalence of home management manuals and guides, and the rise of mothers' magazines and associations,[12] attest to the seriousness with which motherhood is viewed; proper mothering becomes a kind of science, for it is up to the mother to construct the child.

One of the means by which the child's, and here particularly the daughter's, formation is achieved is through textual mediation and literary convention. Prototypes of the domestic bildungsroman, such as Susan Warner's *The Wide, Wide World*, illustrate that the child internalizes the mother as much through a textual as an emotional or spiritual ingestion of values. Little Ellen Montgomery's mother, a devoutly Christian woman, entreats her daughter to submit herself to the will of God and to embrace His commandments. In light of the fact that Ellen's mother is about to embark on an overseas trip for her health, a trip from which she will probably never return, Ellen finds this request difficult to fulfill. Yet in the months after her mother's departure, Ellen does embrace Christianity, and her conversion leads her back to her mother: "When she then undergoes the conversion her mother had covenanted her to, Ellen at once accepts the authority of her mother's religious system and recovers, through participation in that system, felt contact with the mother herself."[13] Yet the covenant between mother and daughter is not first and foremost a verbal one; it is mediated by a text, given from mother to daughter as a substitute for the mother's presence.

One of the last scenes between mother and daughter takes place after Mrs. Montgomery has bought her daughter Ellen a Bible of her own. Into this Bible, Ellen asks that her mother sign Ellen's name, "and any thing else [she] please[s]."[14] On one level, this act foreshadows Ellen's eventual participation in the Christian religion and her metaphorical signature into the sacred Book of Life. But it also illustrates the contract into which Ellen enters with her mother, and her vow to internalize what is written there, to take her mother's inscription to heart:

> Mrs. Montgomery wrote Ellen's name, and the date of the gift. The pen played a moment in her fingers, and then she wrote below the date:
> " 'I love them that love me; and they that seek me early shall find me.'
> This was for Ellen; but the next words were not for her; what made her write them?—
> " 'I will be a God to thee, and to thy seed after thee.' " (42)

The first inscription not only echoes God's promise to his children, but the disciplinary ideology of the day: "I love them that love me" is sounded in subtle and not-so-subtle ways by mother figures throughout nineteenth-century literature. The inscription that follows is a sign of how far and how deep that ideology runs, for it is, as the narrative tells us, not a covenant with Ellen but with Ellen's future—it points toward both the woman Ellen will become and the children she will bear as a result of her maturity. Thus the link between mother and child, here covenanted via the Holy Scripture that writes Ellen's future, extends through multiple generations, a point that is demonstrated in a more symbolic way by her mother's "sacrifice" narrated a few pages earlier in the novel.

The narrative has made no secret of Mrs. Montgomery's spiritual or physical sufferings in relation to her unhappy marriage or of Ellen's own terror at her father's critical and unsympathetic nature. Ellen's mother requests money from her husband to "fit Ellen comfortably for the time they should be absent; and in answer he had given her a sum barely sufficient for [Ellen's] mere clothing." Unwilling to let her daughter rest wholly on the care of others, however, Mrs. Montgomery buys Ellen's independence with the one tangible asset she owns—her own mother's ring:

> " 'Mamma,' said Ellen, in a low voice, 'wasn't that grandmamma's ring, which I thought you loved so much?'
> " 'Yes, I did love it, Ellen, but I love you better.'
> " 'Oh, mamma, I am very sorry!' said Ellen.
> " 'You need not be sorry, daughter. Jewels in themselves are the merest

nothings to me; and as for the rest, it doesn't matter; I can remember my mother without any help from a trinket.'

"There were tears, however, in Mrs. Montgomery's eyes, that showed the sacrifice had cost her something; and there were tears in Ellen's that told it was not thrown away upon her." (29)

Ellen's and her mother's tears reveal their bond in the sentimental tradition that draws women together and knits them in a circle of intimacy. This intimacy excludes the father not only in terms of space and situation but in terms of sensibility. Whereas the mother and daughter share caring, warmth, understanding, and even grief, the interactions between Mr. Montgomery and his wife and daughter are devoid of feeling or, more precisely, devoid of the expression of feeling. In his presence, the narrative practically comes to a halt: there is action but no reaction. The novel depends on the sympathy that moves Ellen and her mother to their choices and readers to their observation, participation, and interpretation of those choices. The ring Mrs. Montgomery wears and then sells in order to buy Ellen's independence is a symbol of the eternal circle of intimacy within which generations of women dwell; it is a symbol of the consecration of daughter to mother, even before the daughter's eventual consecration to God the Father. This circle of intimacy proves constricting in its own way, however. The sale of her mother's ring gives Mrs. Montgomery a sum large enough to purchase those things she feels are necessary to Ellen's improvement—a Bible and, appropriately enough, a writing desk and materials. Through the systems of religion and language, Ellen will learn to internalize the authority to which her mother's love has led her.

The purchase of Ellen's desk is one of the most unforgettable scenes in Warner's novel. As Helen Papashvily observes, the narrative seems to linger over the details; everything one could think of went into that mahogany writing desk:

> letter paper, large and small, with envelopes and note sheets to match, an inkstand, steel and quill pens, a little ivory knife and a leaf cutter, sealing waxes in red, green, blue and yellow, lights, wafers, a seal, a paper folder, a pounce box, a ruler, a neat silver pencil, drawing pencils, India rubber, and sheets of drawing paper.

> Many readers have confessed that yearning over these delightful objects they quite missed the intended poignancy and would have counted a mother well lost for such a desk gained.[15]

Papashvily's somewhat ironic comment hits the mark, since it is the desk, as well as the Bible, that is meant to bridge the gap, in some real sense, between mother and daughter. But, for nineteenth-century readers, the list of objects on which the narrative dwells would be a matter of some distinction. By the dawn of the Civil War, countless handbooks on epistolary etiquette had flooded the market, offering hundreds of sample letters to exemplify the art of polite correspondence. Karen Halttunen, for example, notes that "polite men and women were . . . advised to use good paper and fine wafers to seal their letters and to keep their handwriting neat"; after all, "Just as personal appearance reflected character in face-to-face social relations, the appearance of a letter reflected character at a distance."[16] Letter writers were warned that in sending even a note they left " 'written evidence of either your good sense or your folly, your industry or carelessness, your self-control or impatience.' "[17] Letters were nothing if not acts of "emotional self-expression."[18] They were also, however—and paradoxically—a means by which one's gentility was evaluated. As Halttunen observes, the goal became to express oneself sincerely, but with good taste; to write within the boundaries of prescribed epistolary etiquette, patterned after the formulas the writer had before her, and yet to be completely genuine.

How to both express one's true self and yet conform to the dictates of social responsibility and respectability is the contradiction negotiated by Mrs. Montgomery's assertions to her daughter on the benefits of epistolary education. Her motivation in buying Ellen the desk and materials is to ensure that Ellen will always be "neat, and tidy, and industrious; depending upon others as little as possible; and careful to improve [herself] by every means, and especially by writing to [her mother]" (31–32). Though Mrs. Montgomery seems to subscribe to the Victorian belief that by reading her daughter's letters she will be able to discern the state of her heart, she also implies here that by writing these letters at all, in the privacy of her own room and in possession of her own materials, Ellen will become a better person. The relationship of writing to independence, improvement, and maternal influence spelled out here is telling; it indicates that it is through her mastery of literary convention that Ellen will be able to master both language and *herself*. This idea is reinforced a few pages later, when Mrs. Mongomery cautions Ellen about the psychological cost of the desk and its contents: "My gifts will serve as reminders for you if you are ever tempted to forget my lessons. If you fail to send me letters, or if those you send are not what they ought to be, I think the desk will cry shame upon you" (37). These two sentences move from the idea of the mother's gifts as reminders of her presence to their substitution for it. Ellen's writing desk, the instrument of her self-expression, assumes the mother's role as moral detective, indicting her should she waver in her spiritual struggle. "Self-expression" thus becomes the representation of internalized maternal authority—the words of the daughter's heart will become the law that convicts her. In this way, personal sincerity and social respectability once again intersect, as Ellen becomes both the author and the moral interpreter, both the daughter and the mother figure, of her self.

Although the Bible seems at first glance to function as a source for cultivation in Ellen's personal and private life, and the writing desk to initiate her improvement in the public sphere, the ideology of epistolary etiquette reminds us that for a nineteenth-century woman the two spheres are virtually inseparable: the woman's story is a story of the heart made public.[19] Mrs. Montgomery's admonishment to Ellen early in the novel that she "try to compose [herself]" speaks to the dilemma that lies within the metaphor: it is an injunction to repression dressed in the language of articulation. Ellen is literally being told to "put herself together,"[20] and she is to do so in sensual as well as narrative terms. Paradoxically, to "compose" oneself comes to mean curbing those physical, emotional, and psychological urges that inhere in self-expression. The proof of the woman's integrity, in both senses of the word, is made visible through its narrativization. In the domestic novel, daughters are taught by their mothers how to regulate themselves, and this is achieved both by their internalization of the mother's precepts and her method of transmitting them. What the mother bequeaths to her daughter is essentially a version of herself, and the impression she leaves upon her is the stamp of literacy as well as love.

Ellen Montgomery's writing desk in *The Wide, Wide World* can be viewed as a metonym for language itself, for the literary tradition in which Ellen and other domestic daughters try to participate and articulate themselves, only to find that self-expression has turned to convention in their own hands. The figure of the mother not only initiates but disrupts this convention. Her presence signifies the inherent duplicity in romantic plots of love and of domestic conventions themselves: that is, she functions as both a double and an alter ego for the daughter, revealing the daughter's position as at once dual *and* split, with no private center from which to speak.

As a scene from *Ernest Linwood* illustrates, the heroine's attempts to express herself are often met with public disdain and private doubt. When Gabriella is called upon to read an expository essay in class, she must confess that she has instead written a poem about her mother. She begins to read her poem aloud, but her male teacher snatches the pages out of her hands and reads the poem to the class himself, in a tone of derision. Had her professor understood the depth of her emotion (as well as talent), Gabriella says, he might have been more encouraging, and she might have "sang as well as loved" (9). But with such an "Olympian king-god" (5) in power, what use was it to dream of writing, when to write is to "hear the dreary echo of one's voice return through the desert waste"? Why should she "enter the exalted realm of culture," when after entering the temple the woman finds "nothing but ruins and desolation"? (5, 11).

Later in the novel, Gabriella refers to her own authorship with horror: "Book!—am I writing a book? No, indeed! This is only a record of my heart's life, written at random and carelessly thrown aside, sheet after sheet, sibylline leaves from the great book of fate. The wind may blow them away, a spark may consume them. I may myself commit them to the flames. I am tempted to do so at this moment."[21] Although the author relies on a common trope in this passage, her temptation to commit her life's story to the flames nonetheless emphasizes the emotional and psychological cost of her self-expression; it is at the moment when she focuses on her project, and thereby becomes aware of her reader's eyes focused on it as well, that she is tempted to exert the ultimate authority she has over her life—to reduce it to silence. This is the only sure way to keep unsympathetic readers and "Olympian king-gods" from appropriating her textual self. The reference to the record of her "heart's life" connects Gabriella's autobiography with her mother's "heart's history" and reminds us of the unhappy end such histories may have. Although the mother's story is to serve as a cautionary tale, what it ultimately shows is that such histories cannot prevent daughters from following in the mother's footsteps. In fact, as sympathetic readers, daughters are compelled to do so.

Mirroring the Mother Text: *Love's Progress* and *Ernest Linwood*

Filial identification takes on a particularly malignant cast in Caroline Howard Gilman's *Love's Progress* (1836), a story in which a daughter is required to become a literal substitute for the dying mother. Approximately midway through Gilman's novel, the heroine, Ruth, becomes affianced to a young man named Clarendon. At this time, Ruth's mother confides to her daughter the secret that it has been the "aim of [her] existence" to conceal: "Ruth, your father hates me.' " The mother's secret continues in the tradition of domestic ambivalence by laying the mother's unhappy love relationship alongside the daughter's happy one. But rather than run these parallel stories side by side, *Love's Progress* takes them to a critical juncture in which they intersect and become one. The long-term effect of the husband's abuse is his wife's emotional and physical decline. On her deathbed, Ruth's mother makes Ruth pledge that she will take the mother's place in the father's life: "Swear to me that *you will be to him as a child, what I have been as a wife*; that you will conceal his infirmities, and not breathe them to the winds" (126, emphasis mine).[22] After her mother's confession, and Ruth's promise to fulfill her mother's duties in her father's life, Ruth begins to dream that her father's hatred is now "fixed . . . on her until she [becomes] rigid and [is] turned to stone." The father's passion *is* in fact turned on her, but not in the way Ruth has imagined. For, in the ensuing scenes, Ruth's father, aware of Ruth's engagement to marry, becomes insanely jealous and vows murder unless Ruth agrees to run away with him. Ruth dutifully complies. Although Clarendon follows them and attempts to persuade his intended to forsake her father, she adamantly refuses. She has come to take her position as her father's helpmate quite seriously.

In the end, the father's passion overwhelms him and the story reaches its climax. The father drowns in a torrential river and Ruth is saved by Clarendon's timely arrival. Undaunted by recent events, Clarendon interprets Ruth's service to her father as a confirmation of her good character: " 'I have traced the self-sacrificing progress of your heart's love through life's varied duties, and I know that the tender daughter will be the faithful wife' " (171). What Clarendon's final proclamation does not acknowledge is that his words not only predict the future but narrate the past, for Ruth has already proven the "faithful wife." The dynamics of triangulation between mother, child, and father speak to the dangers of sympathetic identification as well as to the way in which such identification reinforces an ethos of seductive paternalism.

The daughter's assumption of the mother's place in *Love's Progress* makes explicit the dual role played by mother and daughter figures, while the reintroduction of desire and betrayal from the mother's past reveals her as the unconscious dis-covered. Such a reading shows the extent to which the domestic heroine is a woman divided and calls into question the normative experience of women that the domestic novel formula would perpetuate. The happy ending gives final assent to the myth of the transforming power of love, but, within the story's telling, the mother has not only invaded the daughter's life history, she has made her for a time the main character of an earlier unhappy plot. Baym's claim that the domestic authors had no interest in the negative example of seduction plots proves to be beside the point, for regardless of intention seduction does intrude into "woman's fiction" and, by implication, into her psyche as well. Seduction fiction is not only alluded to in the daughter's quasi-incestuous bond with her father, but in the question the reader is forced to ask in the face of such a bond; that is, how does one differentiate between what is an "appropriate" and "inappropriate" object of desire? If the answer lies in "education," as so many seduction novels claimed, then the mother's story as moral exemplum ultimately fails. For just as the seduction narrative is said to foster those very desires in the telling of the story that it purports to suppress, so the mother's confessions to her daughter ironically invoke a future they are trying to forestall. As the daughter "reads" her mother's desire, she is taught to desire what she should avoid. In a repetition of the seduction novel's dilemma, what is meant as "education" becomes a form of seduction.

We encounter a near perfect example of the mother's *seduction*, as both noun and verb, when, in *Ernest Linwood*, Gabriella finally reads her mother's history and loses herself in the story: "Thus far had I read, with clenching teeth and rigid limbs, and brow on which chill, deadly drops were slowly gathering, when my mother's shriek seemed suddenly to ring in my ears,—the knell of a broken heart, a ruined frame,—and I sprang up and looked wildly round me. Where was I? Who was I?" (184). Gabriella reads the manuscript literally hunched over her mother's grave and, when she finishes, she finds herself in another world: "I did not become insensible, but I was dead to surrounding objects, dead to the present, dead to the future. The past, the terrible, the inexorable past, was upon me, trampling me, grinding me with iron heel, into the dust of the grave" (185). Gabriella becomes so involved in her mother's seduction that she herself loses all sense of her body, mind, and even personal history. After reading the narrative, Gabriella questions why she should wish to live, as if it were her own future and not her mother's past that she has just been reading. In this, as in so many domestic stories, we see that the attempt to put violation in the past proves unsuccessful—the past may always return, if not through the body of the mother herself, then through the text with which she entraps her daughter-reader.

As if to emphasize the connection between mothers and lovers, Gabriella's swoon is interrupted by the entrance of her future lover and husband, Ernest Linwood. Linwood lifts his future bride up off the grave and out of the past with an assurance that her history is nothing, a clouded name is nothing; his name can absorb it. And absorb it he does. For the autobiography Gabriella writes is under the lover's signature, *Ernest Linwood*, subtitled vaguely, "or, The Inner Life of the Author." Linwood offers Gabriella a new name—his own—and thus ostensibly a new destiny: the mother's sad history of wrongs and disgrace will be subsumed in the lover's identity. The mother's text is thus replaced by the lover's text that bears his name, and it is a story that proves equally engrossing: for Linwood's entrance into the mother-daughter dyad prompts Gabriella's turn from her mother to her new lover; now seduced by

his words, Gabriella admits that she "forgot the sad history of wrongs and disgrace which [she] had just been perusing; — [she] forgot that such words had
breathed into [her] mother's ear, and that she believed them" (188).

Gabriella's marriage to Ernest Linwood reveals itself as yet another relationship meant to keep the woman's ego boundaries permeable and her identity undeveloped. Her husband's desire to "enshrine [Gabriella] like a crystal
vase in his heart," to fashion her after one of his classical statues and to paint
her into the image of the flower girl whose portrait hangs in his study, attests
to Linwood's proficiency in the objectification of women so central to nineteenth-century lovemaking, but he falls far short of satisfying his bride's desire:
Gabriella wants only to be loved as flesh and blood. Instead, Gabriella is
housed within her husband's fortress of marble and burnished gold, where she
dwells as his most priceless object. And, as if to emphasize that such a state is
the necessary outcome of becoming a woman, Gabriella describes the setting
of her leisure space as that room "lined with mirrors, [where] I could not turn
without seeing myself reflected on every side; and not only myself, but an eye
that watched my every movement, and an ear that drank in my every word"
(244). When taken to the extreme, domestic ideology proves more of a prison
than a sanctuary, and the romantic lover a panoptic disciplinarian who can
penetrate, not only the woman's every deed, but her every thought as well:
"Beware then, Gabriella, — I may be one of the genii, whose terrible power no
mortal can evade, who can read the thoughts of the heart as easily as the
printed page. How would you like to be perused so closely?" (243). Once the
daughter-reader of her mother's text, she is now turned into a text by her lover,
a text for him to read, and read into, whatever his jealous and paranoid imagination may conjure up.

Gabriella's reduction to textual object reconfirms the uneasy alliance
between mother and daughter, but, as if to underscore the point, Gabriella's
long-lost father, Henry Gabriel St. James, mysteriously appears. His entrance
into Gabriella's life signals, once again, a resurfacing of her mother's unhappy
past; however, it is also the necessary precondition to a happy domestic ending. The repressed past must be brought to light and dealt with before the new
daughter-hero can go forward in her story.[23] Since the domestic novel aims to
convert the seduction story to its own ends, all criminal actions of the past must
be rectified and the damage contained; order must be restored. And this,
somewhat ironically, is managed through the familiar plot device of the evil
twin brother. It was, it turns out, St. James's profligate brother who married
and deserted the woman in New Orleans, not Gabriella's father. The news is
doubly significant: in rewriting the mother's history, even after her life has

ended, there is an attempt to presage the daughter's felicitous end, since Gabriella's fate has all along been inextricably linked with the mother's. However, what this plot twist succeeds in doing on another level is to drive home the paradigm of the duplicitous nature of love as well as the duplicitous nature of men. The man you marry, like the mother you adore, has two faces; this is a fact Gabriella, as well as the reader, has seen all too clearly in the charismatic but unpredictable Ernest Linwood.

In her attempt to write the woman's end differently from the old eighteenth-century story, the nineteenth-century woman is confronted again and again by her mother's image, often in the shape of herself. Such an illustration is furnished by yet another of our heroine's encounters with her own reflection, this time coming after she has read her mother's history and pledged her future to Ernest Linwood: "As I passed and repassed the double mirror, my reflected figure seemed an apparition gliding by my side. I paused and stood before one of them, and I thought of the time when, first awakened to the consciousness of personal influence, I gazed on my own image." This time the mother's face is absent from the reflection; it is Gabriella herself who forms the double, foreshadowing her own coming struggle to reconcile the image she holds of herself with the way she is read by others, particularly her husband. However, in standing between the double mirror and mirroring a reflection of herself, Gabriella also constitutes herself as the reader of her own story and so a mother to herself. Her gaze recalls the figures of absorbing influence—mother and lover—and dramatizes her own participation in, or rather her own assumption of, the model. It is neither past nor future, neither mother nor lover, that holds her attention now. It is the vision of herself that enthralls her.

The domestic novel's idealization of womanhood ultimately leads us back to earlier repressed modes of feminine sensibility, in which the seduction of the woman, and the emotional suggestibility it signifies, is represented as both redemptive and all-consuming. The American ethos of seductive paternalism characterized by sentimental fiction is complemented by the image of the seduced and seducing mother, bringing to light once more the potentially stultifying effects of a virtually incestuous filial identification. In the end, we see that while the mother may offer an example of how to write one's own story she cannot tell how to avoid being imprisoned by it: sympathetic identification, the cornerstone of sentimental education, converts readers and characters alike into reflections of each other. The sentimental world of familial intimacy, though seductively alluring, suggests the disturbing possibility that, for the reader enshrined within, there is no way out of the house of mirrors.

Conclusion:
Billy Budd and the Critique of Sympathy

I have been arguing that sympathetic identification provides one of the principal modes by which eighteenth- and nineteenth-century readers are taught to see themselves as part of a unified political body, a body made familiar to readers by its associations with the feelings and attachments of a family. As this statement suggests, rhetorical constructions of sympathy serve to make imaginable a body simultaneously public and private, collective and individual. They do so by representing the feeling self as the locus of authority in a democratic society. As Enlightenment philosophers like Adam Smith present it, sympathy creates affective bonds between individuals through vicarious experience and projection: we sympathize with others by imagining what *we* would feel if put in the other's position. In the sympathetic scenario, the individual self—its feelings and responses—becomes the measure for understanding and evaluating the experiences of others. The more like oneself others can be made to appear, the greater the possibility for sympathy. At its most successful, then, sympathy converts otherness into sameness, organizing sentiments around the perception of familiarity and constructing a community of like-minded individuals.

Thomas Paine's *Common Sense* made the correlation between sympathy, democracy and familial feeling a popular concept in the postrevolutionary period by arguing for national unity based on the shared sentiments of a sympathetic American "family." A hundred years and two wars later, Thatcher Thayer's *The Vicarious Element in Nature and Its Relation to Christ* (1888) completes Paine's argument by idealizing the individual's role in constructing a national family. What his work fails to account for—and what Melville's

Billy Budd makes explicit—is the cost to the individual in playing such a role. Thayer's treatise serves as a coda to the arguments we have been tracing. Through it, we can see just how pervasive the politics of sympathy have become in the years between the Revolutionary and Civil Wars. Albeit unwittingly, Thayer's work makes manifest the ways in which the material concerns of late eighteenth-century seduction fiction—concerns with the body, with sexuality, with economic and gender differences—are sacrificed to a less tangible, more ethereal cause. Whereas in the early novel, "the power of sympathy" was evidenced through the body and the blood, by the end of the nineteenth century both blood and body are shed for the sake of the idealization of sympathy, made perfect in the sentimental construction of a Christian state. Once denoting the particularity of biologically related bodies, sympathy now denotes a process by which the limits of the individual body are transcended for the good of the whole—for the collective, political, or national body.

The Vicarious Element in Nature is essentially a Christian apology; its ultimate goal is to present Christ's atonement—his vicarious suffering and death on behalf of sinful humanity—as a logical, though supernatural, extension of the "natural" relations between human beings. The majority of the work, however, is devoted to arguing the manifold ways identification and representation inform all aspects of social life, from the family to the government. According to Thayer, human relations are, by their very nature, vicarious. In learning to live with others, we naturally resort to imagining how others must feel or how we would feel in their place: "It is safe to state, generally, that men, in the natural course of [their] instinctive feelings towards their fellow creatures, do bear in themselves, much of what belongs to others. Thus in the relation which is the beginning of human society, the truer the union, the more there is of reciprocal assumption" (26).[1] Vicariousness thus partakes of the elements of sympathy so central to the nineteenth-century American imagination. And, like sympathy, the vicarious can be expressed in either practical or affective terms: *vicarious* is defined as both the *act* of taking another's place and the *feeling* that one has done so. Thayer's construction of vicarious relations, like the sentimental construction of sympathetic identification, blurs the boundary between action and emotion to suggest that sympathetic feeling itself is an act that holds society together.

Thayer's assertion that "affection cannot express itself to the utmost, without assuming thus another, almost to identity" sums up the sociological implications of the sympathetic imagination: society is first structured and then perpetuated by a reciprocity of feeling, "the willing taking upon self, what is anothers [sic]" (26). In keeping with the sentimental ethos of the age, Thayer offers familial attachment as the strongest instance of a reciprocity of feeling, amounting in some cases to a virtual "substitution": "Within the sphere of home an almost identification of persons is formed through the working of natural affection" (18–19). In a sentiment reminiscent of Stowe, maternal feeling gets cast as the prime example of such identification: "The mother's relation to the child affords the climax of the vicarious element in the sphere of natural affection. Here the identifying of self with another, is something wonderful. The mother lives, as it were, the life of the child" (27). Thayer's "as it were" is telling, for it signals the confusion between the material and the emotional life as well as the potential conflation of representation and appropriation. In feeling *for* her child, the mother virtually eclipses the child's identity by her own. In other words, the sympathizing subject, in taking on the experience of another, may substitute her own experience for the one with whom she identifies.

Although Thayer himself concedes the potentially dangerous effects of vicarious relations, he sees the threat lying in sympathy's capacity to engender pain as well as joy. One may become so identified with another as to take on the other's suffering. Yet despite its potential harm, for Thayer, the vicarious remains a natural, and thus unavoidable, structure in human relations. It is what makes personal interactions possible; it is also what gives nations their own distinctive identities. In a move that parallels Paine's, Thayer compares a parent's obligation to represent the interests of his or her child to the responsibility of politicians to serve their constituents' needs. According to Thayer, citizens of a nation, like members of a family, are bound together by a common sensibility. Vicariousness takes active shape in a politics of representation that defines American democracy:

> In every community two opposing forces, integrating and disintegrating, come in conflict, and on the issue turns the question whether or not there shall be a nation. But when at last a real nation has come to be, it has a unity of its own. It is possessed of an organic life. A national sentiment is formed. . . . Now, in this great form of society, where so much of human history is embodied, representativeness prevails. The men of one time in this national life, act for those of another to all intents, as if they stood in their place. They determine for them nationally. Their counsels, their actions, often their sufferings; are, in large part, for those who come after. Nay, in one sense, they are more for others than for themselves. (20–21)

Thayer's idea of a political structure resembles a family tree. By acting "for those who come after," elected officials effectively play the role of metaphorical fathers to their imagined descendants. For Thayer, politicians and parents share the common trait of representation, a vicarious position in relation to their charges that compels them to act more in the other's interest than in their own. But, then, in Thayer's depiction of vicarious relations, otherness hardly exists. Writing out of a sentimental tradition of democratic sympathy, Thayer represents vicariousness as equivalent to "unity."

Thayer's treatise reinforces Smith's idea that it is the individual's affective and imaginative powers that allow him or her to care for others; yet Thayer is careful to reject the notion that such powers result in the individual's autonomy. On the contrary, the vicarious structure inherent in all relationships exposes the "great lie" of democratic capitalism, the idea that one's life is "wholly individual": "In our day, men are giving great attention to what are termed 'The laws of society.' Now these laws, by their quiet resistless action, teach as really as by voice, that men are so related to each other, as in a very full sense, to be 'their brothers' keepers' " (33). According to Thayer, nature itself functions as "a vast pedagogy" to teach individuals how intimately their lives are connected. Put another way, one could say that nature functions as a vast sentimental text, dispensing lessons whose personal truths are constantly reflected in the political realm: "The loosest democracy is no more independent individualism at last, than the closest autocracy. Millions depend in matters of property and life, and character, on the government acting for them, and there is no other way" (29). In making his argument for the fundamental principle of vicariousness, Thayer offers an apology not only for Christian theology—for the extraordinary power of individual sacrifice—but for republican government as well. For though Thayer does not distinguish here between a democratic and autocratic government, he assumes a ruling body that, ostensibly at least, represents its people through consent rather than coercion.

The ruling tenets of republicanism and liberalism, seen by most twentieth-century critics as competing ideologies of the postrevolutionary and antebellum eras, respectively, are brought together in Thayer's vision of vicarious relations. Thayer simultaneously depicts the individual body—and the senses attached to it—as the epistemological center of a national universe and yet dissolves the individual into a larger body, a body constituted "more for others" than for oneself. Reading the political body through the individual one, the former becomes, as the metaphor of the body suggests, "possessed of an organic life." It is the individual body writ large, producing, as if of one accord, a "national sentiment." Thayer's rhetorical transition from the political to the spiritual, from the vicarious element in nature to its supernatural incarnation in Christ, marks the crowning achievement of sympathy's sociopolitical work. For Christ becomes the ideal representative whose ability to identify completely with all humanity signifies the unifying power of sympathy. In Christ we get not only a theological but a *political* model for the unification of diverse individuals into one corporate body—Christ's own.

The Vicarious Element in Nature and Its Relation to Christ reflects the spiritualizing of sympathy made popular in nineteenth-century domestic fiction; it also makes explicit, through the example of Christ, the ultimate goal of sympathetic identification: to convert the foreign into the familiar. "We cannot truly understand Christ's morality without an appreciation of his sympathy," writes Thayer; it is a sympathy manifested in Christ's "identifying himself, with others" (78). To be a Christian is to be like Christ, and to be like Christ means to partake of his willingness to put himself, literally, in the place of others. If resemblance to Christ is the goal of a Christian life, it is also, somewhat tautologically, the precondition for recognizing who it is one is to resemble. Thus Thayer contends that a self "blinded by sin to any clear perception of its own sinfulness, forms a medium in which an imperfect, untrue representation of Christ will appear" (68). Moral rectitude, by contrast, provides individuals with an untarnished view of Christ based on their similarity to him: "By the very aptitude of like to apprehend like, [regenerate souls] recognize with awe indeed, and humbling consciousness . . . the perfection and greatness of vicarious love in Christ" (70). In keeping with the principles of sentimental sympathy, *The Vicarious Element in Nature* reinforces the idea that representation relies on likeness. It does so by articulating the progress of human society in what has by now become familiar terms: the conversion of difference—and its concomitant associations with division—into sameness.

Considering the political in light of the spiritual, we see that, for Thayer, democracy is but a reflection of a greater sympathy in action—that of a Christian state where individuals become like Christ and, through him, more sensible of their relation to each other. Christ thus epitomizes the ways in which disparate individuals are brought together into one corporate or collective body through the sympathetic dynamic, a dynamic that simultaneously depends on and reproduces likeness. However, as we have seen in the shift from seduction to domestic fiction, the materiality of the body becomes compromised by the very sentiments used to represent it. When feelings come to stand for bodies, the body itself becomes superfluous. Perhaps nowhere is this made clearer than in the fact that it is Christ's death that proves the measure of his identificatory and substitutionary greatness. Thayer argues the perfection of Christ's sympathy by pointing to his willingness to sacrifice himself for humanity. His sufferings, claims Thayer, "are on account of those, into whose unity he came" (51). In other words, Christ's atonement signifies the obliteration of the individual body for the sake of its power of representation. Unity, or rather a democratic *sense* of unity, can only be perpetuated by the systematic sacrifice of individual difference. This suggests that in a perfectly sympathetic state the ideal individual is exceptional in his *typicality*, representing in the body not himself only but also those others in whose place he stands.

The Vicarious Element in Nature participates in a tradition of depicting Americans as unique, but unique in that they exemplify what is common to humanity. Given this paradox, it is no wonder that the literature of the eighteenth and nineteenth centuries so often evinces a tension between individualism and that which the individual is meant to represent—a national community sharing a common sense. Though distinctly political in agenda, American literature habitually depicts national values as a reflection of what is most "natural" in human relations. It is a pattern that appears in numerous American narratives: Eliza in *The Coquette*, Hester in *The Scarlet Letter*, Tom in *Uncle Tom's Cabin* all represent a uniquely "American" individualism that is ultimately sacrificed for the moral edification of America's impressionable members. The fact that the American novel grows out of a tradition of reading fiction as ideally pedagogical in intent only exacerbates the conflict between "individualism" and the individual. For what readers are to learn—through their own sympathetic identification—are two seemingly contradictory lessons: that the self is constituted by its relation to others and that the price of those relations is the alienation of selfhood.

Written after the heyday of sentimental fiction, *Billy Budd* (1868–1891) employs the conventions of sentimental sympathy—epitomized in the trope of vicarious substitution—to critique the assumptions upon which those conventions are based.[2] Specifically, *Billy Budd* underscores what Melville sees as the irreconcilable ideals of individualism and patriarchal democracy. Where the former denotes the right of each individual to pursue life, liberty, and happiness, the latter concept puts the father figure in the position of mediating the individual's goals. In a patriarchal democracy, the father rules as a "representative"; when his "children's" wills are aligned with his, their choices have the appearance of freedom. Christian tropes and structures help reinforce a patriarchal system: in the Christian scenario, fatherhood retains its sovereignty while also conferring it on individuals who are to become one with the Father through his Holy Spirit. Billy Budd explores American culture's idealization of sympathy, epitomized in Christian works like Thayer's, to show the cost of sentimental equations. Melville's "handsome" but naive hero, executed for accidently killing Claggart, the master-at-arms who falsely accuses him of treason, paints the internalization of patriarchal authority in its darkest hue. For, in acquiescing to the fate to which the paternalistic Captain Vere condemns him, Billy sacrifices more than his life; he sacrifices the best that humanity has to offer.

Billy Budd has been read by many critics as a Christian allegory, and, as Frederick Busch notes, it is with good reason:

> Billy, impressed from the merchant, *Rights-of-Man*, does, after all, cry out "Good-bye to you too, old *Rights-of-Man*." Vere does, after all, stand for verity. Billy, as he is hanged, does die as sun shoots through clouds to create "a soft glory as of the fleece of the Lamb of God seen in mystical vision." Melville does liken Claggart to Satan ("the scorpion for which the creator alone is responsible"). And he does liken Billy much to Adam as well as to Christ. (xi)

Though Busch concedes that Melville must have meant much of the type-casting that critics ascribe to the novel, he himself prefers to read the narrative in a more personal vein—as the author's attempt to work through the issue of his own paternal guilt in the suicide of his son.[3] In fact, I would argue that both critical positions are accurate: Billy represents not only Christ, but all sons, while Vere stands for both the heavenly and earthly father. Melville uses the archetypal Christian story to expose the dangers of a sentimental view of patriarchal authority. In this reading, the issue of paternal guilt is not simply personal; it serves to underscore the political implications of this Christian allegory. Melville employs the sentimental concepts of unity, filial sympathy, and identification to demonstrate the destruction of the individual that results from one's subscribing to a sentimental view of politics. *Billy Budd* makes explicit the implications of texts like Thayer's by demonstrating that a sentimental concept of democracy must reject exceptionalism in favor of an ordered mediocrity.

Billy Budd is set against the backdrop of late eighteenth-century revolutionary Europe, a time when, as we have seen, the politics of patriarchalism and democracy are particularly at odds. Rather than reconcile the two concepts, as much American fiction attempts to do, *Billy Budd* complicates both. The story takes place in the aftermath of the Nore Mutiny (1797), an event as devastating to the British Empire, the narrator tells us, as "a strike in the fire brigade would be to London threatened by general arson" (303). The potential for mutiny is raised not only by the spirit of revolution that pervades the North Atlantic but also by the policy of impressment practiced by the British following its own Revolutionary War. Under this policy, both Americans and Englishmen could be physically taken from a ship and forced into the service of the King's navy. Legitimate authority thus becomes indistinguishable from the criminal actions it sets itself against. Billy Budd himself is a victim of impressment. He is made captive to a paternal figurehead whose right in turning sailors into slaves belies the democratic system it ostensibly means to protect. Although, in terms of the allegory Melville sets up, Billy's transfer from his merchant ship, the *Rights-of-Man*, to the king's man-of-war, the *Bellipotent*, would seem to symbolize his move from a democratic to a coercive state, Melville makes clear that the *Rights-of-Man* and the *Bellipotent* are but two sides of one coin. The former can only be protected by the presence of the latter, while the actions of the latter render the principles of the former null and void. And this, essentially, is the gist of Melville's moral tale. Democracy can only be preserved through violence, a violence that, by its very nature, constantly threatens to unravel a democratic system.

Though set aboard an English ship upon the British seas, *Billy Budd* incorporates the issues and anxieties concerning patriarchal authority characteristic of American literature from the end of the eighteenth through the nineteenth century. In fact, Melville never makes clear whether Billy is British or American. What is clear is that the "foundling" Billy, whose "entire family was practically invested in himself" (300, 198), is an innocent; his naïveté is reminiscent of Melville's other quintessentially "American" characters: Ishmael and Captain Delano. And as in these cases, Billy's innocence protects him from realizing the magnitude of the evil happening around him. His innocence, however, is also the trait that contributes to Billy's becoming, in Vere's unhappy words, a "fated boy" (350). Unable to articulate his defense because of a "vocal defect"—a tendency to stammer—Billy strikes Claggart a fatal blow out of sheer frustration. Later, when asked before the drumhead court to explain his actions, Billy can only turn a look of "dumb expressiveness" toward Vere, a look "not unlike that which a dog of generous breed might turn upon his master, seeking in his face some elucidation of a previous gesture ambiguous to the canine intelligence" (359). Billy, finding the discussion around him incomprehensible, turns for assurance to the man who will seal his fate. But, in this, Melville assures us, Vere took no pleasure. The narrator comments that "the condemned one suffered less than he who mainly had effected the condemnation" (367). It is the wise, suggests Melville, who suffer the sin of knowledge, while the innocent sail placidly along in the comfort of their faith and trust.

In the midst of revolutionary chaos, Captain Vere represents a patriarchal authority that, according to Vere himself, remains the ship's only hope of order. But, in Vere's claim that "in feature no child can resemble his father more than [the Mutiny Act] resembles in spirit the thing from which it derives—War" (363), the question arises as to whether fatherhood itself signifies stability or revolution, a consensual or a coercive mode of politics. And, in the end, it is impossible to tell. For, although Vere's one concern is to prevent mutiny, he must kill Billy in order to secure his position as father. Moreover, while Vere exercises his patriarchal right as captain in demanding Billy's execution, at the same time he rejects the affective privileges associated with fatherhood—that of acting out of personal regard for his child. In trying to convince the reluctant officers adjudicating Billy's case that Billy must die, Vere disclaims the personal in favor of the political. When war is declared, asks Vere, "are we the commissioned fighters previously consulted?" "No" is the obvious answer. "We fight at command," says Vere:

> So now. For suppose condemnation [of Billy] to follow these present precedings. Would it be so much we ourselves that would condemn as it would be martial law operating through us? For that law and the rigor of it, we are not responsible. Our vowed responsibility is in this: That however pitilessly that law may operate in any instances, we nevertheless adhere to it and administer it. (362)

Vere describes himself as a tool of law; he is not his own man but a vehicle through which forces greater than himself operate. He reminds his officers that their allegiance is not to Nature or to personal sentiment but to the king. By invoking the figure of the king, however, Vere underscores the idea that the political is always already personal. Vere's logic, borne out of a moment of revolutionary crisis (a crisis Melville implies is always upon us), displays the seductive machinations involved in making personal decisions appear executed by an inexorable law.

Billy's power to pacify the crew through his own virtue and innocence becomes perceived by Vere as a power to unite the crew against his own authority. Thus Claggart's false claim that Billy is involved in a mutinous plot registers an echo of truth in the story, although it is dramatically opposed to the way the "Handsome Sailor" is characterized by others—as "peacemaker." The captain of the *Rights-of-Man*, for example, tells the *Bellipotent*'s lieutenant that he is loath to give Billy up, for "before I shipped that young fellow, my forecastle was a rat-pit of quarrels. It was black times, I tell you, aboard the *Rights* here. . . . But Billy came; and it was like a Catholic priest striking peace in an Irish shindy. Not that he preached to them or said or did anything in particular; but a virtue went out of him, sugaring the sour ones" (295). Billy's virtue acts like a balm to his shipmates; he becomes representative of a moral superiority the crew is quick to perceive and admire. The crew's affection for

Billy leads Vere to fear that if Billy is shown mercy after killing Claggart the rest of the crew will follow Billy's lead. Thus, addressing the council, Vere speculates,

> "The people" (meaning the ship's company) "have native sense. . . . The foretopman's deed, however it be worded in the announcement, will be plain homicide committed in a flagrant act of mutiny. What penalty for that should follow, they know. But it does not follow. *Why?* they will ruminate. You know what sailors are. Will they not revert to the recent outbreak at the Nore? Ay. . . . They would think that we flinch, that we are afraid of them — afraid of practicing a lawful rigor singularly demanded at this juncture, lest it should provoke new troubles. What shame to us such a conjecture on their part, and how deadly to discipline." (364)

In other words, Billy must die in order to perfect the role he has played all along — the role of unifying and pacifying the crew. Vere must solidify his own role as patriarchal father by sacrificing his most perfect son. But whereas Vere is willing to reaffirm his authority through negative example — offering a kind of cautionary tale to "the people" — Billy succeeds in converting fear into sympathy and rebellion into consensus.

Immediately following the drumhead court's decision, Vere assembles the crew and tells them the basic facts of the case: Claggart is dead and Billy Budd is to hang at daybreak: "Their captain's announcement was listened to by the throng of standing sailors in a dumbness like that of a seated congregation of believers in hell listening to the clergyman's announcement of his Calvinistic text" (368–369). Like Billy, whose stammer renders him inarticulate, the crew stands "dumb" before their captain. At the close of the announcement, however, "a confused murmur went up. It began to wax." Before the crew has a chance to communicate their unified objection, "shrill whistles" go off and "the word was given to about ship" (369). It is clear that Billy's execution has the potential to destroy the hierarchical order Vere has been so careful to protect. Only Billy has the power to quell a possible rebellion. And this he does with his final words:

> Billy stood facing aft. At the penultimate moment, his words, his only ones, words wholly unobstructed in the utterance, were these: "God bless Captain Vere!" Syllables so unanticipated coming from one with the ignominious hemp about his neck . . . had a phenomenal effect. . . .
>
> Without volition, as it were, as if indeed the ship's populace were but the vehicles of some vocal current electric, with one voice from alow and aloft came a resonant sympathetic echo: "God bless Captain Vere!"

And yet at that instant Billy alone must have been in their hearts, even as
in their eyes (375).

Billy's benediction redirects the flow of feeling from rebellion into common
sense. Although Billy "alone must have been in their hearts," he becomes one
with the father figure whose name the crew speaks. Billy's will is aligned with
the parent, and the crew, identifying with Billy, becomes a reflection of that
will—aligned with the parent through the son. Such a moment of sympathy
signifies the consummation of individual and patriarchal authority at the heart
of a sentimental culture. Billy's acquiescence completes the image of democracy that only his death can accomplish. Through his death, Billy makes manifest the redemptive politics of identification: he creates in the crew a new
political body. Speaking as if "without volition," and with the "sympathetic
echo" of "one voice," the crew registers the seductive manipulations of a patriarchal democracy—a power not only to unify but to render indistinguishable
the will of the parent from one's own.

Like Christ, Billy becomes the representative body through which others are
brought together. But, also like Christ, he must die in order to transform what
is otherwise exceptional—his virtue—into what is typical and thus truly representative. Speaking to his officers of Billy's case, Vere puts their doubts into
his own words:

> "But the exceptional in the matter moves the hearts within you. Even so too
> is mine moved. But let not warm hearts betray heads that should be cool.
> Ashore in a criminal case, will an upright judge allow himself off the bench
> to be waylaid by some tender kinswoman of the accused seeking to touch
> him with her tearful plea? Well, the heart here, sometimes the feminine in
> man, is as that piteous woman, and hard though it be, she must here be
> ruled out." (362)

There is no place for the exceptional in a patriarchal order, unless the exceptional, the "feminine in man," be assimilated into the collective body.

It is no coincidence that Billy himself is compared to a woman throughout
Melville's tale. His "as yet smooth face" is said to be "feminine in purity"
(299). Elsewhere, the narrator compares Billy to one of Hawthorne's beautiful
women (302). In many respects, Billy embodies the feminine as we have come
to know it in sentimental stories. He is virtuous, pure, susceptible to filial
influence. Moreover, he enacts the conversion of sentiments from an Old
Testament mindset to a New by turning feelings of rebellion and vengeance
into a state of peace and unanimity. The catch, of course, is that he can only

do so by sacrificing the material body for a more spiritual cause. But then, according to the sentimental agenda, this has been the function of the "feminine" all along.

Melville uses Billy not to reproduce a sentimental reading of patriarchal authority but to critique it. In the final analysis, fathers prove more takers than givers of life. Speculating as to what took place in Vere's last interview with Billy, the narrator observes that "[Vere] was old enough to have been Billy's father"; thus the "austere devotee of military duty" may have let himself "melt back into what remains primeval in our formalized humanity, may in end have caught Billy to his heart, even as Abraham may have caught young Isaac on the brink of resolutely offering him up in obedience to the exacting behest" (367). Sacrifice is not only a dominant theme in *Billy Budd*, Melville seems to imply, but in any founding patriarchal order. Vere, typecast as both God and Abraham in Melville's novel, is represented as both the earthly father who mourns and the heavenly Father who demands, the sacrifice.

In the end, Melville depicts a patriarchal order as one in which the thing that we most cherish becomes the thing we must give up. This is a truth obscured by a sentimental view of filial relations, one in which the sacrificial act functions both to redeem the collective body and to preserve the image of what that body stands for: the individual. Divorced from the body of the individual, the idea of individualism can live on. The exceptional remains in our collective memory, its influence spreading over those who strive to identify with it. The lesson Melville leaves us with, however, is that the virtue we aspire to may be cast out as too good, not representative enough. Only by translating the individual into an idea will we able to live with what we have made. Once rendered less exceptional and more typical—more familiar—we can take the other to our hearts. We can, in the terms of sentimental literature, make the other our own.

Notes

1. The Politics of Sympathy

1. The union of private and public privilege is epitomized in the double duty "self-government" is meant to signify.

2. The rhetorical strategy of consensus making implicit in the Declaration of Independence has been addressed by political and literary theorists alike. See for example, Bonnie Honig's "Declarations of Independence," where she discusses Hannah Arendt's and Jacques Derrida's theories of the performative language in the *Declaration*. "Declarations of Independence," in Frederick M. Dolan and Thomas L. Dumm, eds., *Rhetorical Republic: Governing Representations in American Politics* (Amherst: University of Massachusetts Press, 1993), 201–225.

3. See Thomas Paine, *Common Sense*, in Michael Foot and Isaac Kramnick, eds., *The Thomas Paine Reader* (New York: Penguin, 1987), 85.

4. Philip Fisher, for example, argues that "the political content of sentimentality is democratic in that it experiments with the extension of full and complete humanity to classes of figures from whom it has been socially withheld." *Hard Facts: Setting and Form in the American Novel* (New York: Oxford University Press, 1985), 99.

5. See Karen Sanchez-Eppler, *Touching Liberty: Abolition, Feminism, and the Politics of the Body* (Berkeley: University of California Press, 1993), 3. Sanchez-Eppler cites in particular the work of Carole Pateman, *The Sexual Contract* (Stanford: Stanford University Press, 1988).

6. Susanna Haswell Rowson, *Charlotte Temple*, ed. Cathy Davidson (New York: Oxford University Press, 1986), 5. The 1794 date for *Charlotte Temple* corresponds to the first American edition, published by Matthew Carey. The novel was originally published in England by William Lane in 1791 under the title *Charlotte. A Tale of Truth*. See Davidson's introduction to *Charlotte Temple*, xi–xxxiii.

7. Adam Smith, *The Theory of Moral Sentiments*, ed. D. D. Raphael and A. L. MacFie (Oxford: Clarendon Press, 1976 [1759]), 9.

8. Although it is tempting to read Enlightenment treatises on sympathy as an affirmation of universal "fellow-feeling," I agree with David Marshall's assertion that "Enlightenment desires to discover universal principles" should not cause us "to overlook the implications of a perspective that casts people as spectators to each other." *The Figure of Theatre: Shaftesbury, Defoe, Adam Smith, and George Eliot* (New York: Columbia University Press, 1986), 169. The idea that sympathy is essentially "theatrical" in nature, a characterization present in the moral philosophy of David Hume and Francis Hutcheson as well as Smith, forces us to view sociopolitical attachments through the eyes of the individual subject. In a formulation crucial to the interests of sentimental fiction, Smith's theory places the affective and imaginative self at the heart of sympathetic fellow feeling.

9. The latter notion complicates twentieth-century views of sentimentality as synonymous with melodrama—the exaggeration or overindulgence in emotion. Novels like *Charlotte Temple* might seem to warrant this reputation by repeatedly attempting to direct the reader in his or her response: "Oh my friends, as you value your eternal happiness, wound not, by thoughtless ingratitude, the peace of the mother who bore you. . . . You must love her; nature, all-powerful nature, has planted the seeds of filial affection in your bosoms" (54). For most twentieth-century readers, novels like Rowson's epitomize the vulgarity of mediated emotion, whereby the ideal spontaneous outpouring of feeling becomes corrupted by the narrative's self-conscious in(ter)ventions. Yet, considered in its psychological and philosophical context, one could argue that sentimental fiction *realistically* describes the imaginative operations of sympathy at the heart of all social interactions. Insofar as the reader's own affective experiences serve as the basis for sympathy, sympathy proves an inherently mediated dynamic.

10. Ross C. Murfin, ed., *Case Studies in Contemporary Criticism: Nathaniel Hawthorne's "The Scarlet Letter"* (Boston: St. Martin's, 1991), 23. Citations hereafter will appear in parentheses following the quotation.

11. In this idea, Hawthorne seems to reflect Adam Smith's own doubts about the power of sympathy to relieve us of our isolated conditions. Although lack of sympathy represents for Smith, as for Hawthorne, the greatest evil, we are yet constantly put in the position of imagining to ourselves how others imagine us, and internalizing that perspective. As David Marshall puts it, "For Smith, sympathy depends upon a theatrical relation between a spectator and a spectacle, a relation that is reversed and mirrored as both persons try to represent the other's feelings." *The Figure of Theatre*, 190. We are thus constantly under threat of being alienated, not only from others, but from ourselves.

12. Cathy Davidson, *Revolution and the Word: The Rise of the Novel in America* (New York: Oxford University Press, 1986), 46.

13. See for example Richard Brodhead's "Sparing the Rod: Discipline and Fiction in Antebellum America" in *Cultures of Letters: Scenes of Reading and Writing in Nineteenth-Century America* (Chicago: University of Chicago Press, 1993).

14. For an extended treatment of gender and sensibility from the seventeenth through the nineteenth centuries, see G. J. Barker-Benfield, *The Culture of Sensibility: Sex and Society in Eighteenth-Century Britain* (Chicago: University of Chicago Press, 1992). For a treatment of the subject in the eighteenth century, see Janet Todd, *Sensibility: An Introduction* (London: Methuen, 1986).

15. Reprinted in *Short Stories from Another Day: Eighteenth-Century Periodical Fiction*, ed. Keith J. Fennimore (East Lansing: Michigan State University Press, 1989).

16. See Jay Fliegelman, *Prodigals and Pilgrims: The American Revolution Against Patriarchal Authority, 1750–1800* (Cambridge: Cambridge University Press, 1982).

17. Carole Pateman, *The Disorder of Women: Democracy, Feminism, and Political Theory* (Stanford: Stanford University Press, 1989), 39.

18. Carroll Smith-Rosenberg, "Domesticating 'Virtue': Coquettes and Revolutionaries in Young America," in Elaine Scarry, ed., *Literature and the Body* (Baltimore: Johns Hopkins University Press, 1988), 170.

19. Smith-Rosenberg, "Domesticating 'Virtue,' " 171.

20. The nature and definition of republicanism became particularly unstable at the turn of the nineteenth century. As Carroll Smith-Rosenberg observes in "Domesticating 'Virtue,' " while classical republicanism had identified the virtuous citizen as one whose economic privilege allowed him to work for the good of the common man, middle-class definitions of republicanism tended to associate virtue with frugality, hard work, and the absence of economic luxury. Yet despite these contrasting definitions, classical and middle-class republicanism have in common their reliance on hierarchical structures to maintain social order. Rejecting the class-based differentiation of groups inherent in the classical republican tradition, middle-class representations of virtue still clung, or perhaps clung more strongly, to the ideological division based on gender. In support of this point, Stephanie Coontz argues that "republican ideology obscured the differences between producers and employers by stressing their common opposition to aristocracy and dependence and by identifying people on the basis of their household relations rather than their class" (133). The result, according to Coontz, is that the male head of the household tended to "represent his wife and children in public just as propertied community leaders had formerly represented less socially powerful males" (133). Such a division was often made to appear *fortuitous* for women, for in the heterosexual model of affective relations, a woman's rights could be protected through the man who represented her. *The Social Origins of Private Life: A History of American Families, 1600–1900* (London: Verso, 1988).

21. Nina Baym, *Woman's Fiction: A Guide to Novels by and About Women in America, 1820–1870* (Ithaca: Cornell University Press, 1978), 27.

22. Susan Warner, *The Wide, Wide World* (New York: Feminist Press, 1987).

23. Davidson, *Revolution and the Word*; Michael Warner, *The Letters of the Republic: Publication and the Public Sphere in Eighteenth-Century America* (Cambridge: Harvard University Press, 1990); Gillian Brown, *Domestic Individualism: Imagining Self in Nineteenth-Century America* (Berkeley: University of California Press, 1990); Brodhead, "Sparing the Rod"; Jane Tompkins, *Sensational Designs: The Cultural Work of American Fiction, 1790–1860* (New York: Oxford University Press, 1985).

24. An example in the twentieth century would be Ann Douglas's *The Feminization of American Culture* (New York: Anchor, 1977), which assumes sentimentality and femininity to be virtual synonyms and posits both as largely responsible for the erosion of rigorous intellectual exchange in the nineteenth century.

I believe one problem attending criticism of sentimental fiction has been the "separate sphere" phenomenon so fundamental to nineteenth-century American thinking. While the criticism often begins by critiquing conventional antebellum views of white middle-class men's and women's roles in American society (the idea that men inhabit the public sphere, associated with the antisympathetic market values of competition, capitalism, and greed, while women become the guardians of the private sphere, characterized by Christian morality, self-sacrifice, and maternal love), the analysis often ends by reproducing the dichotomies it is purportedly seeking to investigate. Although feminist attention to the nineteenth-century "woman's sphere" has helped readers better understand various women's experiences since the American Revolution, it has sometimes kept both readers and critics alike from examining the rhetorical strategies by which such categories as "men's" and "women's" spheres are developed and maintained.

25. Nancy Armstrong, *Desire and Domestic Fiction: A Political History of the Novel* (New York: Oxford University Press, 1987), 4. Armstrong has successfully shown that the rise of the domestic woman signals a "major event in political history" (3). In contrast to her contentions about the English novel, however, I would argue that the American novel does not seek to "disentangle the language of sexual relations from the language of politics" (3). As my discussion of incest and seduction will reveal, family, politics, and sex are inextricably connected in the imagination of this fledgling nation.

26. See Tompkins, *Sensational Designs*.

27. Quoted in Gordon Wood, *The Creation of the American Republic, 1776–1787* (New York: Norton, 1972), 60.

28. Smith, *The Theory of Moral Sentiments*, 110.

29. According to Smith, sympathy is also disciplinary in the sense that it forces us to lower our passions to that pitch where others "are capable of going along with us." Ibid., 22. As David Marshall says, one of sympathy's social functions is to force us "to moderate our passions in order to create a 'harmony and concord with the emotions' of those who are watching us." *The Figure of Theatre*, 173.

30. Smith, *The Theory of Moral Sentiments*, 145, 156.

2. Natural and National Unions

1. Herman Melville, *Pierre, or The Ambiguities* (New York: Dutton, 1929 [1852]), 380–381.

2. Adam Smith, *The Theory of Moral Sentiments*, ed. D. D. Raphael and A. L. MacFie (Oxford: Clarendon Press, 1976 [1759]), 109. Citations hereafter will appear in parentheses after the quotation.

3. "Fellow feeling" denotes the projection of our feelings outward, but outward only onto those subjects who, by virtue of their likeness to us, inspire us to put ourselves in their place.

4. We can find this idea in the work of other eighteenth-century philosophers as well: David Hume, Francis Hutcheson, Lord Kames, the Earl of Shaftesbury.

5. As Jay Fliegelman observes, the phrase was one of the rhetorical markers of the Scottish Common Sense school, which assumed "the sociable character of man" and "extolled 'soul kinship,' 'affinity,' 'sympathetic attachments,' and 'the power of sympathy.'" Fliegelman goes on to note that "for Locke such subrational and noncontractual relationships endangered the sacred principle of moral independence." *Prodigals and Pilgrims: The American Revolution Against Patriarchal Authority, 1750–1800* (Cambridge: Cambridge University Press, 1982), 26.

6. See, for example, Lawrence Stone, *The Family, Sex, and Marriage in England, 1500–1800* (New York: Harper and Row, 1977); and Fliegelman, *Prodigals and Pilgrims*. Fliegelman specifically addresses the importance of new "affectionate" and "non-coercive" methods of child rearing and their impact on revolutionary and postrevolutionary attitudes toward authority.

7. For an excellent analysis of Locke's theory of "liberal patriarchy," as well as its implications for the gendering of individualism, see Mark Kann's *On the Man Question: Gender and Civic Virtue in America* (Philadelphia: Temple University Press, 1991).

8. John Locke, *Second Treatise of Civil Government*, reprinted in *Locke on Politics, Religion, and Education*, ed. Maurice Cranston (New York: Collier, 1965 [1690]), 38.

Locke's gender-specific term here is of course intentional. His reference to "man" is significant not only in terms of political clout but also contemporary attitudes toward the gendering of character. As Barker-Benfield points out, whereas men were considered self-fashioners, women were believed to be at the mercy of their delicate sensibilities. See G. J. Barker-Benfield, *The Culture of Sensibility: Sex and Society in Eighteenth-Century Britain* (Chicago: University of Chicago Press, 1992), xvii–xviii.

9. See Fliegelman, *Prodigals and Pilgrims*, 12–29.

10. Locke, *Second Treatise*, 19.

11. Alfred Young, for instance, quotes Carl Becker, who argued in 1909 that the Revolution "was the result of two general movements; the contest for home rule and . . . of who should rule at home." Alfred Young, ed., *Beyond the American Revolution: Explorations in the History of American Radicalism* (Dekalb: Northern Illinois University Press, 1993), 4.

12. For a discussion of Americans' mixed sentiments surrounding the British parliamentary model, see Bernard Bailyn's *The Ideological Origins of the American Revolution* (Cambridge: Harvard University Press, 1967). Bailyn makes the point that the "leaders of the Revolutionary movement were radicals — but they were eighteenth-century radicals concerned, like the eighteenth-century English radicals, not with the need to recast the social order nor with the problems of economic inequality and the injustices of stratified societies but with the need to purify a corrupt constitution and fight off the apparent growth of prerogative power" (283).

13. John Locke, *Some Thoughts Concerning Education, The Works of John Locke,* 10 vols. (Germany: Scientia Verlag Aalen, 1963 [1693]), 9:34.

14. Until relatively recently the term *sentimental* was more or less a pejorative one when applied to the novel, denoting an overindulgence in emotion. See, for example, Ann Douglas's *The Feminization of American Culture* (New York: Anchor, 1977), in which Douglas chronicles the decline of rigorous intellectual thought in the face of a growing sentimentalism. Critics such as Philip Fisher, Jane Tompkins, Cathy Davidson, and Gillian Brown have persuasively argued for the social and political agendas behind much American sentimental fiction in the nineteenth century.

15. David Marshall, *The Surprising Effects of Sympathy: Marivaux, Diderot, Rousseau, and Mary Shelley* (Chicago: University of Chicago Press, 1988), 3.

16. Ibid., 5.

17. For a discussion of the fundamental opposition between Lockean and Scottish views on the relationship of the individual to society, see Garry Wills, *Inventing*

America: Jefferson's Declaration of Independence (Garden City, N.Y.: Doubleday, 1978).

A twist on the relationship between Locke's empiricism and the more affective-oriented approach of the Scottish moralists such as Hutcheson appears in Barker-Benfield's book on sensibility. Barker-Benfield writes that the third Earl of Shaftesbury (1671–1713), considered by many historians to be "the originator and celebrant of the existence of an innate 'moral sense'," may have been influenced by the "high evaluation of good nature he had learned in his childhood from Locke." Locke was the "employee and close collaborator of the first earl of Shaftesbury [and] because of his son's degenerative illness, this Shaftesbury delegated to Locke the task of rearing his grandson, and Locke was thus enabled to implement the 'permissive' childrearing precepts that followed logically from his sensational psychology." *The Culture of Sensibility*, 105.

18. The subtitle to Fliegelman's *Prodigals and Pilgrims*.

19. The extent to which patriarchalism suffered a terminal blow in the eighteenth century has been debated by various historians and political theorists. Carole Pateman, for instance, argues persuasively that political theorists can represent the victory of contractualism over paternalism only because they are silent about the conjugal aspect of patriarchy. See *The Disorder of Women: Democracy, Feminism, and Political Theory* (Stanford: Stanford University Press, 1989), especially chapter 2.

20. Locke, *Some Thoughts Concerning Education*, 6–7. Citations hereafter will appear in parentheses following the quotation.

21. Hutcheson was influenced by Shaftesbury, whose influence can be seen in the thinking of David Hume and Adam Smith as well. I discuss Adam Smith in detail later in the chapter.

22. Francis Hutcheson, *An Inquiry Into the Original of Our Ideas of Beauty and Virtue, Collected Works of Francis Hutcheson*, 7 vols. (Hildesheim: Georg Olms Verlagsbuchhandlung, 1971 [1725]), 1:127, 129. Citations hereafter will appear in parentheses following the quotation.

23. I should note here that Hutcheson saw the duration of parental responsibility in much the same light as Locke, which the following excerpt will show:

The manifestly disinterested nature of [parental] affection shows at once the nature and duration of the parental power. . . . The generous nature of this affection shews that the power committed by nature is primarily intended for the good of the children, and, in consequence of their happiness. . . . The right therefore cannot extend so far as to destroy the children, or keep them in a miserable state of slavery. When they attain to mature years, and the use of reason, they must obtain that liberty which is necessary to any rational enjoyment of life. The parental affection naturally secures to them this emancipation, as the reason God has given them intitles [sic] them to it. (189–190)

A System of Moral Philosophy, Collected Works of Francis Hutcheson (Hildesheim: Georg Olms Verlagsbuchhandlung, 1969 [1755]), vol. 6.

24. The phrase is Fliegelman's. Fliegelman, after quoting a passage from the first edition of the *Encyclopaedia Britannica* (1771), sums up the sympathetic contract between parent and child in the following line: "God has designed this reciprocal sympathy to serve as the ideal paradigm for all future social relations." *Prodigals and Pilgrims*, 25.

25. Bailyn quotes Paine delineating *two* ancient tyrannies: "monarchical tyranny in the person of the King . . . [and] aristocratical tyranny in the persons of the peers" (285). *The Ideological Origins*. In my view, the connection between the two shows how the "prerogative power" and self-interest of the king has become a dangerous political (and thus personal) model for those closest to him.

26. Thomas Paine, *Common Sense*, in Michael Foot and Isaac Kramnick, eds., *The Thomas Paine Reader* (New York: Penguin, 1987), 79. Citations will herafter appear in parentheses following the quotation.

27. For a discussion of Paine's "political vernacular prose," see Olivia Smith, *The Politics of Language, 1791–1819* (New York: Oxford University Press, 1984), 39–67; and Eric Foner, *Tom Paine in Revolutionary America* (New York: Oxford University Press, 1976), 79.

28. In addition to Fliegelman, *Prodigals and Pilgrims*, see Louis Schneider, ed., *The Scottish Moralists* (Chicago: University of Chicago Press, 1967). In his introduction, Schneider notes that "the view of human nature entertained by the Scottish moralists is marked in general by an emphasis on uniformity in that nature. The idea of the constancy of man's psychic makeup was indeed a familiar notion of the Enlightenment" (xxi).

29. As I have indicated, the positive aspects of sensibility and sympathy were generally associated with men in the eighteenth century. Not until the nineteenth century, with sensibility's decline into "sentimentality," did sentiment become synonymous with "woman."

30. William Hill Brown, *The Power of Sympathy* (New York: New College and University Press, 1970), 29.

In an effort to legitimate his work, Brown includes a full-scale debate in the first volume of *The Power of Sympathy* wherein the "excellent Mr. Worthy" lectures on what kind of novels are and are not suitable for young ladies. Brown also devotes his preface to admonishing those novels that "*expose* no particular vice, and which *recommend* no particular virtue." In *The Power of Sympathy*, by contrast, "the dangerous consequences of seduction are exposed, and the advantages of female education set forth and recommended" (29).

The specificity of the education — that it is directed toward women — is explained in part by publishers' understanding of their target audience: while both men and women read novels in this period, women were considered the more critical audience (in both senses of the term). However, the assumption that *impressionable* readers were *female* readers also serves to feminize the reader, whether male or female, and to underscore the "seductive" nature of the novel's pedagogical strategies.

31. For a discussion of the critical debates surrounding the early novel in America, see Cathy Davidson, *Revolution and the Word: The Rise of the Novel in America* (New York: Oxford University Press, 1986), especially chapter 3. See also Cathy Davidson,

ed., *Reading in America: Literature and Social History* (Baltimore: Johns Hopkins University Press, 1989); and Nina Baym, *Novels, Readers, and Reviewers: Responses to Fiction in Antebellum America* (Ithaca: Cornell University Press, 1984).

32. In "Domesticating 'Virtue': Coquettes and Revolutionaries in Young America," Carroll Smith-Rosenberg addresses this problem briefly by discussing how the seduction novel permits illicit liaisons to be vicariously *enjoyed* as well as vicariously punished (167). In Elaine Scarry, ed., *Literature and the Body* (Baltimore: Johns Hopkins University Press, 1988). See also David Reynolds, *Beneath the American Renaissance: The Subversive Imagination in the Age of Emerson and Melville* (New York: Knopf, 1988).

33. The family involved was actually that of the American poet Sarah Wentworth Morton. Sarah's sister, Frances (Fanny), had an affair with Sarah's husband, Perez Morton. Fanny later committed suicide.

34. Daniel Wilson's "Science, Natural Law, and Unwitting Sibling Incest in Eighteenth-Century Literature" points out that the "intuition which could attract siblings to each other has come to be identified by the term 'voice of blood.' " *Studies in Eighteenth-Century Culture* (1984), 13:255.

35. Like Smith, David Hume saw sympathy as the basis of social harmony. As Janet Todd claims, in "his *Treatise of Human Nature* (1740) [Hume] makes community a spontaneous formation, a combination of self and other through sympathy and tenderness that elide individual differences" (27). See *Sensibility: An Introduction* (London: Methuen, 1986). But whereas for Hume sympathy elides individual differences, for Smith sympathy actually throws them into relief.

36. David Marshall, *The Figure of Theatre: Shaftesbury, Defoe, Adam Smith, and George Eliot* (New York: Columbia University Press, 1986), 172, 173.

37. The claim is Marshall's: "Sympathy must stop short of total identification: if we really changed persons and characters with the people we sympathize with, we might not feel sympathy." *The Figure of the Theatre*, 179.

38. Martha Nussbaum rightly qualifies this assertion when she points out Smith's omissions from the list of feelings with which readers can identify. The omissions are sexual desire and romantic love. To quote Smith, the "true cause of the peculiar disgust which we conceive for the appetites of the body when we see them in other men, is that we cannot enter into them." On the subject of romantic love, Smith makes a similiar, though less negative claim: "The passion appears to every body, but the man who feels it, entirely disproportioned to the value of the object; and love, though it is pardoned in a certain age because we know it is natural, is always laughed at, because we cannot enter into it."

For Nussbaum, these two categories are exceptions to the rule, and she explains the apparent contradiction by positing that, to Smith, any emotion that the reader cannnot be moved by is "morally suspect": "The fact that he cannot enter into love is not a sign that points beyond itself to some independently existing inappropriateness in the relation. It is the very fact that he cannot enter in, that *makes* the passion inappropriate."

As I see it, Nussbaum attributes value judgment to what is an epistemological dilemma at the heart of Smith's theory of sentiment. Romantic love is not qualitatively different from sympathy but merely magnifies the dilemma of affective feeling: that is, in attaining one's desire—whether it be sexual or affective union—desire is extinguished; and with it goes the illusion of comprehensive sympathy. While desire seems at first to bridge the gap between subjectivities, ultimately one finds oneself confirmed in one's epistemological autonomy. Smith himself makes this point with regard to sexual feeling when he asserts that a person once gratified in his passion will soon cease to be affected: "[The lover] looks round to no purpose for the charm which transported him the moment before, and he can now as little enter into his own passion as [if he were] another person." Martha Nussbaum, *Love's Knowledge: Essays on Philosophy and Literature* (New York: Oxford University Press, 1990), 338–346.

39. This was a relatively common theory about the reading experience in the late eighteenth century. See Todd, *Sensibility*, 30–31.

40. Fliegelman, *Prodigals and Pilgrims*, 26.

41. It is unclear whether Brown means to depict his protagonist as a revolutionary or a conventional hero at this point. On the one hand, Goethe's unconventional life — and by extension his work—led him to be strongly associated with sexual immorality for Anglo-American readers. On the other hand, the tragedy resulting from the power of narrative influence was itself already a literary convention by this time. The *"independency of spirits"* Harrington claims must therefore be qualified, if not made ironic, by his participation in a model already familiar to eighteenth-century readers.

42. Johann Wolfgang von Goethe, *The Sorrows of Werther*, 2 vols. (Litchfield, 1789), 2:85.

43. Marshall, *The Figure of Theatre*, 192.

44. These quotations come from Smith's *The Theory of Moral Sentiments*, reprinted in Schneider, *The Scottish Moralists*, 72–76.

3. Seductive Education and the Virtues of the Republic

1. See Janet Todd, *Sensibility: An Introduction* (London: Methuen, 1986), 30–31.

2. See Tony Tanner, *Adultery in the Novel: Contract and Transgression* (Baltimore: Johns Hopkins University Press, 1979).

3. Joseph Allen Boone, *Tradition Counter Tradition: Love and the Form of Fiction* (Chicago: University of Chicago Press, 1987), 7–8.

4. Jan Lewis, "The Republican Wife: Virtue and Seduction in the Early Republic," *William and Mary Quarterly* (October 1987), 44(4):6.

5. Mason Weems, *The Life of Washington* (Cambridge: Harvard University Press, 1962), 145. Citations hereafter will appear in parentheses following the quotation.

6. Brown's allusion to Goethe's novel adds yet another dimension to the framing of literary influence: that is, the question of American fiction's relationship to English and European literature. For even this "first American novel," a work whose advertisements were printed to coincide with the inauguration of the first American president, must acknowledge its partipication in a widespread ideological battle that encompassed Britain and much of Western Europe. The conflict between individual rights and community demands was a central thematic in eighteenth-century Western literature. As James Donald asserts, the late eighteenth-century German bildungsroman takes from Rousseau "his view of the disjuncture between the growth of individual capacities and desires and social codes of behavior." Such a disjuncture appears in Goethe's *The Years of Apprenticeship of Wilhelm Meister* (1795–1806), the "founding text" of a tradition

that offers protagonists who must learn to "make choices that weigh the *authenticity* of the self against the demands of *convention*" (8). *Sentimental Education: Schooling, Popular Culture, and the Regulation of Liberty* (New York: Verso, 1992), 8.

7. Novels differ from other genres such as conduct manuals and letters to children precisely in the way that makes novels most seductive: that is, they typically require that readers identify with protagonists in order for the narrative's moral lessons to be internalized.

8. See Robert Weisbuch's discussion of English influence on major American writers in *Atlantic Double-Cross: American Literature and British Influence in the Age of Emerson* (Chicago: University of Chicago Press, 1986).

9. Sacvan Bercovitch, "Hawthorne's A-Morality of Compromise," in *Case Studies in Contemporary Criticism: Nathaniel Hawthorne's "The Scarlet Letter,"* 345.

10. Gordon Wood, *The Creation of the American Republic, 1776–1787* (New York: Norton, 1969), vii.

11. For a discussion of the tremendous influence that the rise of print culture had on the shape of middle-class thinking, see Michael Warner, *The Letters of the Republic: Publication and the Public Sphere in Eighteenth-Century America* (Cambridge: Harvard University Press, 1990); and Cathy Davidson, *Revolution and the Word: The Rise of the Novel in America* (New York: Oxford University Press, 1986).

12. Such concerns arose even hundreds of years ago regarding cautionary fiction. Medieval romances on the abuse of parental power, illustrated in stories of seduction and incest, were initially conceived as exemplary tales for the education of young women. Caxton, translating such works into English in the fifteenth century, defended both the conception and the reproduction of the stories on the grounds of their social efficacy, asserting that anyone with daughters should read them. Many English readers, on the other hand, denounced the titillating tales, declaring that they showed less virtue than "vyces, subtletye, and crafte." Fitzherbert, *Book of Husbandry,* quoted in Caxton's *Book of the Knight of the Tower,* ed. M.Y. Offord (London, 1972 [trans. 1483]), xviii.

13. Quoted in Lawrence W. Lynch, *Eighteenth-Century French Novelists and the Novel* (York, S.C.: French Literature Publications, 1979), 176.

14. Aldous Huxley, from *Ends and Means,* reprinted in Marquis de Sade, *The Crimes of Love,* trans. Lowell Bair (New York: Bantam, 1964). All quotations from "Florville and Courval" and "Eugenie de Franval" come from this edition and citations herefater will appear in parentheses following the quotation.

15. Eric Partridge, *Origins: A Short Etymological Dictionary of Modern English* (New York: Macmillan, 1958), 169–170.

16. His success at creating the perfect woman leads Franval to challenge the premise upon which "natural" attraction is denied to fathers and daughters: "Is it reasonable to think that I can't be tempted by a pretty girl simply because I brought her into the world? Must I be repelled by the very fact that ought to unite me more intimately with her? Because she resembles me, because she sprang from my blood, in other words, because she combines all the elements capable of producing the most ardent love, must I look on her coldly?" (23–24).

17. Charles Brockden Brown, *Wieland and Memoirs of Carwin,* ed. Sydney J. Krause and S. W. Reid (Kent State University Press, 1990), 5. All citations hereafter will appear in parentheses following the quotation.

18. Warner, *The Letters of the Republic*, 175.

19. Brown, preface to *Wieland*, 3.

20. Mark Kann catalogues women's sins as follows:

Western tradition had it that women, by nature, were a tempestuous, whimsical, erratic, unpredictable, impassioned, irrational, mysterious, lusty, and powerful sex. . . . Women were said to usurp men's powers, rob them of autonomy, lure them from labor, distract them from public life, and corrupt their courage. Women allegedly played on men's failings, toyed with their emotions, addled their thinking, and manipulated their actions. . . . In the battle of the sexes, women were considered the most treacherous combatants.

On the Man Question, 66–67.

21. Through the discourse of early medical treatises, Foucault addresses eighteenth-century readings of the female body as that which is "riddled by obscure but strangely direct paths of sympathy; it is always in an immediate complicity with itself, to the point of forming a kind of absolutely privileged site for the sympathies. . . . The sympathetic sensibility of her organism, radiating through her entire body, condemns woman to . . . diseases of the nerves." Diseases of the nerves were thought to arise from organs in close contact with one another, producing a sympathetic resonance among them. The idea that a woman's body is "always in an immediate complicity with itself" betrays a kind of awesome wonder at women's physiognomic autonomy, her organic self-communion. But it is a wonder that is immediately translated into negative terms: "From one extremity of its organic space to the other, [the female body] encloses a perpetual possibility of hysteria." Michel Foucault, *Madness and Civilization: A History of Insanity in the Age of Reason*, trans. Richard Howard (London: Tavistock, 1967), 153–154.

For a treatment of nineteenth-century constructions of feminine sensibility and their relation to Victorian narratives, see Athena Vrettos, *Somatic Fictions: Imagining Illness in Victorian Culture* (Stanford: Stanford University Press, 1995); see also Todd, *Sensibility*, 19.

22. According to Barker-Benfield, the same Lockean theories of self-fashioning that depicted men as "willfully engaged" with the world and with their own emotions were eventually invoked to establish women's inability to govern themselves due to their "finer sensibility." G. J. Barker-Benfield, *The Culture of Sensibility: Sex and Society in Eighteenth-Century Britain* (Chicago: University of Chicago Press, 1992), xviii, 3.

23. Charles Francis Adams, *Familiar Letters of John Adams and His Wife Abigail Adams, During the Revolution* (Cambridge: Riverside, 1876), xix.

Abigail Adams's own opinions on the significance of women's patriotism is evidenced in a letter to her husband where she proclaims it "the most disinterested of all virtues." Whereas women's exclusion from honors, offices, and the natural rights of property should tend to make women indifferent to the public welfare, yet "all History and every age exhibit Instances of patriotic virtue in the female Sex." Considering women's situation, reasons Adams, such virtue "equals the most Heroick." Abigail Adams to John Adams, June 17, 1782. *Adams Family Correspondence*, ed. L. H. Butterfield, 6 vols. (Cambridge: Harvard University Press, 1963), 4:328.

24. The force and unpredictability of a woman's passions automatically disqualified her from any political position. Ironically, at a time when female chastity was aligned with national integrity, the feminine signifed all that was potentially threatening to republican virtue. As Linda Kerber observes, female characteristics were often made the measure of what a good republican society should *avoid*: " 'Luxury, effeminacy, and corruption' was a recurrent cautionary triad; so was 'ignorance, effeminacy, and vice.' " Effeminancy was associated with "timidity, dependence, and foppishness . . . with luxury and self-indulgence." Kerber concludes her analysis by remarking that "if Americans lived in a world of the political imagination in which virtue was ever threatened by corruption, it must be added that the overtones of virtue were male, and those of corruption, female." *Women of the Republic: Intellect and Ideology in Revolutionary America* (Chapel Hill: University of North Carolina Press, 1980), 31.

25. Abigail Adams is, in one sense, an exception, as is clearly demonstrated by her letters that follow. However, even Adams herself never acquired any formal schooling and thus must endure, according to her biographer, the anxieties of imagination that only reason can dispel.

26. John Bennett, *Strictures of Female Education* (Philadelphia: Spotswood, and H. and P. Rice, 1793), 5.

Catharine MacCauley and Mary Wollstonecraft are, of course, two exceptions to the rule, declaring that the problem lay not with women themselves but with the *type* of education women received. In *Vindication of the Rights of Woman* (1792) Wollstonecraft takes issue with writers like Rousseau who tow the party line in asserting that female education exists in order to mold women into proper helpmeets for men: "The education of the women should be always relative to the men. To please, to be useful to us, to make us love and esteem them, to educate us when young, and take care of us when grown up, to advise, to console us, to render our lives easy and agreeable—these are the duties of women at all times, and what they should be taught in their infancy." To fail in this regard, concludes Rousseau, is to "contribute neither to [women's] happiness nor our own." Quoted in Mary Wollstonecraft, *Vindication of the Rights of Woman*, ed. Miriam Brody (New York: Viking Penguin, 1985), 175.

27. Hitchcock, *Memoirs of the Bloomsgrove Family*; Bingham, "Oration Upon Female Education, Pronounced by a Member of One of the Public Schools in Boston," quoted in Davidson, *Revolution and the Word*, 47, 49, 63.

28. Davidson, *Revolution and the Word*, 63; see also Kerber, *Women of the Republic*, 189–231; Mary Beth Norton, *Liberty's Daughters: The Revolutionary Experience of American Women, 1750–1800* (Boston: Little, Brown, 1980), 256–299.

29. Judith Sargent Murray, "Desultory Thoughts Upon the Utility of Encouraging a Degree of Self-Complacency, Especially in FEMALE BOSOMS," in *The Heath Anthology of American Literature*, ed. Paul Lauter et al., 2 vols. (Lexington: D.C. Heath, 1990), 1:1028.

30. Lyman Cobb, *Cobb's Spelling Book* (Ithaca: Mack and Andrus, 1829), 164.

31. Christopher Newfield, "Emerson's Corporate Individualism," *American Literary History* (Winter 1991), 3(4):660.

32. Warner, *The Letters of the Republic*, 72.

33. Ibid., 73.

34. Rowson was born in England but spent much of her life in America. The setting of her story—moving between England and America—reflects the transatlantic nature of her career as well as the flexible boundaries of Anglo literary influence.

35. Cathy Davidson, introduction to *Charlotte Temple*, xi. I rely on Davidson's statistics and historical documentation throughout my discussion of this novel. All quotations come from Susanna Haswell Rowson, *Charlotte Temple*, ed. Cathy Davidson (Oxford: Oxford University Press, 1986). Citations hereafter will appear in parentheses following the quotation.

36. Terry Eagleton notes a similar phenomenon with regard to Samuel Richardson's novels, and argues that, though the characters are fictional, "nothing could be more insistently real than the ideological practices to which [the heroine's experiences] give rise. The national crisis which Clarissa's"—or in this case, Charlotte's—"death seems to have triggered is not to be ascribed to the heart-flutterings of gullible females; it is a measure of the material urgency of the themes which that death embodies." *The Rape of Clarissa* (Minneapolis: University of Minnesota Press, 1982), 17.

37. Quoted in Davidson, *Revolution and the Word*, xiv.

38. See Nina Baym, *Woman's Fiction: A Guide to Novels by and About Women in America, 1820–1870* (Ithaca: Cornell University Press, 1978), 21; J. Brooks Bouson, *The Empathic Reader: A Study of the Narcissistic Character and the Drama of the Self* (Amherst: University of Massachusetts Press, 1989); Vrettos, *Somatic Fictions*.

39. Janice Radway, *Reading the Romance: Women, Patriarchy, and Popular Literature* (Chapel Hill: University of North Carolina Press, 1984), 8.

40. As Radway notes in her revised introduction to *Reading the Romance* (1991), David Morley advocates a "genre-based theory of interpretation and interaction" in his book *The Nationwide Audience*. According to Radway, Morley contends that such a theory might better be able to explain "why certain sets of texts are especially interesting to particular groups of people (and not to others) because it would direct one's attention to the question of how and where a given set of generic rules had been created, learned, and used" (10).

41. Davidson, introduction to *Charlotte Temple*, xiii.

42. Davidson's summary of Gordon Wood's argument in "The Democratization of the American Mind." *Revolution and the Word*, 159.

43. J. L. Austin, *How to Do Things with Words*, ed. J. O. Urmson (Cambridge: Harvard University Press, 1962), 2–8.

44. Emphasis mine. Quoted and translated in John Lechte, *Julia Kristeva* (New York: Routledge, 1990), 24, 25.

45. See Austin, *How to Do Things with Words*. Austin himself excluded literary language from his analysis of speech acts, because "it cannot invoke conventions and accepted procedures, and because it does not link up with a situational context which can stabilize the meaning of its utterance." Wolfgang Iser, however, persuasively counters Austin's assumptions. See *The Act of Reading: A Theory of Aesthetic Response* (Baltimore: Johns Hopkins University Press, 1978), 60–62.

46. Davidson, on the other hand, writes that "the novelist's critique of illicit sexual behavior often had a feminist import and emphasized the unfortunate consequences of seduction for the individual woman, not the social mores (although these were in the novel, too) against which she had offended." *Revolution and the Word*, 116.

47. *The Royal American* (January 1774), 1:9, and (March 1774), 1:9, quoted in Jay Fliegelman, *Prodigals and Pilgrims: The American Revolution Against Patriarchal Authority, 1750–1800* (Cambridge: Cambridge University Press, 1982), 127.

48. Stephanie Coontz, *The Social Origins of Private Life: A History of American Families, 1600–1900* (London: Verso, 1988), 133–134.

49. Carole Pateman, *The Disorder of Women: Democracy, Feminism, and Political Theory* (Stanford: Stanford University Press, 1989), 37.

50. Fliegelman chronicles such a shift in sentiment toward patriarchalism in *Prodigals and Pilgrims*, arguing that the "revolution against patriarchal authority" ushered in a "new paternalism" in America, based on Lockean and Scottish views of non-coercive, affectionate discipline and rule (25–26). The emphasis on individual liberties—the right to happiness among them—prompted perceptual shifts toward romantic relationships as well, resulting in both a more relaxed attitude toward divorce and an increased dedication to the idea of voluntary marriage.

However, according to Fliegelman, one of the effects of this liberal trend was the potential for undermining filial obedience in the act of promoting romantic attachment. Citing Milton's *Paradise Lost* and Rousseau's *Julie* as literary examples, Fliegelman makes the point that Protestant republican devotion to voluntary wedlock "set the claims of Romantic love against the claims of patriarchal authority" and "extend[ed] the issue of individualism in the marriage choice to a justification for familial revolution," (130–131). My contention in this chapter is that, in fact, the claims of romantic love usefully served to bolster the claims of patriarchal authority.

51. Jan Lewis,"The Republican Wife," 710.

52. Ibid., 711.

53. The English noun derives from the Medieval French adjective *coquet*, meaning "as vain and swaggering as a cock." See Partridge, *Origins*, 108.

54. Carroll Smith-Rosenberg, "Domesticating 'Virtue': Coquettes and Revolutionaries in Young America," in Elaine Scarry, ed., *Literature and the Body* (Baltimore: Johns Hopkins University Press, 1988), 168.

55. Hannah Webster Foster, *The Coquette*, ed. Cathy Davidson (New York: Oxford University Press, 1986), 22. All citations hereafter will appear following the quotation.

56. Put in terms of reception theory, the "interpretive norms" formed by readers of seduction fiction become so familiar as to render the novel's messages virtually meaningless.

57. The phrase comes from Hans Robert Jauss in *Toward an Aesthetic of Reception*, trans. Timothy Bahti (Minneapolis: University of Minnesota Press, 1982).

58. Nina Baym reports in *Woman's Fiction* that seduction novels decline after the turn of the century. By the mid-nineteenth century, the domestic story is the most popular.

4. Changing the Subject: Domestic Fictions of Self-Possession

1. For the phrase "virtual incest," I am indebted to my student, Mako Yoshikawa.

2. Nancy Armstrong, *Desire and Domestic Fiction: A Political History of the Novel* (New York: Oxford University Press, 1987), 8. Citations hereafter will appear in parentheses after quotations.

3. Nina Baym, *Novels, Readers, and Reviewers: Responses to Fiction in Antebellum America* (Ithaca: Cornell University Press, 1984), 39.

4. The other is the masterpiece of sentimental sympathy, *Uncle Tom's Cabin*. See ibid., 245.

5. Emphasis mine. Quoted in ibid., 119.

6. Baym reports that in the first half of the nineteenth century, an ability to evoke readers' sympathies was viewed as the single most important criterion for a successful novel.

7. Such a model necessarily challenges assumptions found in both traditional histories of "classic" American fiction celebrating an autonomous (and particularly male) individualism and newer noncanonical histories that address but often reinforce the fiction of male and female separate spheres.

8. David Ramsay, *An Oration on the Advantages of American Independence* (1788), 20.

9. America's lofty intentions had been frustrated by the Napoleonic conflict in Europe, with its attendant restrictions on American commerce, as well as by British refusal to let trade be carried on between continents without passing through England. Tensions with Britain ultimately led to America's declaration of war in 1812, but even after America's victory, or its political vindication in the eyes of the world, trade relations with Britain remained strained at best.

10. Leslie Fiedler, *Love and Death in the American Novel* (New York: Dell, 1966), 27.

11. As Nancy Cott and others have shown, material circumstances also helped to shape and perpetuate the notion of separate spheres. The movement of production out of the household and into the factories between 1780 and 1835 signaled a social transformation that eventually distinguished men's from women's work and the domestic arena from the marketplace. "Women's sphere," writes Cott, "was 'separate' not only because it was at home but also because it seemed to elude rationalization and the cash nexus, and to integrate labor with life. The home and occupations in it represented an alternative to the emerging pace and division of labor" (62). Whereas the man's involvement in commercial transactions and capitalist ventures called his republican ethics into question, the woman's retirement from economic production raised her status to the level of a saint. The price the woman paid for this otherworldly position, however, was to be often alienated from the man to whom she was committed. Like the "home" itself, the middle-class woman was "idealized, yet rejected by men—the object of yearning, and yet of scorn. . . . Women's work (indeed women's very character, viewed as essentially conditioned by the home) shared in [a] simultaneous glorification and devaluation" (62). Nancy Cott, *The Bonds of Womanhood: "Woman's Sphere" in New England, 1780–1835* (New Haven: Yale University Press, 1977).

12. Mary Ryan, *Cradle of the Middle Class: The Family in Oneida County, New York, 1790–1865* (Cambridge: Cambridge University Press, 1981), 2. Ryan is quoting from Talcott Parsons and Robert F. Bales, *Family, Socialization, and Interaction Process* (Glencoe, Ill.: Free Press, 1955).

13. An exception in literary studies is Gillian Brown's *Domestic Individualism: Imagining Self in Nineteenth-Century America* (Berkeley: University of California Press, 1990). Historians have also been revising the standard equation between women

and the private sphere in the nineteenth century. See, for example, Mary Ryan, *Women in Public: Between Banners and Ballots, 1825–1880* (Baltimore: Johns Hopkins University Press, 1990); and Glenna Matthews, *The Rise of the Public Woman: Woman's Power and Place in the United States 1630–1970* (New York: Oxford University Press, 1992).

14. See Nina Baym, *Woman's Fiction: A Guide to Novels by and About Women in America, 1820–1870* (Ithaca: Cornell University Press, 1978).

15. Domestic fiction's representations of women inevitably refers to a middle-class ideal of femininity. If middle-class women found themselves precariously positioned in a capitalist and male-centered culture, this dynamic was often reproduced in their relationships to their working-class sisters. Christine Stansell notes that after "the disappearance of productive households . . . families increasingly needed women's cash earnings to get by." In addition, "The exodus of men to the Revolution and, later, to the War of 1812 precipitated a crisis of female poverty from which many . . . never recovered" (11–12). Yet inspite of these economic realities, and the fact that much of the "domestic service" women provided was for families other than their own, the educated woman with a home of her own served as the paradigm for nineteenth-century notions of femaleness. In a cultural maneuver not unlike the separation of the "competitive" from the "nurturing" sphere, class differences were annulled by an image of American homogeneity partly produced and perpetuated by the domestic woman. Such an influential member of society, while offering financial and spiritual relief to those less fortunate, had the power to negate the existence of women not her equal. So Stansell tells us that "in confronting the working poor, [women] reformers created and refined their own sense of themselves as social and spiritual superiors capable of remolding the city in their own image. From the ideas and practices of domesticity they drew many of the materials for their ideal of a society that had put to rest the disturbing conflicts of class" (xii). Unfortunately, the very ideals supposed to liberate working women from their onerous lives became the standards of femininity to which they did not measure up. Working-class women were not only poor, but, by the middle-class criteria of womanhood, they were not really women. See Christine Stansell, *City of Women: Sex and Class in New York, 1789–1860* (New York: Knopf, 1986).

16. Ryan, *Cradle of the Middle Class*, 98. In addition to Ryan's *Cradle of the Middle Class*, see Cott, *The Bonds of Womanhood*; and Stephanie Coontz, *The Social Origins of Private Life: A History of American Families, 1600–1900* (London: Verso, 1988).

17. Sedgwick first began this novel as a small pamphlet protesting religious intolerance. Recognized as among the first novels to include authentic American settings, dialects, and situations, *A New-England Tale* became an immediate success.

18. Catharine Maria Sedgwick, *A New-England Tale, or, Sketches of New-England Character and Manners*, ed. Victoria Clements (New York: Oxford University Press, 1995), 33. All citations hereafter will appear in parentheses following the quotation.

19. The name *Methodism* derives from John Wesley's belief that religion should be studied "by rule and method." There is a strong emphasis on social reform in Methodism, which is related to Wesley's commitment to evangelicalism. Wesley began his evangelistic preaching in the Church of England in 1758; a separate Wesleyan

Methodist Church was established in 1791. The Methodist Episcopal Church was founded in the United States in 1784.

20. Sedgwick's Unitarianism is clearly evident in her fiction. The fundamental principles of the Unitarian Church are akin to Christianity; however, the church rejects the doctrines of the Trinity and the divinity of Christ. Unitarians profess no creed, emphasize social and ethical ramifications of religion, and promote the search for religious truth through the exercise of freedom of religion.

21. For example, working in his capacity as a lawyer, Erskine successfully defends a known seducer in a breach-of-promise suit.

22. Luke 20:35. The entire quotation reads as follows: "And Jesus said to them, 'The sons of this age marry and are given in marriage; but those who are accounted worthy to attain to that age and to the resurrection from the dead neither marry nor are given in marriage, for they cannot die any more, because they are equal to angels and are sons of God, being sons of the resurrection" (Luke 20:34–36). *Holy Bible*, rev. standard ed. (Grand Rapids: Zondervan, 1946).

Mary Wollstonecraft's feminist novel, *Mary*, ends with this same biblical quotation.

23. Maria Cummins, *The Lamplighter*, ed. Nina Baym (New Brunswick: Rutgers University Press, 1988), 1–2. All citations hereafter will appear in parentheses following the quotation.

24. Gerty's desire to go to heaven, and her subsequent efforts to be "good" so she will get there, are linked to her feelings of family. Her growing awareness that she is different both in temperament and in faith from True, the Sullivans, and Emily signals a future—and eternal—separation from them. What she seeks is a home where there is no shadow of parting. It is not an objective acceptance of religious doctrine that initiates Gerty's conversion; it is sympathy. In order to remain with those she loves, she must first be *like* them. Sustaining a family—even after death—necessitates a consanguinity of mind and spirit in its members.

25. Adam Smith, *The Theory of Moral Sentiments*, ed. D. D. Raphael and A. L. MacFie (Oxford: Clarendon Press, 1976 [1759]), 110.

26. C. B. MacPherson, *The Political Theory of Possessive Individualism: Hobbes to Locke* (New York: Oxford University Press, 1962).

27. Brown, *Domestic Individualism*, 2.

28. MacPherson, *Democratic Theory: Essays in Retrieval* (Oxford: Clarendon, 1973), 126–127. MacPherson observes that it is in the modern conception of a full capitalist market society that "the idea of common property drops virtually out of sight" (125). So David Hume can state that property constitutes "such a relation betwixt a person and an object as permits him, but forbids any other, the free use and possession of it, without violating the laws of justice and moral equity" (128).

29. Lawrence Stone, *The Family, Sex, and Marriage in England, 1500–1800*, 22. The other two characteristics Stone lists are "a weakening of the association of sexual pleasure with sin and guilt; and a growing desire for physical privacy" (22).

30. Shirley Samuels, *The Culture of Sentiment: Race, Gender, and Sentimentality in Nineteenth-Century America*, ed. Shirley Samuels (New York: Oxford University Press, 1992), 5.

31. According to Ann Douglas, it was the Compromise of 1850, which included the

Fugitive Slave Law, that motivated Stowe to write *Uncle Tom's Cabin*. See Douglas's introduction to Harriet Beecher Stowe, *Uncle Tom's Cabin, or, Life Among the Lowly* (New York: Penguin, 1985), 8. All citations hereafter will appear in parentheses following the quotation.

32. Karen Sanchez-Eppler, *Touching Liberty: Abolition, Feminism, and the Politics of the Body* (Berkeley: University of California Press, 1993), 32.

33. Emphasis mine. Ibid., 27, 26.

34. Adam Smith, *The Theory of Moral Sentiments*, 9.

35. In contrast to Fisher, Gillian Brown identifies *Uncle Tom's Cabin*'s sentimental sympathy as fundamentally possessive in nature. She demonstrates that the novel's attempts to deobjectify personhood—namely, its attempt to reverse slavery's process of making a "man" into a "thing"—results in a "romance of possession," whereby slaves become—not people—but "properly owned property . . . better-placed things." *Domestic Individualism*, 42. While Brown quite rightly critiques Stowe's romance of sentimental possession, I am arguing that the problem lies in the particular way sympathetic identification was thought and made to operate in the hundred years preceding Stowe's sentimental novel.

36. Philip Fisher, *Hard Facts: Setting and Form in the American Novel* (New York: Oxford University Press, 1985), 102.

37. Ibid., 99.

5. Mothers of Seduction

1. Jane Tompkins, "Sentimental Power: Uncle Tom's Cabin and the Politics of Literary History," in *Sensational Designs: The Cultural Work of American Fiction, 1790–1860* (New York: Oxford University Press, 1985).

2. Baym, *Woman's Fiction: A Guide to Novels by and About Women in America, 1820–1870* (Ithaca: Cornell University Press, 1978), 26.

3. Tompkins, *Sensational Designs*, 125.

4. The idea of a cooperative network of female relations is most persuasively argued by Carroll Smith-Rosenberg in her chapter "The Female World of Love and Ritual," in *Disorderly Conduct: Visions of Gender in Victorian America* (New York: Knopf, 1985). Smith-Rosenberg emphasizes the close bond between mothers and daughters and between sisters in the nineteenth century. Her research and analysis, taken mainly from diaries and letters of eighteenth- and nineteenth-century women, reveals the existence of a "female world" in which women enjoyed with each other great intimacy, love, and passion, characteristics often lacking in their relationships with men. My reading of domestic fiction attempts to complicate Smith-Rosenberg's findings, to demonstrate the degree of emotional ambivalence that arises from such a closed world.

5. Caroline Lee Hentz, *Ernest Linwood, or The Inner Life of the Author* (Boston: John P. Jewett, 1856), 81. Citations hereafter will appear in parentheses following the quotation.

6. *Charlotte's Daughter* was also printed under the title *Lucy Temple*. See Susanna Haswell Rowson, *Charlotte Temple; and, Lucy Temple* (New York: Penguin, 1991).

7. An idea proposed by Sandra Gilbert and Susan Gubar in *Madwoman in the Attic:*

The Woman Writer and the Nineteenth-Century Literary Imagination (New Haven: Yale University Press, 1979).

8. Richard Brodhead, "Sparing the Rod: Discipline and Fiction in Antebellum America," in *Cultures of Letters: Scenes of Reading and Writing in Nineteenth-Century America* (Chicago: University of Chicago Press, 1993).

9. Brodhead, "Sparing the Rod," 18.

10. Ibid., 20.

11. Lydia Sigourney, *Letters to Mothers* (New York: Harper, 1839), 128.

12. See Mary Ryan, *Cradle of the Middle Class: The Family in Oneida County, New York, 1790–1865* (Cambridge: Cambridge University Press, 1981).

13. Brodhead, "Sparing the Rod," 34–5.

14. Susan Warner, *The Wide, Wide World* (New York: Feminist Press, 1987), 175. All citations hereafter will appear in parentheses following the quotation.

15. Helen Papashvily, *All the Happy Endings* (New York: Harper, 1956), 7–8.

16. Karen Halttunen, *Confidence Men and Painted Women: A Study of Middle-Class Culture in America, 1830–1870* (New Haven: Yale University Press, 1982), 121.

17. Quoted in Halttunen, *Confidence Men and Painted Women*, 121.

18. Ibid., 122.

19. Mary Kelley addresses this issue in *Private Woman, Public Stage: Literary Domesticity in Ninteenth-Century America* (New York: Oxford University Press, 1984).

20. The word *compose* comes from the Latin *componere*, literally meaning "to put together." See Eric Partridge, *Origins: A Short Etymological Dictionary of Modern English* (New York: Macmillan, 1966), 515.

21. *Ernest Linwood* is the fictional autobiography of the main character, Gabriella Lynn. However, Mary Kelley links Hentz's own history with the events of this novel. See *Private Woman, Public Stage*.

22. The idea of the daughter as an object of both spiritual and erotic attachment for disturbed fathers is documented in Koren Sanchez-Eppler's fascinating study of nineteenth-century temperance fiction, "Temperance in the Bed of a Child: Incest and Social Order in Nineteenth-Century America," in *American Quarterly* (March 1995), 47(1):1–33.

23. Catharine Sedgwick's *Redwood*, like *Ernest Linwood*, has the heroine facing her mother's past before she can pledge herself to her beloved. In *Redwood*, Ellen Bruce must read her mother's letter and be assured of her "virtue" before she can contemplate marriage. Her mother's story assures Ellen of her legitimacy, but also reveals the deception and betrayal that lay at the heart of that marriage.

Conclusion: *Billy Budd* and the Critique of Sympathy

1. Thatcher Thayer, *The Vicarious Element in Nature and Its Relation to Christ* (Newport, R.I., 1988), 26. All citations hereafter will appear in parentheses following the quotation.

2. Frederick Busch puts the starting date earlier, at 1855: "probably between the time of his retirement as a customs inspector in 1855 and his death in 1891, he worked on a poem that became the ballad 'Billy in the Darbies' ('Billy in Irons') that sparked a

short novel—it concludes with the ballad and began as a headnote to it—that we know as *Billy Budd, Sailor (An Inside Narrative)." Billy Budd and Other Stories*, ed. Frederick Busch (New York: Viking Penguin, 1986), xxi. *Billy Budd* was published posthumously. Citations hereafter will appear in parentheses following the quotation.

3. In 1867 Melville's son Malcolm committed suicide at the age of eighteen. In support of his point that the Vere-Budd relationship works by a father-son analogy, Busch observes that Billy is called *"Baby* Budd" by Dansker, "the voice of insight in the novel." Moreover, "The mutiny act, which necessitates Billy's death, is described as 'War's child,' which 'takes after the father.' " And Captain Vere, responsible for the make-shift jury's guilty verdict in Billy's case, is described as "old enough to have been Billy's father" (xxii).

Index

Adams, Abigail, 57–58, 137n22, 138n24
Adams, Charles Francis, 57
Adams, John, 41–42
Affinity, 22, 38, 130n5; politics of, 4, 92, 98
"Amelia, or the Faithless Briton" (anonymous), 9, 45
American literature: as "classic," 13, 141n7; as different from British novel, 3, 45, 130n25, 135n6; and the exemplary, 43–44, 120; and feeling, 2, 13, 22, 98; and individualism, 13–14, 120; and patriarchal politics, 121–22; and reading, 2–3, 120; and sentimental ideology, 25
American character, 47, 74; as exceptional, 44–47, 120, 125–27; as innocent, 122; as relationally constructed, 77, 120; in *Uncle Tom's Cabin*, 98–99
Armstrong, Nancy, 13, 75–76, 130n25
Austin, J. L., 64, 139n44

Bailyn, Bernard, 131n12, 133n25
Barker-Benfield, G. J., 128n14, 131n8, 132n17, 137n21
Baym, Nina, 11, 76, 78, 103, 111, 134n31, 140n57

Bennett, John, 138n25
Bercovitch, Sacvan, 46–47
Billy Budd (Melville), 116, 120–26, 145n2
Body: as related to political body, 1, 8, 38, 92, 115, 118; and seduction fiction, 116; sentimental representations of, 92–96, 126; and sympathy, 116, 134n38; and tears, 95; as text, 37, 70–71, 113; women's bodies as political symbols, 8, 10, 11, 41, 60; in *Uncle Tom's Cabin*, 92–96
Boone, Joseph, 42
Britain, as "parent country," 3, 24, 29
Brodhead, Richard, 13, 104–5, 128n13
Brown, Charles Brockden, 14, 52–55
Brown, Gillian, 11, 13, 131n14, 141n13, 144n35
Brown, William Hill, 14, 19, 25, 31–41, 44, 67
Busch, Frederick, 121, 145n2

Capitalism, 118; and domestic fiction, 11–12; in *The Lamplighter*, 89–90
Cautionary tale, 35, 45, 54, 71, 124, 136n12; *see also* Seduction novel
Charlotte Temple (Rowson), 4, 8, 15, 45, 61–65, 103, 127n6, 128n9, 139n35

Christianity: in *Billy Budd*, 120–21,
125–26; and capitalism, 90; and *The
Lamplighter*, 84–88; and marriage,
82–83; in *A New-England Tale*,
80–83, 143n20; as paradigmatic, 79,
118; and patriarchy, 120–21; and sentimental culture, 78–80, 116; and
sympathy, 87, 116; in *Uncle Tom's
Cabin*, 97; and vicarious suffering,
116; in *The Wide, Wide World*, 105–6
Clarissa (Richardson), 41–42, 45,
139n35
Common sense, 14, 16, 27–28, 31, 32,
38, 55, 120, 125
Common Sense (Paine), 3, 25–26, 27–31,
93, 97, 115
Consensus, 1, 46–47, 54; of sensibility,
61
Convention, 33, 47, 52, 109, 136n6; literary conventions, 44–47, 96, 105,
108–9, 135n41; and patriarchal fan-
tasies, 56
Conversion, 75; of feminine suggestibility, 100; in *The Lamplighter*, 85, 87,
143n24; as narrative model, 80, 97; in
A New-England Tale, 78–80; and
puberty, 88; of reader, 94; of sentiments, 125; of sympathy, 91; in *The
Wide, Wide World*, 105
Coontz, Stephanie, 66, 129n20
The Coquette (Foster), 10–11, 15, 45,
67–72, 103, 120
Cott, Nancy, 141n11
The Crimes of Love (de Sade), 48–52
Cummins, Maria, 15, 87

Davidson, Cathy, 12–13, 59, 61–62,
131n14, 133n31, 136n11, 139n45
Declaration of Independence, 1–2, 10,
46, 127n2, 139n34
Democracy: versus affinity, 98; in *Billy
Budd*, 120–25; and capitalism, 89,
118; and individualism, 118–20; preserved through violence, 122; rejecting exceptionalism, 121; and representation, 60, 117–20; and sameness,

16, 92; and sympathy, 2, 3, 25, 30,
115; as vehicle of seduction, 41, 125;
and vicarious relations, 117–18
De Sade, Marquis, 48–52, 55–56
Desire and Domestic Fiction
(Armstrong), 75
Discipline: and love, 27, 104, 113; and
mothers, 104–6; and reading, 8, 14,
20, 104; and sympathy, 21
The Disorder of Women (Pateman), 10
Domestic: as distinct from commercial,
77, 82; domestic ambivalence, 110;
domestic ideology, 75–78, 101, 113;
domestic manuals, 76; as opposed to
"foreign" literature, 31; as geographical space, 24–27, 38, 77–78
Domestic novel, 11, 15–16, 73, 78,
100–4, 111, 142n15; and capitalism,
11–12, 89–90; and Christianity,
79–80; and daughter-readers, 112; as
"daughter-text," 102–3; and discipline,
12, 13; and *Ernest Linwood*, 109–10,
112–14; and the idealization of womanhood, 114; and identification, 76,
99; and *The Lamplighter*, 84–91; and
mothers, 101, 109, 144n4; and *A New-
England Tale*, 78–84; as paradigm of
self-production, 76; and patriarchal
politics, 16, 75; as rejection of cautionary tale, 81–82; and self-possession, 73; and "virtual incest," 74; and
virtue, 12
Donald, James, 135n6
Douglas, Ann, 129n24, 131n14, 143n31

Eagleton, Terry, 139n35
Education, 4, 26–27, 45, 56, 58–59, 61,
108, 133n30, 136n12, 138n25; and
men, 41, 59, 64; and mother's example, 112; in *A New-England Tale*,
80–81; and parenting, 51; as prevent-
ing seduction, 59, 72–73; romantic
education, 53; as seductive, 15,
40–43, 47, 48–52, 56, 112; in
Wieland, 53–55
Empathy, 21

Enlightenment, 26, 115, 128n8, 133n28
Ernest Linwood (Hentz), 17, 101–2, 104, 109–10, 112–14

"Fall of the House of Usher" (Poe), 19
Familial feeling (familial love, sympathy, attachment): in domestic novels, 78; as eroticized, 19–20, 38, 75; as fatal, 15; as forbidden, 32; and nationalism, 27, 30, 77, 115; and politics, 2, 3, 15, 91; as romantic ideal, 83–84
Family: as democratic social model, 97, 117; nuclear family, 3, 78; as political analogue, 10, 14, 16, 18, 19–20, 23, 25, 27, 41, 117
"Female education," 4, 8–9, 14, 15, 31, 41, 46, 49, 56, 58–59, 61–62, 65, 68–72, 133n30, 138n25
Feminine sensibility, 56–58, 64, 72, 100, 107, 114, 131n8, 133n29; in Billy Budd, 125; in The Coquette, 70; and democracy, 98–99, 138n23; married vs. single women, 58, 62–63; and reading, 8, 59, 67, 75; and sympathy, 137n20
Feminism: and political theory, 4, 10; and sentimental literature, 13, 130n24
Filial identification, 17, 100–1, 11, 114
Filial sympathy: as American obsession, 101, 114; fostering self-discipline, 89; and its perversions, 55; as requisite for becoming a Christian, 79; as romantic ideal, 84; and seduction, 17; sociopolitical implications, 14, 20, 23, 25, 27, 74, 97–99
Fisher, Philip, 97, 127n4, 131n14
Fliegelman, Jay, 10, 23, 129n16, 130n5, 131n6, 133n24, 140n49
Foster, Hannah, 10, 15 , 67–68, 103
Foucault, 18, 46, 104, 137n20

Gilbert, Sandra, 144n7
Gilman, Caroline, 17, 110
Goethe, 36, 44, 135nn41, 6
Gubar, Susan, 144n7

Halttunen, Karen, 108
Hawthorne, Nathaniel, 5–8, 46–47, 125, 128n11
Hentz, Caroline Lee, 17, 101
Hitchcock, Enoch, 58
Hope Leslie (Segwick), 81
Hume, David, 128n8, 130n4, 132n21, 134n35, 143n28
Hutcheson, Francis, 14, 25, 27–28, 29, 128n8, 130n4, 132nn17, 21, 23

Identification, 32; models of, 1–2, 25, 33, 34, 60–61, 86, 94–97, 117–20; and reading, 2, 15, 22, 25, 35–36, 76, 94, 114, 120; and embodiment, 4, 92, 96; in The Scarlet Letter, 6; and materiality, 7–8, 12; and suggestibility, 8, 57; and eliding difference, 17, 37, 114; in The Theory of Moral Sentiments, 20–22, 34; in The Power of Sympathy, 32–39; and seduction, 35–39, 99, 111; resistance to, 37; and its sociopolitical benefits, 57, 60, 62, 74, 92–99, 115, 125–26; in Charlotte Temple, 61–64; in The Lamplighter, 86–87, 89; and mothers, 17, 99, 117; and women, 100; and vicarious relations, 116; and family, 117; and substitution, 117; in Billy Budd, 125–26; and the exceptional, 126
Incest, in American literature, 3, 19, 22, 45; sociopolitical implications of, 3, 74; in The Power of Sympathy, 14, 32–38; in Pierre, 19; as metaphor for relating to others, 20; in The Crimes of Love, 49–51; as cultural ideal, 74–75; legitimized by domestic fiction, 78; "virtual incest," 74, 114
Independence 32, 33, 35, 43, 44–45, 67, 69–70, 91, 100, 103, 135n41; and domestic literature, 75; versus autonomy, 77; and relational model of selfhood, 85; and possessive individualism, 85; in The Wide, Wide World, 106–8; in writing, 108
Inquiry Into the Original of Our Ideas of

Inquiry Into the Original . . . (*Continued*)
  Beauty and Virtue, An (Hutcheson),
  27–28
Iser, Wolfgang, 139n44

Jefferson, Thomas, 1–2, 41–42, 77

Kann, Mark, 131n7, 137n19
Kelley, Mary, 145n21

The Lamplighter (Cummins), 15–16, 78,
  84–91
Letters of the Republic (Warner), 60
Lewis, Jan, 42, 67
Liberalism, 12, 17, 60–61, 62, 72, 75;
  and vicarious relations, 118
Life of Washington (Weems), 14, 43–44
Locke, John, 14, 23–26, 29, 130n5,
  131n8, 132nn17, 23, 137n21
Love's Progress (Gilman), 17, 110–11

MacCauley, Catharine, 138n25
MacPherson, C.B., 89, 143n28
Marriage, 10, 57–58, 140n49; as ideological tool, 42; as protecting women, 10,
  65; as symbol of sociopolitical union,
  11, 15, 65–67; and seduction, 11, 66;
  as microcosm of the republic, 66–67;
  in *The Coquette*, 69, 71; as goal of
  familial love, 75; marriage market, 78;
  and Christianity, 82–83, 143n22; as
  man-made institution, 83; in *A New-*
  England Tale, 82–84
Marshall, David, 25, 34, 128nn8, 11,
  130n29
Maternal influence, 102, 108; as seductive, 100–1; mother as the failed feminine, 103; and identification, 117
Melville, Herman, 19, 115, 120–23,
  125–26, 145n3
Modeling, as method of child development, 24; as narrative method, 24;
  and Locke, 24–25
Murray, Judith Sargent, 59

Narrative education, 5, 18, 40; and *The*
  Scarlet Letter, 5–8, 46; as reformed,

16, 20; in *The Power of Sympathy*,
  33–36; in *Wieland*, 55
Nature, 31, 33, 34, 55, 123; in *The*
  Crimes of Love, 48–52; in *A New-*
  England Tale, 81–82; as "vast peda-
  gogy," 118
A New-England Tale (Sedgwick), 15,
  78–84, 90, 91, 142n17
Newfield, Christopher, 60
Nussbaum, Martha, 134n38

Paine, Thomas, 3, 25, 27–32, 38, 115,
  117, 133n25
Pamela (Richardson), 45
Papashvily, Helen, 107
Pateman, Carole, 10, 66, 127n5, 132n19
Paternalism, and eroticism, 20, 38; and
  Locke's theories of education, 26–27;
  and narrative authority, 36; and marriage, 42, 66; as seductive, 42, 56, 66,
  84; and patriotism, 43; and contractualism, 10, 132n19; "new paternalism,"
  140n49
"Power of sympathy," 23, 31, 33, 34, 36,
  37; as model of seduction, 32; and its
  social benefits, 83; and the body, 116,
  130n5
The Power of Sympathy (Brown), 14,
  19–20, 23, 25, 31–40, 44–45, 49, 67,
  133n30
Prodigals and Pilgrims, 23, 129n16
Psychology, Lockean, 24

Radway, Janice, 63, 139n39
Redwood (Sedgwick), 81, 104, 145n22
Republican independence, 8, 10, 12
Republican marriage, 10–11, 66–67; and
  domesticating authority, 67
Republican virtue, 8, 18, 69, 129n20;
  and marriage, 15; and seduction, 43;
  and sentimental ideology, 60, 74
Republicanism, 17–18, 62, 66, 68–69,
  75; and vicarious relations, 118
Reynolds, David, 134n32
Richardson, Samuel, 45, 139n35
Rousseau, Jean-Jacques, 135n6, 138n25,
  140n49

Rowson, Susanna, 4, 15, 61–62, 68, 103
Ryan, Mary, 78–79

Samuels, Shirley, 92
Sanchez-Eppler, Karen, 95
The Scarlet Letter (Hawthorne), 5–8, 46–47, 120
Schneider, Louis, 133*n*28
Scottish moralists (or Common Sense philosophers), 20, 27, 38, 130*n*5, 132*n*17, 133*n*28
Sedgwick, Catharine, 15, 80–81, 85, 104, 142*n*17, 143*n*20, 144*n*22
Seduction, in American literature, 3, 23, 31, 53; as a model for politics, 3, 9, 42–43, 74; and education, 4, 9, 14–15, 31, 39, 40–43, 46–47, 48–52, 53–56, 59, 112; and marriage, 11, 42; in *The Power of Sympathy*, 14, 31–39; and paternalism, 15, 42, 48, 51; and mothers, 17, 99, 112; as performed by the text, 32, 50, 74, 136*n*7; in *The Crimes of Love*, 48–52; in *Wieland*, 53, 55; as performed by the author, 52, 55; and patriarchal culture, 56; and masculinity, 56; in *Charlotte Temple*, 61–65; in *The Coquette*, 66–72; as redemptive, 70, 114; and consent, 9, 11, 43, 71–72
Seduction novel, 8, 9, 15, 42, 79, 83, 88, 100, 102, 111, 139*n*45; and patriarchal politics, 9–11, 23, 60, 64; as "mother-text," 17, 102–3, 111; and the problems of influence, 9, 14, 40, 31, 36, 39, 71; as cautionary tale, 35, 45, 54, 71; feminizing readers, 41, 60, 64, 133*n*30; and literary convention, 45; and obsession with female innocence, 48; constructing their readers, 63–64; and its pedagogy, 64–65, 74, 112; and "gender trouble," 67; and private desires, 70; and choice, 71–72; as return of the repressed, 104; and material concerns, 116
Self-scrutiny, and *The Theory of Moral Sentiments*, 21
Self-possession, 12, 73, 76, 85, 88–90

Sensibility, 29, 37, 117, 137*n*21; *see also* Feminine sensibility
Sentimental education, 4, 14, 37, 39, 114
Sentimental literature, and democracy 4, 17, 61, 98; modeling sympathy for readers, 5, 23, 31, 37, 74, 76, 87, 94–96; and its seductive arts, 8–9, 20, 42–43, 114; and patriarchal authority, 24; and mediation, 5, 39, 94–95; and republican education, 43; teaching readers to read, 63, 96; and the shift from seduction to domestic fiction, 15–16, 73–74, 94, 100; and Christianity, 75; and importance of self-interest, 76; reforming sympathy, 80; and tears, 87, 95, 107; and affinity, 91; and the body, 95; and representation of selfhood, 95; and identity politics, 98; and realism, 128*n*9; and separate spheres, 130*n*24, 141*nn*7, 11
Sentimental politics, 1, 3, 38, 41, 44, 98, 101
Sentimentalism, purpose of, 1; definition of, 5, 23, 25, 131*n*14; and representation, 2, 60–61, 93–94, 117; and the family, 2; and patriarchalism, 121; and the body, 126; as synonymous with melodrama, 128*n*9
Second Great Awakening, 75, 79
Sibling attraction, 33
Smith-Rosenberg, Carroll, 10–11, 129*n*20, 134*n*32, 144*n*4
Smith, Adam; and sympathy, 4–5, 18, 20–22, 33–36, 38–39, 85, 88, 95, 118, 128*n*8, 132*n*21, 134*nn*35, 38; and "fellow feeling," 5, 21, 22, 128*nn*8, 11, 130*nn*29, 3; and "the man within the breast," 18, 21, 38, 39, 85, 88
Some Thoughts Concerning Education (Locke), 26–27
The Sorrows of Young Werther (Goethe), 36, 44
Stansell, Christine, 142*n*15
Stone, Lawrence, 91, 131*n*6, 143*n*29
Stowe, Harriet Beecher, 3, 16, 92–99, 117, 144*n*31, 144*n*35

The Surprising Effects of Sympathy
  (Marshall), 25
Sympathetic identification, *see*
  Identification
Sympathetic imagination, 3
Sympathy, definition of, 2, 25, 32; and
  political loyalty, 3; danger of, 4, 14,
  17, 25, 31, 35–36, 117, 120; as mode
  of relating, 4, 5, 20–22, 35, 76, 94–99;
  and the imagination, 4–5, 7, 21–22,
  34, 35, 95–96, 115; theatrical nature
  of, 7, 34–35, 37, 64, 128n8; and
  nationalism, 14, 25, 30, 57, 76–77,
  115–17, 118; and eighteenth-century
  moral philosophy, 19–28; as method
  of reading, 20, 23, 34, 35, 37, 60, 62,
  92–99; as socially organizing sentiment, 20–22, 25, 115–16, 130n29; as
  a method of exclusion, 22; as alienat-
  ing, 25, 34–35, 85, 88, 120; as crucial
  to sentimental literature, 22, 125; and
  masculinity, 30, 62, 97–98; as undermining free will, 33; as force of
  nature, 34; and doubling, 35, 83;
  erotic aspect of, 35; mirror of, 34, 38;
  as disciplinary, 16, 64, 85, 130n29; in
  A New-England Tale, 80–84; as
  learned behavior, 81; love as perfect
  sympathy, 81; legitimizes incest, 91; as
  narcissistic model, 92, 95–98, 117;
  negating distinction between physical
  and fictional bodies, 95–96; and its
  homogenizing function, 97; based on
  likeness, 115; and vicarious experience, 115–17, 120; the politics of,
  116; and the body, 116–18, 134n38;
  and the construction of a Christian
  state, 116, 120; as expression of typicality, 120; as mediated dynamic,
  128n9; and romantic love, 134n38

Tanner, Tony, 42
Thayer, Thatcher, 115–20
The Theory of Moral Sentiments (Smith),
  4–5, 20–22, 33
Todd, Janet, 128n14, 134n35, 135n39
Tompkins, Jane, 13, 16, 100–1, 131n14

Two Treatises of Civil Government
  (Locke), 23

Uncle Tom's Cabin (Stowe), 16, 78,
  90–99, 100, 120
Union, sociopolitical, 1–2, 3, 14, 25, 61,
  117; subversion of, 11; sentimental
  idea of 13, 23, 74 ; and marriage,
  65–67; "unity of spirit," 83; and vicarious relations, 116–18; and eliding
  difference, 120; in *Billy Budd*,
  123–25

*The Vicarious Element in Nature and Its
  Relation to Christ*, 115–20
Vicariousness, and Christianity, 116; and
  human relations, 116–17; and sympathy, 115–17; and identification,
  116–17; and motherhood, 117; and
  democracy, 117–18; and representation, 118
Virtue, in *Pierre*, 19; and Locke, 27; and
  Hutcheson, 27–28; and self-love, 27;
  and love of others, 27; in *The Crimes
  of Love*, 48–49; in *Wieland*, 53; and
  identification, 62; in "Amelia," 72; in
  Billy Budd, 123, 126
"Voice of blood," 33, 82
Vrettos, Athena, 137n20

Warner, Susan, 12, 17, 76–77, 104–5
Warner, Michael, 12–13, 60, 136n11
Washington, George, as quintessential
  American, 43–44
Weems, Mason, 14, 43–44
The Wide, Wide World (Warner), 12, 17,
  78; as "national" novel, 76–77, 104–9
Wieland (Brockden Brown), 14, 45, 52
Wills, Garry, 132n17
Wollstonecraft, Mary, 138n25, 143n22
Woman's Fiction (Baym), 11
Women's writing, and self-expression,
  108, 110; in *The Wide, Wide World*,
  108–9; in *Ernest Linwood*, 109–10
Wood, Gordon, 17, 47

Young, Alfred, 131n11